My Navy

My Navy

The voyage of

a submarine cook

A Naval Autobiography

By Clay Westfall

The Wind in my Sails

This book is dedicated to my beautiful mother, Irmgard Westfall. Thank you for so many years of love and support.

Chapter One

I remember the first time I thought about joining the Navy. I was walking through the local mall in town one day and I saw this poster on the wall of the military recruiting office. At the top of the poster was the word "Heritage" in bold white letters. Just under the lettering was the picture of a sailor in his dress blue uniform, holding the hand of a small boy. They were looking out over Boston harbor, at the USS Constitution. Whenever I would look at that poster, and how great that guy looked in that cracker-jack uniform, I knew then that this was what I wanted to do with my future. I wanted to wear that uniform, and that's what I was going to do. To this day, I still love that recruiting poster.

As my high school graduation day came closer, my excitement grew at the thought of finally being able to do my own thing. I was so tired of school. I wanted to see the world and make my mark on it, however it would be. I loved my family, and liked living at home, but it was time for me to get a life of my own.

The first step was to find a recruiter. Something about this process just seemed so final. I was pretty nervous, but I wanted to do it by myself. As I walked into the Recruiting Office in Opelika, Alabama, I couldn't help but to stare at all the pictures on the wall. Mighty ships, fighter jets and uniforms... it was so exciting! A tall man in a khaki uniform walked up to me, smiled and stuck out his hand. "Hi, I am Chief Reynolds. Welcome to the United States Navy!" I was very impressed, and quickly introduced myself. So far, so good!

Before you can join the military, you have to see what jobs you qualify for. To do this, applicants must take the Armed Services Vocational Aptitude Battery test, or the ASVAB for short. When I joined back in 1983, you needed to score at least a 31 to get into the Navy. If you scored 50 or above, you were eligible to work in a technical field that required extensive school and training. For example, a Radioman, a Sonar Technician or a Fire Control Technician required a six year enlistment. This way the Navy could get their money's worth out of all the schooling they paid for. When I took my test it brought back many haunting memories of days spent lost in Algebra and Geometry class. I had no clue as to what I was doing, or so I thought. The test took about two hours, and I didn't think I did very well. Oh well... I guess there is always barber collage.

After quickly grading the test, Chief Reynolds smiled and said "Wow... you scored a 89! That qualifies you for the Nuke Program!" After he saw the bewildered look on my face, he quickly explained that anyone who makes an 80 or better qualifies for the nuclear field program, which means a better job, more money and faster advancement. This all sounded great to me, until he mentioned the three years of school involved in the process. Three years of school? Are you kidding me? I am just graduating high school by the skin of my teeth, and this guy wants me to go back to school? No way! I told him I was not at all interested in going to school for three more years. It was obvious that the Chief was a bit annoyed with me, but that was alright. It's my life, not his. I asked him to show me other jobs that only required a four year contract and very little school.

Chief Reynolds reached into his desk drawer and pulled out a catalog with lots of pictures to look through. He told me to take it home, look through it, and try to find a job that I would be happy with. I took that as my cue to leave and went home. After a day or two of going through the catalog, I decided on a job that looked like fun, without being too hard or time consuming. I wanted to be a cook! I was very excited to see Chief Reynolds the next day and tell him of my decision.

After school the next day, I borrowed my dad's truck and headed back to the Recruiting Office. Chief Reynolds was less than thrilled with my choice, but it was just that... my choice. He did offer me something else that I had not considered; Submarines! Now I had seen a lot of old time movies where twenty men or so would ride around in an old World War II diesel sub, but I thought that was only in the movies. I never even dreamed that there were real people in real submarines. He went on to tell me that the submarine service was totally voluntary, and if I volunteered, I would get an extra sixty dollars every month. Now that's sounded more like it!

Ok, so now I know what I will be when I grow up – a submarine cook. Now all I have to do is finish up this high school thing and life will be good. The only question was when would I go into the Navy? Chief Reynolds told me that the best plan would be to go into the Navy Delayed Entry Program (DEP). That meant that I could join up now, but go in at a later date. Since my parents also thought that this was a good idea, I decided to wait until after the summer (my last summer as a free man) and then join.

I graduated from high school in late May, and had an awesome summer. As I watched my friends moving away, going off to college or starting their new careers, I couldn't help but be excited about my future. I was going to join the world's finest Navy! I entered the Delayed Entry Program at the end of August. The agreement was for me to leave for boot camp in February, and that was still six months away. I couldn't wait!

I remember arriving at O'Hare Airport in Chicago, Illinois about one o'clock in the morning. I was so excited and terrified all at the same time. The snow was coming down so hard it started to pile up on the window ledge. As I sat there, I started wondering if I had done the right thing or if I had made a terrible mistake by joining the Navy. What was going to happen next? Right now, everyone back home was all snug in their beds while here I was a million miles away not knowing what was around the corner.

Just outside the window where I was sitting, a busy street ran along the length of the airport. On the other side of the street were two pretty girls, just standing there beside the road. It looked to me like they were waiting for someone. They looked so cold in their short skirts and low cut shirts. I wanted to walk out to them and offer one of them my jacket, but then I realized that they must be hookers. I had never seen a hooker before, but I had heard of them. I decided that since I didn't know anything about them, I would let well enough alone.

After what seemed like forever, I looked at the clock again and saw that it was quarter to two. Just when I was thinking about walking home, I heard a yell coming from the other side of the room. A tall man dressed in a blue uniform started calling for anyone who was heading to the Great Lakes Navy boot camp. It starts right now. This was the beginning of the rest of my life.

The bus ride from the airport was long and quiet. There were about sixty other guys with me, and they all seemed to be sleeping. How could they sleep? Didn't they realize that in just under an hour their lives would change forever? There was no way that I was going to be able to sleep on that bus. I couldn't stop thinking about my family, or what my life was going to be like from here on out. Resting my head against the cold window, I silently prayed as I watched the streetlights go by. I had a feeling that I was going to need all the help the good Lord could give me.

After what seemed like forever, we arrived at the Great Lakes Naval Training Center. The bus passed through a very large chain linked gate guarded by four sailors in uniform. We slowly drove around building after building; finally coming to a stop between two identical buildings that I would later come to know as the Division twenty-two. Just then, a short man with a pot belly climbed aboard the bus and looked at us with an odd smile on his face. Then he stood up as tall as he could and said "Hello, and welcome to the United States Navy". Just as I was thinking about how nice he seemed, he started screaming at us. "Get off this bus RIGHT NOW! You will form two lines next to the bus and you had better keep your pie holes shut!" Once we were outside and in line, the man introduced himself as Chief Harris, our senior Company Commander. He was just over five feet tall and was almost as wide. He had a very full black mustache, and wore thick glasses that made his eyes look huge. One thing that was very obvious to me was how pleased Chief Harris was with himself. I knew right then that our relationship was going to be a stressful one.

After briefing us on a few housekeeping items, Chief Harris had us march single file through the front door of the 22nd Division building. We followed a very long hallway and came to a huge room lined on both sides with bunk beds. For the next two months, this was our home. Chief Harris started yelling again. "Alright you misfits, everyone grab a bunk and then throw your gear into the locker directly behind that bunk. After you have done that, get into your bunks and get some sleep. Morning will be here in a few minutes". Then he turned off the light and slammed the door. Then, there was silence.

I remember lying there, thinking about what was going to happen the next morning. The last thing I remembered was the smell of old wool blankets and dirty socks. About an hour later, I was ripped out of my sound sleep by the crashing of a garbage can. At first I thought it was only a dream, but I soon found out differently. As quick as I could, I climbed out of my rack and tried to make sense out of what was happening. Walking quickly down the center of the room was a short, very angry looking Philippine man in a Navy Cracker Jack uniform. He looked like he was mad at the whole world and he just kept yelling. "Good morning and welcome to the Navy. My name is Petty

Officer Aquino and I am not your friend." Well, I guess that was one thing I didn't have to wonder about.

"For the next eight weeks, you belong to us. Your parents must hate you, or they would never have sent you here. Your girlfriend was on the phone with your best friend as soon as you were on the airplane. Now she is his girlfriend. If you have a problem, I don't care. If you miss home, I don't care. If you think you have made the worst mistake of your life, well, you are probably right. But none of that matters now, because you are here, and you are mine. If you have a problem with the way I am talking to you right now, I don't care."

My dad told me what to expect in boot camp, and I could see that everything he told me was correct. He also told me to shut up and get through it. It might seem like forever, but it would be over in a couple months. I just had to be strong.

Petty Officer Aquino told us what we were to expect while we were at Great Lakes. From what I was hearing, it sounded pretty much like hell on earth. My first look into the bathroom, or the 'head' as the Navy called it, was shocking. There were no doors on the stalls! OK, now I was having flashbacks of every prison movie I had ever seen.

About an hour later, Chief Harris showed up. He and Petty Officer Aquino took turns teaching us about everything we needed to know to survive the next eight weeks. They kind of slipped into a 'good cop, bad cop' routine, which made it much easier to ask questions. We just had to avoid the bad cop. Then, he told us that our day was going to be a busy one, and we needed to get started. After forming us all up in one long line, we left the barracks and marched over to the other side of base.

On the other side of the base was the recruit processing area. As we entered the huge building, we were told to get into a long line. Everywhere you looked there were scared, hungry looking recruits standing in line. First, they would stand in one line, and then they were hurried over to another line. It was a never ending cycle of lines. There were so many things that had to be done.

The first thing that had to be done was the background questionnaire. This had hundreds of questions to fill out, like your birthplace, and the names and birthdays of your immediate family. God help you if you knew anyone in another country! I was an Army brat, born on an Army base in Heidelberg, Germany. I had a German mother, German grandparents, German cousins, and several German friends. Of course, the Navy had to know everything about them. Since I was a Bubblehead (submariner), I needed a Top Secret clearance, so there was even more questions.

One of the biggest issues for me was my one time use of marijuana. It was pretty stupid, actually. My buddy and I had never tried marijuana before, but we had heard about it. One evening when we were running around in Auburn, we decided to buy a dime bag (ten dollars' worth) from some kid we had just met named 'Stony'.

Once we had made our big purchase, we rolled the whole bag into about twenty joints (marijuana cigarettes) and attempted to smoke all of them. Since we were on a back street with our windows opened, the police car that was sitting just downwind from us easily sniffed us out. Before we knew it, we were sitting in the back of that same police car. Well, since we were just kids who obviously had no idea of what we were doing,

the Police Officer gave us a stern warning an
on our way, minus our marijuana.

Now, when my recruiter, Chief Reynolds, asked
me about marijuana usage, I should have kept my
mouth shut. But, being the scared to death Recruit I
was, I confessed my big crime to the Navy, and that
brought forth paperwork. I had to get a waiver from the
Navy, and see a couple extra counselors before I could
be placed into the submarine program. I have also been
repeatedly questioned about my marijuana usage for
every reenlistment and every time I needed my clearance
renewed.

After the paperwork was started, the haircuts
commenced. Now, I did have long hair that I was fond
of, but I had already adjusted to the idea of losing it.
There were some guys there who were actually crying
and asking for a 'hair waiver'. This started as a cruel
joke one of the Company Commanders decided to play
on the group. They said if you asked for a hair waiver,
the Navy might agree to let you keep your hair. These
guys didn't share the CC's sense of humor.

The next thing that happened was my most vivid
memory of the whole process... uniform issue. We were
led into a very large, open building. There were long
tables running the length of the building, and we were
directed to strip down to our socks and underwear.
Since we were instructed to wear underwear when first
coming to Great Lakes, the four men who were not
wearing them stood there naked, in their socks. We
were each given a large cardboard box and told to walk
down the table from station to station. On the other
side of the table were several women, all looking mean
and annoyed with us.

The first station had a stool for us to step on, so we could be measured by the first unhappy lady. I remember how uncomfortable I felt when she measured my inseam, but when I thought about how the guys with no underwear would feel, I started feeling a bit better. It was all pretty humiliating, being treated like we were cattle, but I knew it would be over soon. After passing though the entire gauntlet, we were led to a changing area and told to put on our new jogging suits. This would be our only clothes until out uniforms were tailored and returned to us.

Next, we had to pack up everything that we brought with us to boot camp, and send it home. It was not easy mailing off the only remnants of the way life used to be. After this, it was all Government Issue.

Once we mailed all of our clothes and personal items home, we went to the Navy Exchange. This is the Navy everything store. Since money was not allowed, we were issued a coupon book. This coupon book had a coupon for everything you could imagine. Haircuts, laundry service, cigarettes, or just small amounts of money. For example, if I need a comb and a bottle of shampoo, I would use a five dollar coupon, and the Company Commander would write the remaining value on the coupon and sign it. The cost of the coupon book was deducted from our first paycheck.

After a day or so, our uniforms arrived. Now, we had to stencil everything, and that was an experience in itself. We had to put our last names on all of our shirts, pants and everything else we owned. For some of us, it wasn't so bad. But the guy who slept in the rack next to mine's name was Michael Martinkovicova. When you compare his name to Amos Tu who was in the rack just down the line, it just didn't seem fair.

The next couple of days were spent learning how to fold underwear and march around in circles. I never realized that there was a correct way to insert a roll of toilet paper (the roll must pull from the bottom) or a right way to tie your shoes. I still remember the letter that I wrote to my mom that week, telling her how miserable I was:

Sunday, 13 February 1983

Dear Dad and Mom,

How is everyone? I think I am going to die. We ran one and a half miles yesterday, and then we did calisthenics for two hours, then we ran two more miles. Today, every muscle, bone and organ in my body hates the Navy. Friday I get to have real fun. I get to do twenty-five push-ups, twenty-five sit-ups, twenty-five body builders, fifty jumping jacks, fifty back breakers, and then run two and a half miles in twenty minutes. One of the Company Commanders left his car running outside, and I really thought hard about 'borrowing' it, but I resisted the temptation. I gotta go for now... I will write more tomorrow. Love, Clay

Well, I'm here again, and life is still lousy. This morning life looked good. The weather was just beautiful. Now, there is eighteen inches of snow on the ground and it's about minus five degrees outside. My eyelids froze shut coming from dinner. We also have several cases of frost bite. It is so cold here, and windy. I don't know when I can write again, but if I am still alive, I will write soon. I love you all. Clay

The Company Commanders got pretty angry whenever someone would ask a dumb question. I remember what my Dad told me just before leaving home a few days earlier. He had just cracked open the seal on a jar of moonshine someone had given him. Now, my dad wasn't a heavy drinker, and I had never seen him drink anything like moonshine before, so I knew this was a special occasion. He took a drink from the jar, and then he handed it to me and said "Son, when you go to Great Lakes don't ask any stupid questions. If you have a question, someone else will most likely have the same question, so let them ask it. That way, if it seems like a dumb question, they will get beat up, not you". This advice served me well, not only at boot camp but also in the years to follow.

Another great piece of advice my Dad gave me was to go to church as often as I could. Now, being brought up in a Christian home, we went to church regularly. I wasn't quite sure why Dad would say that, until that first Sunday. Chief Harris came into the bay and called everyone to attention. "For anyone who would like to go to church this morning, we will be lining up in two minutes". I had always had a very close relationship with God, and I really needed His help to get me though the next few weeks. As a small handful of us were getting into line, we could hear the comments of the guys who decided not to go. They were saying things like "I'm not wasting my morning in a church... I can write home." Or "Not me, I'm sleeping in." I wasn't really sure what they would be doing while we were gone, but I was pretty sure they wouldn't be sleeping in.

As we marched across the base to the church service, I couldn't help but notice the huge piles of snow everywhere. It is very cold in Illinois in February, and I knew first hand why Chicago was called the 'Windy City'. I had never been so miserable in my life.

We soon marched up to a big airplane hangar that had been transformed into a drill hall. These were the biggest buildings I had ever seen! Just inside of the drill hall was the area where they were having the Catholic Mass Service. There was a small stage set in the middle of the drill hall with a couple hundred folding chairs neatly placed around it. Since there were only a few people there, they were all sitting in the same section.

The service was good, and the Chaplain, a full bird Captain, preached about how we should allow God to bring us through this challenging time in our lives. It sounded like good advice to me. On the way back to the barracks, I felt much better. I knew then that I was going to be alright, no matter how bad it got. When we arrived back 'home' at Division twenty-two, I noticed the windows were all fogged up. It seems that the Navy frowned on men who didn't go to church, and decided that the ones who stayed behind should do pushups until the rest of us got back. My father became wiser and wiser each day I was there. Incidentally, the next week, everyone got religion.

Whenever we marched anywhere at Great Lakes, we had to carry our 'pieces'. A 'piece' was an old World War II M-1 carbine rifle with no firing pin and a slide that was spot welded in the closed position. It looked kind of cool, but unless you were smacking rats with them, they were totally useless.   Whenever we would march to the chow hall, we would have to stack the pieces in a tee-pee shaped stack with the barrels pointed up. One lucky person would get picked to stand at attention for the next twenty minutes guarding these useless firearms. I remember how stupid I felt when it was my turn. There I was, standing at attention looking out over the parade field as snow piled up on my nose. It was so cold and uncomfortable, but I didn't dare to move, even to wipe the snow off my nose. After a few minutes, one of the guys from my company would come to relieve me so I could go and eat. Such was my life.

Navy chow was excellent! I had heard people complain and warn me about it, but I thought it was great. Lots of variety and all you could eat. But there was one problem. We had to be finished in five minutes. That was quite the challenge at first, but I soon mastered it. To this day I still eat my dinner in record time. When I was home, Mom always cooked excellent, nutritious meals. Even when times were tough and meat was scarce, our meals were wonderful. My problem was taking the time to eat the wonderful meal. When I graduated from boot camp, I had gained twenty nine pounds.

Our barracks was very long and rectangular. Running down the middle of the room was a painted walkway, about ten feet wide. Along each side of the walkway were two perfectly straight rows of bunk beds, approximately fifty down each side. At the end of the bay were two large rifle racks that held our numbered pieces. Whenever we would leave the barracks, we would march by the piece rack and pick up our pieces.

Now, one of the main jobs of the Company Commanders was to make sure the recruits are mentally able to conform to the Navy. Every now and then, they would weed out a problem child, such as Wong.

Chi Wong was Chinese - American, and he was a bit of a loner. He slept in the rack right across from me, so I tried to reach out to him. As it turned out, he didn't want to make friends, and would never turn his back on anyone. The guy gave me the creeps from day one. I remember the night before he lost it. I had asked him if he was alright, because he had a weird look in his eyes. He just ignored me and never blinked once.

At four o'clock the following morning, Petty Officer Aquino came through the bay yelling and kicking his garbage can like he did every morning. As he passed in front of my rack, he looked at Wong who was still lying in his bed. (For the sake of my mother who will be reading this book, I have softened the language a bit) "Wong!" He screamed at the top of his voice "You had better get your gosh darn butt out of that rack right now! Who do you think you are? The mostly feathered Admiral?"

Wong threw back his blanket and jumped out of bed. Then he pointed his finger right at Petty Officer Aquino and said "Westfall, go get your rifle! Shoot this piece of soap right in the gosh darn head. He is evil!" Then Wong started walking slowly, side to side and making weird sounds, kind of like the wind blowing. Petty Officer Aquino looked like he had seen a ghost. He jumped back and said "Get this crazy man away from me! Someone call the Shore Patrol!"

A few minutes later, three men came in from the hospital. As soon as Wong saw them, he started jumping from top bunk to top bunk. The whole time he was screaming "Kill those mother flakers... they will destroy us all!" A couple of minutes later, he over shot his mark and fell to the deck. The guys in the white coats quickly jumped on him and shackled him. As they were carrying him out, he looked at me and said "Westfall, don't let them take me. Tell my mother where I am" And that was the last anyone ever saw of Wong.

The time I spent at Great Lakes was very challenging. I couldn't figure out why it was so important to fold my underwear in a Navy fashion. Then one day it dawned on me... they didn't care about my underwear, they cared about how I followed directions. Once I realized this, life got much better. The last couple weeks of boot camp seemed easier. I couldn't believe it... I was actually going to survive.

Finally, graduation day arrived! I was so excited. I had no idea where exactly I was going after boot camp, but at that time I did not care. I just wanted to leave Great Lakes. The ceremony was going to be held in the big parade hanger, and all the family members and guests we going to be there watching us march by.

For the past two months, we have been learning how to march. Back and forth, round and round the drill hall. We marched and marched and marched. "By the left flank, march" Petty officer Aquino would yell. Then "Right oblique, march!" I can still hear him yelling twenty five years later. On several occasions, some of the company would miss a command and turn the wrong way. It was pretty funny when everyone would walk into each other, kind of like the keystone cops. Whenever we would do that, Petty Officer Aquino would get so angry, he would turn red!

At the graduation ceremony, there were eight companies celebrating the completion of boot camp. One by one, we would march by the Admiral, waiting for him to salute. We knew that we were all going to be able to leave the base that night, but if the Admiral gave you a double salute, your company would get two nights off. This is where it paid off to be good. As we were marching by, I was so sure we were the best! That is, until Seaman Corpavelli dropped his piece. Yep. That was just dandy. No double salute for us. After thinking about it, it really didn't matter, as long as I was leaving that awful place.

I graduated from boot camp in early April, and went directly to the Naval Submarine School in New London, Connecticut. I was so happy to be anywhere but Great Lakes! Connecticut was very enjoyable during the summer months. The air was crisp and refreshing, and the cool breeze seemed to blow constantly. This was my first time anywhere in New England, and I was going to make the best of it. After all, how hard could sub school be anyway? I guess I was about to find out.

The whole purpose for sub school was to get future submariners ready for sea duty. The type of submarine we were learning about was the newest submarine of the United States Navy fleet, the Los Angeles Class Fast Attack. The reason it was called 'Los Angeles' class was because the Navy always refers to the name of the first ship of that class, in this case it was the USS Los Angeles (SSN-688). I was expected to learn everything about it, from the air pressure and hydraulic system, to the trim and drain system, which keeps the sub from sinking to the bottom of the ocean. I was also going to have to learn everything about life on a submarine, and I was going to have to do it in six weeks. It was obvious that there was not going to be a lot of time for partying.

Coming from a good home and a big family, my mom was always taking care of us. She would do everything to ensure we were well taken care of, including all of the family's laundry. Needless to say, laundry was one of the many adventures I was now having to experience. But how hard could it be? You throw in the dirty clothes, dump in some soap and push a button... so easy a monkey could do it.

I remember when I first arrived at the Submarine Base. I wanted to look my absolute best so the instructors would have a good impression of me. My uniforms were starting to look a bit dingy, so a buddy of mine suggested I use bleach. Since all of my summer uniforms were white, it seemed to be a no-brainer. So, I went to the Navy Exchange and bought a gallon jug of bleach. Because I really wanted to impress my instructors, I had to make sure enough bleach was used. After putting all of my white clothes into the washing machine, I carefully poured about ten gurgles on top of the clothes. When that was done, I started the machine and went to watch a movie in the day room.

After an hour or so, I went in to put my clothes in the dryer, but something was wrong. The bottom of the washing machine was filled with soupy looking white stuff. When I reached in to take out my clothes, the only thing that came out was the rubber waist bands from my underwear. I was horrified! I had melted my entire summer wardrobe, about two hundred dollars worth of clothes. I called my mom as fast as I could because I knew she could tell me what to do. Much to my dismay, she said there was nothing that could be done, and she suggested that I call her first before my next experiment with new laundry techniques. Now, I had to run to the Exchange to buy new uniforms...

The first week of sub school was very challenging. The instructor that was assigned to our class was very professional, but a bit scary. I decided to put my best efforts forward, and just get through it. There were four hours of night study offered each night, but that was for losers. I was going to pass without effort!

When Friday came around, I was confident that I would ace the test. How hard could it be anyway? It was a Navy test... After two hours of filling in the blanks, I finished with confidence.

Well, as it turns out, I failed miserably. I wasn't sure exactly what happened, but I decided to stay close to the school that weekend and hit the books. If I were to fail the test the next Friday, I would be set back a week in my training. My buddies did much better than I did, and they seemed to take the test in stride. It did bother me a bit, but I decided to put it behind me and just study harder for the next test.

The next Friday came and I was pretty confident that I knew what I was doing. The test seemed easier than the last one, but I took all the time allotted to make sure I answered each question properly. But, once again, I failed the test. The next morning I was dropped from my class and I received notice that I was to report to the Academic Review Board on the following Monday. I was very upset and had no idea why I kept failing. That weekend I stayed in the barracks and studied. Maybe this submarine duty was not such a good idea after all.

Chapter Two

When Monday morning rolled around, I showed up early for my Academic Review Board. When I was called in, I saw that there were four officers and my instructor sitting at the table. They questioned me on my study habits and asked me how I was getting along since I had come to the Submarine School. I answered all of their questions to the best of my ability, and told them that I was doing well. After the discussion was over, the board had determined that I did everything as I was supposed to, and just needed a bit more time to adjust to this type of school environment. They allowed me to join the next class that was coming through the school the following week.

Once again I started the school, this time with a new attitude. Not only did I spend all of my time studying, I also reported back to the school every evening for four hours of night study. Night study was a voluntary gathering at the main school house where students could compare notes and discuss what they had learned that day in class. Most of the students blew off night study, but I needed to show the Academic Review Board that I was serious about passing my course, and would do everything in my power to do it.

There was always an instructor available at night study to answer any questions that a student might have. He also kept a record of all of the students who showed up, and what time they left.

Friday soon came around again, and I took my third test. I was very careful this time to make sure I understood the questions, and answered them completely. Three hours later, I was pulled into the instructor's officer and told I had failed yet again. I was so angry; I just wanted to catch the first plane back to Alabama. Once again, I was directed to report to the Academic Review Board. I had heard many of the instructors's talking about students and the issues they had, and one thing was certain: Nobody ever survived a second visit to the Academic Review Board.

The following Monday morning I reported back to the Review Board as ordered. As I was sitting in the waiting room, forty-five minutes early, I was wondering what part of the South Pole they would send me too. A couple minutes after eight o'clock, I was called into the board room.

One of the chief's at the table said he had been watching me since the very first week, and he thought he knew where my problem was. He explained to the board that there was only one reason that I would be failing the class, especially after all the extra study time I was putting in. After a few minutes of discussion among themselves, the chief directed me to report to the lower base that evening, and meet him pier side at the USS Groton (SSN-694). A few moments later I was dismissed.

I have to admit, I was pretty excited about that evening. I had never actually been on a submarine, and now I was going to see one in action! As usual, I arrived pier side, half an hour early. When the chief walked up to where I was standing, he asked "Are you ready to see one of the most awesome boats in the world? Follow me," and he started across the gangplank, or as we called it in the sea going Navy, the brow.

This was not only my first visit aboard a submarine; it was also my first time on any Navy ship. There is a certain protocol when boarding or crossing over any Navy vessel. The first thing to remember is that the United States flag, or the ensign as we call it, is posted at the after end (back) of every ship. It's only flown during daylight hours, so you must always salute the ensign first, and then board the ship. Once you had come up to the top of the brow and are actually at the ship, you must salute the Officer of the Deck and say "Request permission to come aboard." Once the OOD gives you permission, you can come aboard.

Another thing that was made clear to me when boarding the Groton was that submarines are not called ships, they are called boats. Back in the early days of the submarine, the vessels were much smaller and resembled a closed fishing boat. During World War II, submarines picked up the name "pig boats". Many people believe this term was used because submarines use dolphins as a kind of mascot, and dolphins were sometimes called "sea pigs." Personally, I believe they were called "pig boats" because at that time the lack of space and ventilation made submarine life very smelly.

The Chief walked me through the boat and showed me how the trim and drain system worked. A submarine is designed to dive or surface rapidly under complete control. It must be able to proceed on the surface and to submerge at the desired rate of speed to the depths required. To do so quickly and efficiently, the submarine must maintain forward and after balance, and stability throughout the boat. The chief function of the trim and drain system is to maintain this forward and after balance by controlling the amount and distribution of water in the various tanks used for this purpose.

Since I had been studying so hard the past three weeks, I understood how the trim and drain system worked, and where it was controlled from.

After walking through the boat and discussing various systems, the chief told me it was time to go. As we walked back to the school house, the chief explained what he was going to do with me.

"Seaman Westfall, the problem is how your mind works. You can understand all the information, and you can see it in your head. But when you take a written test, all the information gets screwed up. Now, as soon as we get back to the school house, I am going to give you the last test you failed orally. Once that is done, we will talk more.

After the chief administered the test to me, he graded it and called my back into his office. "Westfall, you aced it. You scored one hundred percent, and only one other student has done that this year. Tomorrow, you will be put back into your class and every Friday I will be administering your test orally. Since I have been here, you are the only person to ever survive a second trip to the Academic Review Board."

The next day I was put back into my original class, and life was good. The rest of my time at the Submarine School was much more relaxed, and I was able to enjoy myself a bit.

Before I knew it, we had reached the end of the course, and it was our last weekend. Graduation was on Monday, and my buddies and I wanted the last weekend to be a weekend to remember. One of my buddies, Mark Masterson, invited me and a few others from our class to his parents' house on Beacon Beach in New Jersey.

The next day, Saturday, we hit the road. Since there were so many of us going, we had to take four cars to get us all to New Jersey. We raced to see who would get there first, and two speeding tickets later, we all arrived. Since this was really the first road trip any of us had taken since boot camp, we were very excited about being turned lose!

Marks parents house was located right on the beach. It was obvious that they were loaded, and Mark told us that they would be away in New Hampshire for the weekend. When we got there, we had already missed a lot of that day, so we started partying hard.

Since she was home for the weekend, Marks big sister Megan was going to hang out with us. Megan was a model for a major soda company, and very nice looking. She kept walking around in her string bikini, which made it very hard for me to focus on anything else. The huge bucket of margaritas she made for us helped to ease my pain a bit.

The rest of the day was spent on the beach, or as Mark liked to call it, in his back yard. I really hadn't had very much to drink in a while, what with boot camp and sub school, so my tolerance was pretty low. Megan wanted to lie in the sand and work on her very nice tan, and asked me if I wanted to lay with her. Me, being the dummy I was, said "Sure" and laid next to her. That was not a good move.

The next few hours went by kind of fast. Since we had been drinking, I quickly fell asleep in the hot sun. Because I had been studying so hard and really needed some sleep, the next three hours flew by. I didn't think to use any sunscreen, so while I was sleeping I was getting quite sunburned. Megan was sweet enough to wake me and flip me over so I would burn evenly on both sides. By night fall, I had second degree burns over ninety-five percent of my body. Needless to say, my afternoon on the beach with a beautiful model was less than I expected it to be.

We left Beacon beach about two o'clock the next afternoon so we could get back to Groton in plenty of time for the graduation. I was in so much pain, I probably should have gone to the hospital, but if I did, I would have been put on report. The Navy had a strict policy about Sailors who were stupid enough to do what I did. Life sucked.

The following morning at eleven o'clock, I walked in my graduation. I have never been in so much pain in my life, but I did it. Never again would I be so stupid, no matter how pretty she is.

Early in June of that year, I was to report to my "A" school in San Diego, California. An "A" school is the primary school for a Navy job. Later in one's career, they might go to a "C" school, where they would learn the more intricate details of the trade.

I was very excited, especially since I had never even been west of the Mississippi River. California was beautiful! The temperature seems to always be perfect, and it didn't rain for the entire two months I was there.

Our class formed up the following Monday morning, and our lives as Navy Mess Specialists (MS's) began. It was all pretty easy compared to sub school. Since everyone in my class was right out of boot camp, I had about three months seniority over them. Being the most senior person allowed me to be put in charge of the class. It was my responsibility to form them up in the morning and march them all to the training center. Every Friday morning we had a formal dress inspection, and I had to stand out in front of the class and present them to our division officer. The very first time I did this, I was careful to stand as tall and still as I could so I could give the best impression possible.

On that very first morning, as I stood there saluting, just before the Division Officer came to inspect the class, a seagull flew over my head and crapped right down the front of my dress white uniform. Needless to say, everyone had a huge laugh at my expense. As soon as the inspection was over, I was dismissed to go back to the barracks and change my uniform.

MS "A" school was more of a cultural experience than anything else. I remember my first trip out into town with a couple of newly found buddies. We walked out the front gate and just down the road to Rosecrans, the main drag at that time. As we walked down the street I noticed every couple blocks there were pretty girls standing around, and they seemed to like me. Being the friendly guy that I was, I started talking to one of them. Her name was Lisa, and she told me she was from San Francisco, but moved down to San Diego to find work. When I asked her what she did for a living, she laughed and said "You are so sweet". I really didn't know what that meant, until my buddy Sampson explained it to me. He said "She's a prostitute, stupid." Wow! A real live hooker and she was talking to me like she had known me forever. I couldn't wait to call home and tell my brother Toby!

As we were leaving, Lisa made me promise to come back and see her, but I wasn't sure if she was just being friendly or what. Right then I realized just how far I was from Beulah, Alabama.

San Diego is about eighteen miles north of Tijuana, Mexico. Now I had heard stories about Mexico, and especially Tijuana. The stories were always about wonderful music, pretty women and rivers flowing with tequila. I really wasn't looking for women or tequila, but I had never been anywhere in my life, and now I had the chance to see another country. I had to go to Tijuana!

The following Saturday morning I headed out with Sampson and another buddy named Shaun Bateman. We took a taxi and soon we were at the border. A few minutes later, we were walking across into Mexico. Once we were actually in Mexico, we saw hundreds of street venders selling their wares.

I was especially touched by a little boy who introduced himself as Jose'. Jose' was selling little knitted hand towels. They were handmade and each of them had a picture of a humble Mexican home on them. Jose' was dressed in a torn, dirty shirt, and it looked like he had not had a bath in a couple weeks. I wondered where he lived or when the last time he had a good meal was.

"Hi, Jose'. How much are your hand towels?" I asked. "Senior, this are fifteen dollars" he said in broken English. Smiling, I happily handed the boy thirty dollars, and asked for two. He smiled and said "Gracias, Senior." I walked away feeling good about myself, knowing that I helped a poor boy to survive in a sometimes cruel world.

As we walked through the street, I noticed an older woman with a table full of hand towels, exactly like the ones I bought from poor little Jose'. "How much?" I asked the woman. "Four dollars each" she said. Then, I noticed a small boy sitting behind her wagon. It was poor little Jose', and he was eating from a big bag of candy he had just bought. I said "Hey, you tricked me!" He smiled at me and said "Welcome to Mexico, Gringo!"

Our day in Tijuana was wonderful! The beautiful colors and the cheerful music made it seem like the friendliest place on Earth. We found a great restaurant where they served two pound burritos filled with chopped beef and chicken.

Now, the food in Tijuana was excellent, but the water was a problem. In the United States, it's easy to take drinking water for granted. We just turn on the faucet, and there it is clean and delicious. In many countries, the water is not filtered and treated like back at home. Mexico was one of these countries. The Navy made sure we all knew not to drink the water or the locally made beer, which was made from the water. We decided that as long as we were in Mexico, we would drink Bohemia, a wonderful Mexican beer. Whenever we were tired of the beer, we would have a couple shots of tequila.

As the evening came, Bateman decided to head back home. Sampson and I walked him to the boarder, but decided to stay a bit longer. An hour later, we found ourselves in a small cantina operated by a local woman and her four beautiful daughters. Life was good, until I remembered that I had given my wallet to Bateman. Earlier, I had been playing in a fountain with some local children, and asked him to hang on to it for me. Now, Bateman and my wallet were safely back on American soil, and I am stuck in Tijuana, with no way to prove that I am an American Citizen.

The next three hours was spent at the border crossing talking with the Federales (Mexican Federal Police). Just after three o'clock that morning, a very angry chief showed up from the Naval Base to escort me back across the boarder. Such was my first trip to Mexico.

Before I knew it, I was graduating from "A" school, and my 'vacation' in San Diego was over. I made a lot of friends there, and it was hard to leave them behind. That's when I learned that the Navy was all about leaving shipmates behind, and meeting new shipmates. I also knew that I would see many of them again, if I stayed in the Navy. Who knows? If the submarine I am going to is as fun as MS "A" school was, I just may stay in the Navy forever.

In early September, I was ordered to report to the Pre-Commissioned Unit Salt Lake City (PCU-716) in Newport News, Virginia. A real submarine! Well, almost a real submarine. A pre-commissioned unit is a boat that is under construction. Once a boat is completed, it will be commissioned, and then it will be called a United States Ship (USS). Until then, it is a PCU

I was pretty excited about becoming a part of the Salt Lake City, but I had no idea what to expect. The Newport News Shipyard was huge, and the taxi driver dropped me off at this big white three story building. Since it was Friday, most of the crew had already gone home for the weekend. The sailor on watch led me back to where the cooks worked, but there was no galley. As a matter of fact, there was no sign of a submarine at all. I was starting to wonder if I was in the right place.

I asked the watch where the boat was, and he told me it was a short walk from the building in a dry dock. When it was time for the watches to change, I followed the men down to the submarine. Wow! I had never seen anything like this in Alabama. The dry dock was huge... about the size of four football fields. The sub was standing in the middle of the dry dock with several walk boards, or 'brows' allowing the many shipyard workers to come and go from the boat. There were wires, pipes and duct work going everywhere. If you looked really hard, you could see traces of a submarine under all the tarps and plastic.

Before I could go aboard the boat, I had to request permission from the Topside Watch. His job was to protect the ship from unauthorized personnel. Security was the most important function of the Topside Watch. Once he had checked to see if my name was in the topside log, I was allowed to go down.

This boat was unlike anything I had ever seen before. There were no bulkheads (walls) in place at all. I could see from the forward torpedo hatch in the front of the boat all the way to the reactor compartment in the middle of the boat. A 688 class submarine, when fully assembled, has three levels. The Salt Lake City was over a year away from commissioning, so there were no levels at all. From where I was standing, I could see three stories down into the torpedo room bilges. It was very hard to imagine this as a submarine at all.

The biggest jobs going on at that time were all the welding and pipefitting. Every welder needed ventilation and a "hot watch", a second person keeping watch in case a fire was started on the other side of the wall or the deck being welded. There must have been a hundred shipyard workers aboard the ship around the clock. Now I can see why the crew had to live in a building!

The mission of the food service department underway on a sea going ship is to manage and cook nutritional meals for the crew. Since there was no galley in the PCU building, our mission changed a bit. Now we were in charge of taking everyone's order for lunch, ordering the right sandwiches, hoagies and gyros and delivering them to the crew. Not exactly the naval career I had in mind, but the work was easy. We stood duty a couple times a week, and that consisted of sleeping in the PCU building, standing a desk and phone watch, then going home. Life was good.

When I wasn't at work, I stayed out in town at the apartment complex the Navy was leasing for us. It was about ten miles from the PCU building, and the boat had a private bus that ran back and forth to pick up the duty sections. The apartments were pretty nice. They were large, two story buildings with laundry rooms and were located right behind a huge shopping center just off of Mercury Boulevard, one of the major highways in Newport News. I remember that I used to spend my evenings off at a local Chuck-E-Cheese where I could get a medium pizza and a pitcher of beer for like six bucks.

I would sit in the sports room and watch the huge wall size television. That was me, Mr. Excitement.

As the ship was slowly getting put together, the crew had to keep up with all of its training. We had drills constantly, things like "Repel Boarders" where there would be a threat to security and we would have to find the threat and stop it. Since there was only a couple ways to get into a submarine, the easiest way to repel boarders is to shut the hatches. Then, you had to find the "bad guys" who boarded the boat. This was kind of fun because the shipyard workers were suppose to stand still and not move during the drills. If someone was running toward the exit, they would most likely be the "bad guy", so we were duty bound to stop them. Of course, sometimes the yard birds wouldn't hear the alarm due to all the noise, and if it was someone we didn't care for, we would tackle them and slam them to the deck. It was lots more fun than it should have been.

The USS Buffalo (PCU-715) was one of the two other boats in our building. The Buffalo had just returned from "Alpha" Trials and scored pretty well. Alpha Trials included diving to test depth, executing an emergency surface, and testing the ship's propulsion plant performance. The next week they were due to depart on "Bravo" trials, where they will do more testing on speed and depth control. Our Chief had volunteered me and two other junior cooks to go with them to give us some underway experience. Since none of us had even seen a real submarine galley before, this was the perfect opportunity for us to get our "sea legs". I was really anxious to go, so that Sunday night I set my alarm clock and checked it twice. I was finally going to be a real sailor!

The next day I woke up promptly at... ten thirty? The USS Buffalo was scheduled to set sail at eight o'clock that morning. My alarm had been set to go off at six o'clock, giving me plenty of time to take a shower, get dressed and get to the boat. The only problem was the alarm was set to play the radio, like usual, but I had accidentally turned down the volume, and when it went off I couldn't hear it. My heart sank to the floor! My very first underway assignment and I missed movement! This meant that I would automatically be placed on report, and I would probably be busted back to childhood. This was serious. I quickly dressed and ran all the way to the shipyard.

When I arrived (out of breath) at the shipyard, I was praying hard and steady. I have been a praying man my entire life and I was no stranger to asking God for help. But, I honestly didn't think there would be any divine intervention today. As I reached the dock, I couldn't believe my eyes... there was the USS Buffalo! It seems that the forward escape hatch had a problem with its seal, and that pushed the underway time back to noon. Life, once again, was good.

I quickly boarded the boat, and made my way to the galley. I was already nervous since I didn't know anyone, and since I was late reporting aboard I was expecting to get chewed out by someone. Once I found my way to the galley, I met the Leading Chief Petty Officer, Senior Chief Balagtas. He was calmly rolling out homemade dinner rolls. When I told him who I was and apologized for being late, he smiled and said "That's alright... it won't happen again, will it?" I just smiled and nervously shook my head, and then I went to stash my gear.

There are usually seven men in the Mess Department. Two galley day cooks prepare all the food for the crew during the day. That includes Lunch, Dinner and preparations for the eleven o'clock meal known as midrats. Then, there is the Night Baker, who does all the baking and serves midrats and breakfast. Next, there is the Wardroom cook, who feeds the officers. Then there is the jack of the dust, who is in charge of breaking out the food for the next day and all the store rooms and storage tanks. Next, there is the Leading Petty Officer, who usually does all the records and returns, keeping the books just right so the good people at the Pentagon leave us alone. Lastly, is the Leading Chief Petty Officer, who runs the whole mess and coordinates all of the training.

My job this underway would be an assistant to the duty cook, which included washing pots and pans, serving the crew, and TDU operations. The TDU or Trash Disposal Unit was basically a torpedo tube that shoots trash straight down into the ocean. It's a very nasty job, so naturally they chose me to do it. During the cold war, one of the most important day to day things that American or Soviet submarines would do is to dispose of trash properly. During the Second World War, Japanese fishing trawlers would gather up floating trash and go through it, collecting valuable information about allied submarines. They could usually find out the name of the ships patrolling the area, the names of some of the crew members, where they were heading and approximately what time they came past that point.

There were two kinds of garbage. First was the compacted trash, which was compressed into a rolled sheet metal can about three feet tall and about twelve inches wide. Once it was properly weighted and sealed, it was "launched" down to the bottom of the ocean with a vertical torpedo tube. The cans had to weigh more than fifty or sixty pounds, or the trash would float up the surface. The second type of trash was called a "wet bag". Wet bags were for trash that wouldn't compact, like meat scraps or dirty wet rags from the engine room. Once the bag was filled, it also had to be a certain weight before being launched. The whole process was nasty and left you smelling worse than the garbage you had just packed.

When the garbage was too light, you would have to add seven pound steel weights to it, until it was heavy enough to sink. These are called Trash Disposal Unit weights, or TDU weights. One of the most crucial supplies a sea going submarine must have is TDU weights. More than one Supply Officer has been relieved of his position due to leaving port without enough TDU weights.

Running the TDU room properly is one of the most important jobs on the boat. At the time, I thought it was a horrible job, and I hated it. Now, as I look back through the many years of my sub duty, I can see that my time on the USS Buffalo was crucial to my success as a submariner.

The galley on a fast attack submarine is very small, but efficient. In a space that is half the size of most living rooms are two convection ovens, two steam jacketed kettles, one large griddle, one high pressure steamer, three deep sinks, one dish washer, six warming drawers, and a proofing oven. Most of the time there are two cooks and five mess attendants that the crew fondly calls "cranks". The cranks are responsible for all the cleaning on the Crews mess. Out on the mess decks are seven tables that will seat approximately twenty-four men, out of a crew of a hundred and twenty. That means if everyone wants to eat, they have about fifteen minutes to rotate through. It sounds a bit chaotic, but the process is quite efficient.

There were four meals served every day. Breakfast at five o'clock, lunch at eleven o'clock, dinner at five o'clock in the evening and midrats is served at eleven o'clock at night. On a sea going ship, stations are manned twenty four hours a day, so the guys get hungry. Midrats usually consisted of some leftovers, ravioli or maybe pizza. As long as the crew got fed and the food was good, we were doing our jobs. Since I was on the day shift, I worked from about seven every morning until eight at night. At the end of each shift, it was time to do the trash again. My life sucked, but that's alright. I was on a United States Navy nuclear powered fast attack submarine!

Every morning at seven, I was awakened by the night crank. I had just enough time to get dressed, shave, brush my teeth, and get to the galley for breakfast. As soon as breakfast was over, I was expected to start working. There were lots of things to do to prepare for lunch.

When cooking on a submarine, timing and flexibility are everything. Every day during "Bravo" trials there are tests that have to be run throughout the boat. Some of these tests are run to see how quiet the boat is during certain operational evolutions. Other tests are run to see how deep the boat can go. Still more test are run to see how fast the ship can react to things like fire, flooding or collisions. When cooking aboard a sub, you have to be ready for anything, because when the drills are over, the crew still wants to eat.

After five grueling weeks of being underway, we finally arrived back at the shipyard. It was so nice to be back! After spending a month or so under the water, you really miss the sunshine and the fresh air.

Liberty was down as soon as the brow was across, so I was heading to the house. I had three paychecks in my pocket and I couldn't wait to cash them and have a nice relaxing weekend. There was a grocery store right by my apartment that cashed military checks, and once I cashed them I would put most of it in the bank for my next trip home, and keep a bit to 'relax' with.

By the time I got home, it was almost dark. I decided to go ahead and walk to the grocery store, even though we were warned about that side of town. I knew that the grocery store would be opened late, so I quickly walked to the shopping center. After a few minutes, I had cashed my checks and started walking back to the house.

The street that led to my apartment complex had nice, simple houses lining both sides of the street. There were a few street lights, and the occasional car. As I was walking home, I noticed a man had stepped out from between two of the houses just ahead of me. He looked kind of shady, so I decided to cross the street and walk on the other side. A minute later, I saw that he was running toward me. Before I knew it he had stopped in front of me and pulled out a pocket knife. "Give me your wallet" he said in a raspy whispering tone. I was scared to death! I had never been mugged before and I just froze. I could see that the man was white and he was about five feet eight. He was wearing a black ski cap and a long black raincoat.

As I was reaching for my wallet, I started praying that I would live through this. At the same time I was thinking about the money I just got for cashing my pay checks. Slowly, I pulled out my wallet. As I was handing it over to him, I accidentally dropped it on the sidewalk. He quickly reached down to pick it up and without thinking I drew back and kicked him in the center of his forehead as hard as I could! He dropped the knife and before I could react one way of the other he started to run away. I have no idea what I was trying to do, but I grabbed his raincoat and tried to hold him back. He quickly wriggled out of it and ran down the street back between the houses.

For a few moments, I just stood there trying to figure out what had happened. I reached down and picked up my wallet and the knife, and I walked to the seven-eleven down the street to call the police. After answering a few questions, the Police Officer on the phone asked me to look in the pockets of the raincoat for any identification the mugger may have left. I asked him to wait a minute so I could check and then found a roll of small bills in the left pocket. There was thirty-two dollars there, and a gum wrapper, but that was all. As I told the officer on the phone what I had found, he started laughing. When I asked him what was so funny he said "You are the only person I ever knew of who made a profit off of being mugged!" He suggested that I keep the money and the knife, and be more careful next time. It sounded like good advice to me.

Chapter Three

The next Monday I reported back to the Salt Lake City. I was a bit disappointed at the lack of progress over the past few weeks. The boat was still a mess. There were still a million shipyard workers coming and going constantly, and we were still in charge of buying the sandwiches.

On a submarine, everyone must qualify. To qualify, you must learn everything there is to know about the boat, from the sonar dome to the screw. The qualification process consists of about fourteen months of very hard study and testing given by the ships onboard experts. Once a person was qualified, they would receive their dolphins, which is the highly coveted Submarine Warfare pin. Until you were qualified, you were known by the entire world as a "nub" (non useful body). I was a nub.

One of the most fascinating things I found out about submarines was how the reactor worked. Nuclear submarines contain a nuclear power plant within a shielded compartment in the boat. The science and technology of nuclear propulsion is complex, but the basic concepts of it are simple. Within the nuclear reactor, atoms are split, generating heat. This heat is used to create highly pressured steam that is routed to the electricity and propulsion generator turbines, causing them to rotate and create power for both the ship's electronics and propeller. The condensed steam is then routed back through the pipes to be used again for the same process.

The nuclear reactor that powers the submarine emits radiation. In order to protect the crew, the reactor compartment is shielded by steel, water tanks and polyethylene. With this protection, the crew members and the outside world are well shielded from the reactor's harmful radiation. In fact, the crew members are actually exposed to less radiation than the general public. This is because on land there is naturally-occurring radiation, called background radiation, and water acts as a radiation shield. So when a nuclear submarine is submerged in water, the crew is actually being exposed to less radiation than what they would be exposed to on land.

One advantage to being on the Salt Lake City was the fact that the reactor had not yet been installed. The reactor compartment was still empty, as it was just nearing completion. Since there was no reactor, I was able to go into the reactor compartment and really see how it was put together.

Now that I had been around for a sufficient time, I was able to qualify as the Topside Watch. This was the most important watch on the ship up until now. There was a huge book in the topside watches podium called the Top Side Access Log. The name of everyone who was allowed access to the boat was in that book. If their name could not be found in the book, they were not allowed to go down, no matter what. If one of us screwed up and let the wrong person onto the boat, heads would roll.

I remember the very first time I stood the watch. It was about eight o'clock at night, cold and raining very hard. A man I did not recognize came up to me and handed me his ID card. I carefully read it and popped to attention. It was the base Commodore, and he looked very angry. I quickly shuffled through the topside log, but I couldn't find his name. I looked again slower and more carefully, but could not find his name. He started yelling and said "Don't you know who I am? I am your Captains Boss!" I knew who he was, but if his name wasn't in our topside log, he could not board the ship, no matter who he was. I mustered up the courage and said "Sir, I am sorry but your name is not in my topside log." As my Navy career flashed before my eyes, he pointed at me and yelled "I'll be back, and you had better pray that my name isn't in your book or you are in big trouble!"

The rest of my watch was quiet, and when I was properly relieved, I was ordered to report to the Duty Officer in the Ward room. Well, it was a nice eight months. My time in the Navy was brief, but good. Now, all that was left was for the Duty Officer to throw me off the ship for denying access to the Commodore. I just hoped it would be quick and merciful.

I knocked on the Ward Room door and was asked to come in immediately. When I went in, the Duty Officer, Mr. Delphino, asked me what had happened topside. When I told him he smiled and looked through a stack of papers. Then he said "I'm sorry. It's my fault for not having the topside log updated. You did exactly what you were supposed to do." Then he shook my hand and said "Thanks." I just smiled and said "No problem." I still can't believe I lived through that night.

A couple weeks later I was told that I would be loaned out again. This time it was the USS Baltimore (SSN-704), which had suffered the temporary loss of four of its cooks. The ship had recently come into port after a very hard run, and when the cooks took out the trash, well, they didn't come back.

The Baltimore was heading out to an undisclosed location, and I was told it would come back whenever Uncle Sam told it to. That was one of the problems with the cold war... It was not very concerned with people's schedules. I was told to pack for forever, and then we would see.

I arrived the following morning at six o'clock, just as I was supposed to. You see, when I almost missed ships movement on the USS Buffalo, I made sure that was the last time I was late for any ship in my career.

When I reported to the Leading Chief, he told me that I was going to be working in the wardroom for this deployment. The wardroom is where the officers live, and they get treated a bit differently than the rest of the crew.

Submarines are much smaller than most Navy ships, so the Officers eat the same food the crew does. The officers live in Staterooms, which were a very small room with two built in desks and three bunks. The Commanding Officer (CO) had the largest stateroom on the upper deck, just forward of the Control Center. The Executive Officer (XO) had a stateroom just forward of the CO's, and he had an extra bunk in his stateroom for high ranking riders. The CO and the XO shared a bathroom, or as the Navy calls it, a 'head'.

On the middle level is the main wardroom, or the Officers Mess. This was where the officers were served four meals a day. They also held had meetings, training for the Junior Officers (JO's), and played games at times. There were three smaller staterooms by the wardroom, where the JO's slept. There was one officer's head shared by nine JO's. It was a bit cramped at times, but that's what submarine duty was all about.

My job as the wardroom MS was to keep all of it cleaned and organized. I also had to do the officers laundry on Saturdays. The dirty clothes would be put into large mesh bags that would fit into the boats one washing machine. When the wash cycle was completed, the bags would go into the boats one dryer. Once the laundry was done, it was put on the officer's racks for them to fold.

Wardroom duty was not very glamorous, but it did have its advantages. A good wardroom mess attendant would be around the Captain and the XO all day long, thus hearing about ships events long before the rest of the crew. There were also many advantages when it came to eating. The wardroom had first choice of all the crews' food, which meant they also ate better. In the end, it's wasn't so bad.

During the cold war, there were many places that we went that we couldn't talk about. You know, 'we were never there' kind of places. Well, this was one of those places we never went to. Battle stations was called about four o'clock in the morning, but we were not sure why. We weren't scheduled for any drills, so it must have been something unexpected.

As I was bringing the Skipper his coffee, I overheard him talking to the Officer of the Deck. I heard him say that we were in very close proximity to three Soviet submarines, and they were not playing games. The Baltimore was in a very stressful situation, and quite honestly, I didn't think we were going to come back this time. We stayed at battle stations for three days. Every time I heard the JO's talking in the wardroom, they were more serious than usual. I remember seeing one of the youngest officers' praying once, and I noticed he had been crying. Yes, I was nervous. I also remember sitting in my bunk and writing a letter to my mother, one of those letters you know that will never get there. Either you will get through the situation and decide to throw it away, or you won't get through the situation and no one will ever see the letter. In my twenty-two years in the Navy, I was never so sure that I was going to die. Yeah, it was one of those missions.

Submarines are designed to go a certain depth. Normally, a submarine would never go past that depth, unless there was an emergency or something. We went past that depth several times over that three day period. The ship stayed at "Ultra Quiet" over those three days as well. That meant there could be no noise at all. No shutting doors or hatches, no clanking pots and pans, no scrapping the bilges. Everyone had to take off their shoes, whisper and the only food anyone could eat was sandwiches. I remember a couple fights breaking out between some of the guys on the mess decks. The stress was intense, and it was getting to everyone.

The boat pulled back into Norfolk on a Friday. I was under orders to stay with the boat for another week in port, until their new cooks arrived. One thing that I was sure of was my nerves were fried and I needed some relaxation. I needed a drink. Since I really didn't have any good friends aboard the Baltimore, I decided to walk to the base EM club, the "Trade winds".

As I was standing in line to get into the club, I saw an old buddy of mine from sub school standing in line just in front of me. He waited for me and we went in together. At that time, the Trade Winds was set up like a half circle. The band pit was in the center of the huge room, and tables were in horseshoe shaped rows, each row one level above the last. We found a table on the fourth row and sat down. Slowly, I was sipping my beer while listening to the music. I didn't want to talk, I wasn't interested in meeting girls, I just wanted to be left alone and drink my beer.

Timmy Bowen was a good guy, but he loved flirting. He had caught the eye of a girl sitting at a table with about eight Marines, and she was smiling at him. At that time, all the gates on NOB Norfolk were manned by Marines. These guys worked hard, trained harder, and when the day was over, they were out trying to enjoy themselves. Since the girl and the Marines were all behind me, I didn't see Timmy blowing kisses at her. If I did, I would have reminded him that Marines were not particularly fond of sailors, and he was badly outnumbered. But, as I said before, I had my back to them and was in my own world.

I didn't see the Marines getting angry. I didn't realize how drunk Timmy was. All I remember is getting hit in the back of the head with an eight inch glass ashtray which one of the Marines threw at Timmy. I didn't really think about what happened next, I just grabbed the chair next to me, turned around and threw it at the Marines table. Well, those Marines were fast. Every one of them dodged the chair, but the girl wasn't so lucky. She was knocked out of her chair and started screaming. Everything happened really fast after that. I remember getting punched, and punching all kinds of people. Glass was breaking, tables were flipping over, people were running and screaming... it was total chaos.

Just as I was thinking about getting out of there, I was slammed to the floor by a huge Marine. I decided it was probably in my best interest to just stay there and quietly cooperate with him as he placed handcuffs on me. So much for my quiet evening...

That was the first time I had ever ridden in a patty wagon. Riding back to the pier with me was one of the Marines I was fighting with. I remember wanting a cigarette really bad, but my hands were cuffed behind my back, and I didn't have a light. He also wanted a smoke, but he didn't have one. He did have a lighter, but he was also cuffed behind the back. We decided to work together in our drunken stupor, so we both laid on the floor of the patty wagon. Bill, my new best friend, reached into my left pocket and pulled out my pack of smokes. I reached into his pocket and got out his lighter, then after a bit of wiggling, he held out a cigarette for me to grab with my lips. Then, I passed him the lighter and he lit it behind his back, burning his hand in the process. Finally, I got the cigarette in my mouth lit just in time for the back doors to open. There we were back at the USS Baltimore. Once the Duty Officer signed for me, I was off to bed. Tomorrow there would be Hell to pay, but that was tomorrow.

The next morning I heard my name being called over the ships announcement system, the 1MC. It seems I was in a missing status, since I fell asleep in someone else's bunk and they couldn't find me. "MSSN Westfall, report to the ward room." I quickly got up and ran to the ward room where the CO was waiting for me. I opened the door, walked in and popped the sharpest salute I could and said "MSSN Westfall reporting as ordered, SIR!" Just as I had started sounding off, I heard several of the JO's snickering under their breath.

Then I realized why they were laughing at me... I was quite the sight. I had two black eyes, a busted lip, my shirt was missing the left sleeve and my pants were torn right down the front.

The skipper asked me if I had anything to say for myself, and after thinking about it for a minute I said "Sir, I was very stressed out yesterday, and I just kind of unloaded with a few Marines at the club. It won't happen again." The Captain just shook his head and asked "Did you get it all out of your system?" I just smiled and said "Yes sir, I did." Then a smile slowly crossed his face. He said softly "Get out of my wardroom and make me some breakfast."

Everyone on board a United States Navy nuclear submarine has to qualify submarines. Until you are qualified in submarines, your life sucks. As a nub, you had very few privileges aboard ship. No matter what your rank is, if you are sitting in the crew's mess watching a movie, any qualified person can ask you to get up and let him sit in your seat. A qualified person can also take your place in the chow line. If you are doing anything recreational, qualified people will ask you why you are not studying instead. It just sucks to be a nub.

Qualification can take anywhere from ten to fourteen months, depending on your boats schedule. If you are underway on a mission, then opportunities for signatures come often. If your boat is in the shipyard, there are a lot less opportunities. So, my qualification program took a long, long time.

The way to qualify is to first study the system you want to get checked out on. There are five sets of SSM's (Ships Systems Manuals). This is a set of reference books that covers every system on the ship in great detail. If you show up for a signature and didn't study the SSM, bad things would happen. Once, I had an engineer spit his gum into the fold of my qual card and then stomp on it. The problem with this is you can't just throw it away because it has lots of valuable signatures on it. So, there I was using a butter knife and an ice cube trying to salvage my card. I did learn a very important thing that day... never go to another checkout without knowing the SSM first.

The best time to qualify in port is on a duty night. The ship consisted of about a hundred and twenty men and approximately fourteen officers. Most boats are split into four duty sections, each one staying aboard the boat for twenty four hours, then being relieved by the next section on duty. This way the boat is manned all the time, so if there is an emergency or if we have to get underway in a hurry, we could do it relatively fast. Normally, cooks didn't stand overnight duty, but if the cook made a particularly good meal, or maybe gave the guys and extra piece of pie, the checkouts come a lot easier. Life as a nub sucked, but being a cook defiantly made it easier.

Our crew was full of interesting people. First, let me tell you about the wardroom. Our Skipper's name was Daniel McKinley, a heavy drinking Irish man with a thick accent. Our Executive Officer's name was Oleg Khrushchev, who looked and sounded Russian, but we never asked. Our Engineer's name was Willy Henderson, a Redneck from the word go. The Navigator's name was Boris Trapski, from Poland.

Finally, our beloved COB (the Chief of the Boat), MMCM(SS) Rockdale. The very first day I met the COB he was in a wheelchair with two broken legs. He explained to me that he was a Harley riding atheist and when he was at the ships picnic he decided he would try to jump over four picnic tables on his Harley Davidson. Well, it didn't quite work out the way he intended it to, and there we were. What a command!

Another interesting person was Machinist Mate Third Class (SS) Robert McGregor. He was different, to say the least. One Saturday morning he had invited me over to his apartment to go over some checkout material. When someone offers to help you, you don't ever say no, you just go. Bob lived just across the apartment complex from me, on the second floor of his building.

When I arrived, it was just past ten o'clock in the morning. Bob opened the door without saying anything. I started to talk and he put his finger to his lips and said "Shhhh..." then he walked to the balcony door and looked out over the parking lot. I peeked out quickly and saw two young guys changing the oil in their car. I had no idea why they were so interesting to Bob, but he was staring intently at them. Then, without looking at me he said "Reach into the closet and hand me the AK." I had no idea what he was talking about, but I opened the living room closet to see what he wanted, and there in the corner was an old rifle I later found to be an AK-47. The gun had a long clip in it, but it looked like it hadn't been fired since Moby Dick was a minnow. I turned and looked at him and said "Are you kidding me?"

Then he reached over, grabbed the gun and pointed it out towards the parking lot. I was pretty sure he was just trying to scare me, but I started backing up towards the door just in case. Then he screamed and started shooting! I didn't wait to see what was going on, I just ran as fast as I could. The loud 'crack, crack, crack' of the gun could be heard everywhere. As I ran across the yard in front of the building, I looked at the parking lot and saw the two boys running for their lives! I didn't stop until I reached my apartment, then I locked the door and tried to catch my breath.

A few minutes later, I heard a siren and decided to go back and see what was happening. I walked out of my apartment and slowly headed back to Bobs house. As I peaked around his building, I saw him being led out by two Police Officers. His hands were cuffed behind his back and he was saying "They were just blanks... I was only kidding. I was trying to scare a nub." Behind him was another officer carrying out three or four rifles and what looked like some kind of grenade launcher. Obviously Bob had a hobby the Navy didn't know about. I quietly walked back to my apartment and decided to stay in for the day.

The following Monday there was lots of talk about Bob McGregor. We were told he would not be coming back to the boat anytime soon. I just wish he could have signed my card before he wigged out.

Well, the USS Salt Lake City was finally all put together. The boat was starting to look like a submarine now. It had decks, berthing compartments (where the crew slept), and ninety nine percent of its gear had been installed. There were tests going on all the time, and systems inspectors were everywhere. Rumor had it that we were going out in a couple weeks for Alpha trials. We were also being sent to the Caribbean so we could do sonar trials, speed trials and anything else the Navy throws at us. Now we had to load the ship, go through an in service inspection, and if we pass, we will move aboard the boat. Then, its haze gray and underway!

The Board of Inspection and Survey (INSURV) is a U.S. Navy organization assigned by the Secretary of the Navy (SECNAV) and the Chief of Naval Operations (CNO), whose purpose is to inspect and assess the material condition of naval vessels. After a ship has been constructed by a shipyard and turned over to the Navy, an INSURV team must certify the vessel prior to declaring it operational.

As for the crew, INSRV sucks. Our job is hard enough without having to watch our "P's and Q's." But, many INSERV inspections have been failed due to the crew's lack of commitment, and that was something nobody wanted. If your ship failed its INSERV inspection, you were on the Navy's crap list. Every eye in Washington would be on you, and every Admiral within a hundred miles of you would show up on your doorstep. Needless to say, the USS Salt Lake City passed its INSERV! Next stop, sea trials.

When a submarine goes through sea trials, there are usually about forty extra people aboard. All the shipyard workers or yard birds as we called them, which had been installing the various systems, were now going to sea with us to test those systems. This was an uncomfortable period for the crew because we have to share our precious little space with a bunch of overpaid civilians who would usually sit around for ninety percent of the day and do nothing but eat and play dominoes. I remember how angry I would get when they would sit there for hours and then ask me to do things for them. I had no use for yard birds.

The next two weeks were filled with getting the boat ready for trials. Since there are only a certain number of racks or beds on board, temporary racks are loaded into the torpedo room and attached to the torpedo skids. Unusually, the room would be filled with over thirty Mark 48 torpedoes. The Mark 48 is about nineteen feet long, weighs about thirty five hundred pounds and has to be occasionally shifted around the room with hoists and lifts. Obviously, with the yard birds on board there wouldn't be a lot of weapons shifting.

Alpha trials sucked. Being the junior nub on board, I drew a bunk in the torpedo room between two overweight yard birds. Most of the yard birds had nothing really to do all day except to monitor the various systems they had installed. The rest of the time they would sit around and brag about how much money they made, play cards or wait for the next meal.

The crew was exhausted. Everyone worked around the clock making sure the systems were up and running as good as possible. The wardroom was just as tired as the rest of us were. For every yard bird taking notes, there were five crewmen and two officers jumping through hoops. Like I said... Alpha trials sucked. After nine grueling days of testing, we arrived back in Newport News. With a week or so to load more gear and reshuffle, we would soon be going out again for Bravo, Charlie and Delta trials.

One of the things that everyone who was qualifying on a submarine had to do was to drive the boat. Now I had driven a lot of things in my life, but driving a nuclear submarine is unique. It's kind of like flying an airplane with your eyes closed.

There are two operation stations for controlling the boat; the steering station and the dive station. The Diving Officer sits in a seat between and just aft of the steering and diving station. As the Officer of the Deck gives the orders, the Diving Officer makes sure the orders are carried out exactly as they should be. The whole time you are driving boat, you are blindly looking at the controls.

Every now and then, the Officer of the Deck would throw a drill simulation at us. For example, he would yell "jam dive" which means the fairwater planes have failed, and if you don't do something fast, the boat will sink rapidly and be crushed by the pressure of the sea.

The fairwater planes are the planes, or the 'wings' located on the sail of a 688 class submarine. The stern planes are located on the tail end of the boat. If the larger fairwater plains are stuck in the downward position, the boat will go down until it is stopped. If speed is increased, the stern planes will over-ride the fairwater planes, and the boat can be brought under control. At any rate, this is a scary process that every man on the boat will have to master.

The Chief of the Watch sits at the Ballast Control Panel, or the BCP for short. Ballast on a submarine is essentially weight in the form of water, which controls the depth and trim (angle) of the boat. Filling the main ballast tanks at the bow and stern of the boat with water allows the submarine to surface or dive. Pumping water between variable ballast tanks along the submarine's hull, with the help of the planes, controls the water depth once the boat is submerged. To bring the boat to the surface, compressed air blows the water from the ballast tanks.

Controlling the precise depth near or below the water surface is one of the most critical operations on a submarine. Proper depth control allows a submarine to remain exactly deep enough for periscope viewing, avoid obstacles (especially in polar operations), hide from enemies, or dive quickly to avoid interception.

In an extreme situation, the Chief of the Watch may need to conduct an emergency blow, which would immediately start to fill the ballast tanks with air, forcing the water out. The new buoyancy will bring the ship up to the surface fast.

Just as I was ending my shift on the planes, the OOD yelled "Emergency surface!" The Chief of the Watch reached up and hit the emergency blow levers, or as we called them, the "chicken switches." After a few seconds, the boat started to rise to the surface, faster and faster. I remember once when the boat was doing an emergency blow that it was at such an extreme angle that I could stand straight up and if I stuck my arm out in front of me, I could touch the floor.

When the boat hits the surface, it comes out of the water almost half way and then slams back down in a spectacular splash. There is really nothing quite like the feeling of that boat coming to the surface under you. Submarines are quite unique.

After a few weeks, the tests were all over. We passed our trials with flying colors, and the brass was happy. Now all that was left was the bells and whistles of a commissioning ceremony, then we would be a real United States Navy Submarine!

The two weeks before commissioning were spent working toward my qualification board. Finally, after so many months of duty weekends and late night study sessions, it was time. The board had to have at least four senior qualified members of the crew who were experts in various areas. In addition to that, there had to be one Chief Petty Officer and one of the ships Line Officers. The board itself was semi-formal.

The members of the board sat around the table asking specific questions that they had prepared beforehand. If you answered enough of the questions satisfactorily, you would pass your board and get your "dolphins." Dolphins are a warfare insignia that you wear on your uniform to show that you are a qualified expert in submarine warfare.

The board went on for about an hour, and I was having lots of problems remembering everything. They could have asked me my name and I would have given them the wrong answer. The guys on the board tried to help me, but I was so confused. It was no surprise to me that I failed the board. I was so angry I walked all the way home. I decided to put off quals for a while.

After a few weeks, the pomp and glamour of commissioning subsided, and life slowly went back to normal. We were moored at the Naval Operations Base (NOB) in Norfolk, at the end of pier twenty-three, right across from our submarine tender, the USS Emory S. Land (AS-39).

A submarine tender is a type of ship that supplies and supports submarines. Submarines are small compared to most oceangoing vessels, and generally do not have the ability to carry large amounts of food, fuel, torpedoes, and other supplies, nor to carry a full array of maintenance equipment and personnel. The tender carries all these, and either meets up with the submarines at sea to replenish them or provides these services while docked at a port near the area where the submarines are operating. In some navies, the tenders were equipped with workshops for maintenance, and as floating dormitories with relief crews.

Submarine Squadron Eight had about fourteen submarines, and the Land took care of their every need. Tenders had everything a boat could ever need, from food and supplies to a carpentry and upholstery shop. The ship also was the headquarters for the entire squadron, and the Admiral's work center.

One thing that sea going submarines are often tasked with is burials at sea. Every year, hundreds of aging veterans die and their remains are cremated. If they request a burial at sea, the Navy will take the remains anywhere in the world that they want them to be buried. For example, if someone wants to be buried over the sunken wreck of the Titanic, the Navy will wait until there is a ship going in that direction. Once the ship is on location, a short ceremony takes place and the remains are dropped overboard. When the ship returns to port, the Skipper writes a letter to the family telling them of the exact location of the burial.

Each of the individual remains is given to us in a sealed plastic bag, inside of a small black plastic box. What is suppose to happen is the ship or boat would stop over the site, and after a few words were spoken, then the ashes are poured out of the bag and scattered across the water.

On one of our test runs, we were passing over the wreckage of several World War II submarines, so we were assigned to hold the services for three burials. The XO brought the three boxes of remains onto the Crews Mess. Obviously, he had never done this before, because he thought he was suppose to throw the plastic boxes out onto the water and they would sink. The XO had used an electric drill to put some holes in the boxes, so the remains would sink like he thought they were supposed to.

Sitting on the Crews Mess at the time were eight or nine crewmembers playing dominoes. They didn't pay much attention to what the XO was doing until the drill started. When they found out that these were the remains of actual people, they started paying attention. The XO was a pretty big guy, and when he put his weight on the drill, the bit slipped quickly through the plastic box, and into the plastic bag holding the ashes. He pulled the drill up as fast as he could, pulling ashes out with it and sending them all over the mess decks.

Well, when the guys playing dominoes saw those ashes flying everywhere, they scattered like bugs. Most of them didn't come back to the Crews Mess until they were absolutely starving. Then the rumors started about a ghostly figure that could be seen walking down the passageway from the ships office to the escape trunk, looking for a way off the ship. The haunting of the USS Salt Lake City is still talked about in many a Goat Locker on the water front.

Chapter Four

Now that we were finally in the real Navy, we were set to do some tests down in the Caribbean. Because we had been doing such a great job, we were given two liberty ports, Puerto Rico and St. Croix. Since I had never been anywhere before, I was very excited about going. I really wanted to see what a liberty port was like. Besides, I wanted to learn how to snorkel, and I had heard that the water in the Caribbean was the best snorkeling water in the world!

The days on the boat passed by quickly, and everyone was excited about going to the islands. Everyone who had ever been there, or anywhere else for that matter, was telling sea stories. I remember wishing I had some sea stories to tell. I had never really been anywhere before, and now since I was of drinking age with some money in my pocket, I was about to experience life! Yes, I was excited.

The day we were due to pull in to Roosevelt Roads, Puerto Rico, I woke up hours before I needed to. Finally, a liberty port! We pulled into port about noon, and as soon as we were tied up and everything was stowed most of the crew went on liberty. I had the duty, so I would have to stay onboard to receive stores, fresh milk and produce, and to cook dinner. I knew that I would be on liberty soon after evening chow was over, so life was good.

Working aboard a submarine in the eighties was very stressful. When the boat pulled into port, stress relief was a necessity. The cranks that were working with me that evening were all friends of mine, so we had decided to go out together. There were only two things that most sailors were after when going ashore in a liberty port, and that's a stiff drink and a friendly girl. Since I was married at that time, I was not interested in the girl, but I was sure looking for a drink!

Roosevelt Roads, or "Rosie Roads" as the Navy calls it, is a huge base. It was the biggest Navy base in the world as far as size goes, and there was only one shuttle that would take the sailors back and forth. We had decided to walk to the enlisted club, about two miles, but at that time we were blissfully unaware of how long that would take.

At that time there were many threats to United States military personnel in Puerto Rico. San Juan was off limits (black listed) and the Sailors and Marines were not allowed to leave base. The front gate was locked and guarded by four Marines, two of which manned the fifty caliber guns that were mounted there. We were told to stay away from the fence line, because there were threats from the local people surrounding the base. Just six weeks before there had been someone shooting at a bus full of Sailors driving out to the weapons range. While we were looking for excitement, we were not looking for trouble so we stayed clear of the gate and the fence line.

After walking through the thickest patch of hungry mosquitoes I had ever seen, we arrived at the club. There were not too many people there from the boat, but we did see a few of our shipmates. One really nice thing about being in the Caribbean is the cheap rum. I had never tasted rum before, but mixed drinks with rum were only fifty cents so I became a quick fan. After an hour or so, we started getting board so we asked the waitress where all the Navy boys were hanging out, so she pointed us to the Constriction Battalion (CB) base down the road.

The CB base club was more to our liking. There were pictures of ships and stations hanging all over the place. In the middle of the room were a foosball table and two pool tables. There were several Marines sitting around in the back of the room, so not looking for trouble, we decided to hang out at the bar and finish the night out by swapping sea stories.

The next morning a couple buddies and I decided to start out early and see where the wind would take us. It was a beautiful day, so we decided to walk down the beach and go snorkeling. Just down the beach a bit was a small clubhouse where people could drink, throw a game of darts or rent snorkel gear. Since I had never been snorkeling before, I was anxious to get started.

It took me a few minutes to get used to breathing through a tube, but once I figured it out, life was good. The water that I was in was only about six feet deep and a few feet from shore, but I was amazed at how beautiful it was. This was the first time I had ever been in Caribbean water, and I couldn't believe what I was seeing. There were fish of every color, and the coral was unbelievable. Red, green, blue, orange, yellow... no matter where you looked, the scene was miraculous.

After about half an hour, I decided that I needed to get a souvenir for my mother. She would be so impressed with a piece of this beautiful coral. After looking around, I found the most beautiful piece I had seen yet. It was red with orange spots, and the color was spectacular. I swam up to it and reached out for it, but it was soft and I thought it moved. Thinking it was my imagination, I tried to grab it again. This time it pulled away from me, and then it shot out right at me. It was an octopus about four feet long and just as it passed me it squirted ink all over my legs! I was so surprised I almost drowned from all the water I was choking down.

When I finally made my way to the shore, I noticed my legs and feet were a pale green color, and they smelled horrible! I was pretty sure the guys on the boat were not going to like this. I spent that evening taking one shower after another, each one getting rid of a little more of the smell. Finally, around midnight, I was allowed into the berthing compartment. Life was good once more.

A couple days later we departed for St. Croix. It was only a short transit, so everyone was in an excellent mood! I was in the galley chopping up shrimp for shrimp scampi, trying not to slip and slide all over the place. A submarine is round, so when it is transiting on the surface, it rolls a lot. On a submarine, or any ship for that matter, everything has to be rigged for sea. That means the hatches have to be shut, the dishes have to be strapped down and the crew has to hold on or there will be broken bones and concussions.

As I was chopping the shrimp, I was talking to one of the cranks about all the rum and fun we were planning. The next thing I knew the boat had rolled again and I felt a pain in my left hand. While being distracted I had cut the end off of my left index finger!

I looked down and saw the tip of the bone sticking out of my finger. Since I had always been fascinated in medicine, I thought the sight of the bone showing was kind of cool, so I took a minute and studied it.

The next thing I knew, my Chief grabbed me and wrapped my hand in a dish towel and rushed me off to the corpsman's' space. Since the submarine was such a small and cramped place, the Corpsman had to work in the pyrotechnics area, or as we called it the three inch launcher space. The Doc looked at my finger and started to disinfect it, and then he smiled and said "So Clay, did you bring me the tip of your finger or should I just avoid eating the shrimp today?" Smiling, I opened my other hand and handed him the tip of my finger. He then decided that it would be better to not to sew it back on and just treat the wound. The only good thing about getting an injury in the galley is that it usually gets you the rest of the day off, since the wound has to stay dry.

About an hour later the maneuvering watch was set for pulling into St. Croix. Fredricksted, on the west side of the island, had only one pier. The pier was about three quarters of a mile long, and relatively new. Since there was no one on the pier to tie up the boat, we had the very dangerous task of doing it ourselves. Normally, you would use mooring lines to bring the boat in. As the boat slowly nears the pier, a strong thin line is tossed over to the men on the pier. At the end of the rope is a heavy knot called a "monkey fist." Once they catch the monkey fist, they pull the rope which is tied to the much heavier mooring line. Once the pier team has the mooring line, they tie it loosely through the "cleat" on the pier. As the boat drifts closer to the pier, the lines are pulled tighter and tighter, until the boat is "moored," or tied to the pier.

Since there was nobody on the pier this time, the mooring line had to be thrown around the cleat from the boat, and then the capstan was used to pull the boat in. The reason this procedure is so dangerous is because the strain on the mooring lines is much greater when using the capstan. If the lines were pulled to tight, they would break and possibly kill or dismember anyone who was standing near them. As we pulled the boat closer and closer, I noticed the line starting to smoke, which meant it was getting close to the breaking point. Luckily, the boat was pulled in quickly without incident, so everyone made it through safely.

On the pier the Skipper was greeted by old Sadie one leg, the beer lady. Every bubblehead on the East coast knew Sadie one leg. Rumor had it that Sadie used to run on the pier, and one day she got drunk and fell off the end and had her right leg chewed off by a big barracuda. Now she greets every sub that pulls in with a truck full of iced beer, selling them for a dollar each.

As we were getting the boat rigged for in port operations, we heard the Officer of the Decks voice over the 1MC "Liberty call, liberty call. Liberty will commence for all hands with the exception of duty section four." It was time to hit the beach, so we quickly finished what we were doing and went ashore.

The sun was bright and the wind was perfect! The water off the pier was crystal clear and about 100 feet deep. One of the guys dropped a quarter off the end of the pier and we watched it slowly sink to the bottom. The water was so clear you could almost see the outline of George Washington's' head!

I was hitting the beach with two of my buddies, Bucket Head Jennings and Billy Motts. Bucket head was another cook who got his nick name from the Alpha trials. He was so seasick he had to wear a bucket around his neck so he could work and throw up at the same time. Billy was a crank from Oklahoma who we had befriended during the trials.

We decided to take a walk out into the small town and find a watering hole somewhere. At the end of the pier was a store dedicated to selling rum, and only rum. Light rum, dark rum, banana rum, coconut rum, orange rum, tapioca rum, coffee rum... the list goes on and on. The best part was the rum averaged about seventy five cents a bottle. The Captain had already told us that this was a booze cruise, and we would all be allowed to take back six bottles of island rum. They would stash it in the torpedo tubes and break it out again once we arrive back at pier twenty three in Norfolk.

As we walked through the small town, we noticed there were several bars to stop in and have a drink, but they were all empty. We asked one of the locals where the action was, and she told us to try the "Brandy Snifter", a bar on the next block. When we arrived there we saw many of our friends there from the boat, and a few marines who had island hopped in from Cuba for a couple days of leave.

After ordering a round of rum and cokes, we decided to hang out there for the rest of the afternoon. The restaurant around the back of the bar had some great seafood, so there was no need to go anywhere else.

A hour or so later one of our shipmates, Senior Chief Sonar Tech, Hank Bilko, came into the bar and joined us. He was working up a good drunk, and then asked me if I had any tattoos. When I told him I didn't have any, he said he was thinking about getting one while he was in St. Croix. After a few more drinks, we asked him if we could help him pick out the perfect tattoo. He said "If you want to pay for it, I will get any tattoo you want anywhere you want me to get it." After passing the hat around, we had collected about eighty dollars, so we all started walking toward the only tattoo shop on that side of the island.

Once we got there, we saw that the tattoo shop was actually an old barber shop, recently converted to suit the needs of the old Rastafarian man, "Mr. Tat," who just happened to be a tattoo artist. After we all crowded into the shop, we told the man that the tattoo we wanted was a simple set of submarine dolphins. He looked at the picture we showed him and he said "Yes man, it will be thirty dollars. Where would he like it?" We all just smiled and looked at one another, and then one of the Sonar techs said "On his Johnson!" The man looked at Hank and said "Ok, man, but there will be a fifty dollar handling charge." Laughing, I handed the man the eighty dollars we had collected, and pointed Hank to the chair.

Before we could get the ball rolling on the tattoo, Hank said he needed two bottles of rum, one light and one dark. One of the cranks ran to the saloon next door and brought the two bottles. Since Hank already had a pretty good drunk going on, Mr. Tat got started. As soon as the needle touched him, Hank started yelling. I am sure it didn't help much to have thirty crewmen, seven tourists and four barmaids from next door watching as his manhood was being brutalized. The entire process took about two hours, and the end product had great detail, although it was kind of hard to see all withered up like it was. I was sure whenever Hank recovered he would have a great story to tell at the next liberty port!

After the excitement died down, Bucket head, Billy Motts and I decided to wonder back to the Brandy Snifter. It was about an hour before midnight when we got there, and the place started filling up. Most of the tables were filled with guys from the boat, but there were also some Marines and a few locals there. It was a great night, filled with rum, arm wrestling, darts and sea stories.

I noticed Bucket head was making goo-goo eyes at a very pretty local girl sitting at a table across the room. Of course, he was drunk, and did not notice that this lovely young lady was sitting with three men who we later found out to be her husband and two of his buddies. The three of them were local police officers who happened to be off duty.

I saw one of them get up and start walking over, so I elbowed Bucket head and said "Knock it off... you are starting to piss off the locals." The man walked up to our table and said "Is there something you would like to say to my wife?" Bucket head just looked at him and smiled. Then, the cop hauled off and punched Bucket head right in the mouth. I jumped up and swung at him, but one of his buddies grabbed me instead. Just when he was about to punch me, Big John Gannon, a Machinist Mate buddy of mine, caught him with a crushing left hook. I quickly dropped to the floor and crawled under a table so I could get my barring. When I looked around, all I could see were sailors and marines fighting. One of the off duty police officers had called in the local police, and sirens could be heard in the distance.

When I looked for Bucket head, I saw him lying on the floor trying to look unconscious. I quickly motioned to him to crawl towards me and we quietly crawled out the side door.   As we looked back at the chaos, it reminded me of something out of an old western. There were men fighting everywhere!   The police had just arrived, so we hid in the back alley and then when the coast was clear, we headed for the pier.

While all this was going on, one of our shipboard drunks, Quartermaster Second Class Sully Easterman had run back to the boat screaming. "There are sailors dead on the beach! The police are shooting our sailors" Of course, this was not quite accurate, since no one was shooting and no one was dead. Sully just had a flair for the dramatic.

Acting on the news he was receiving, the Duty Officer, Lt. Campbell, ordered the duty section to report to the weapons locker. He then issued weapons and told the duty section leader to go out and bring the ships company back to the boat.

As the duty section headed down the long pier, they were met half way down by several police vehicles. As the vehicles stopped, several men got out and pointed their weapons down the pier toward the boat. The ships duty section formed a line facing them, also with weapons pointing.

When Bucket head and I got back to the pier, it was about two o'clock in the morning. As we looked down the pier, we saw the police and the duty section and decided it would be best to get in the water and swim quietly to the boat. Of course, in our drunken state we didn't think about the sand sharks and the barracuda that constantly swam under the pier. After a lengthy haphazard swim, Bucket head and I arrived at the boat. The Topside watch was distracted by all of the gun pointing, so we were able to quietly sneak onboard, get undressed and slip into our bunks.

About an hour later, all of the lights in the berthing compartments were turned on. Several of the senior members of the crew started pulling back the curtains on the bunks looking for certain people. I was awoken from my drunken sleep by Master Chief Rockdale, the Chief of the Boat. He yelled back through the berthing compartment "I found them. Westfall and Jennings are here asleep in their racks!" When he asked me how long we had been asleep I told him honestly that I didn't know. Then the COB yelled "Everybody up! I want everyone topside NOW!"

What a sight the pier was! Sailors were lying everywhere, drunk and beat up. Several Junior Officer, and two Senior Officers were also drunk and beat up. The police were all standing just down the pier, and the Skipper was taking to an important looking man in a white car, whom I later found out to be the Governor of the island.

After a couple minutes, the Skipper stood at the top of the brow and yelled "Attention!" As the entire crew tried to stand at attention, the very angry Skipper started talking. "As of now, the Governor of St. Croix has asked us to leave the island. Never, in my thirty three years in the Navy have I ever been asked to leave a port because of the crew's actions. You will pay dearly for this embarrassment! As of this minute, the entire crews, including the Officers, are all restricted to the boat!"

Well, that was St. Croix. They never did figure out how Bucket head and I got back to the boat, since we had basically started the whole incident. Although no shots were ever fired, and nobody was seriously injured, St. Croix would forever be a black spot on the record of USS Salt Lake City.

When we arrived back at good old pier twenty three, we were greeted by all the families of the Salt Lake City. Obviously, some had called ahead and told the wives club about Hank's new tattoo. High over the crowd was a banner written in huge letters that read "SHOW US YOUR CRANK, HANK." It was all in fun, but I heard later that Hank's wife was not as entertained as the rest of us were. I think Hank lived in the doghouse that year.

Since we were home now, I knew it was time to hit the studies again. I had been working tirelessly for some time now, and every system expert on the boat had walked me through the systems over and over again. My problem was the board itself. Whenever I am being asked questions with people staring at me and waiting for an answer, I just seem to wig out and get all flustered. It was starting to look like I would never get my dolphins.

That evening when I got home, Henry Logins, the leading nuke mechanic on board, was waiting for me at my apartment. He asked me if I wanted to go out for a pizza and beer. Hoping to pick his brain, I grabbed my coat and followed him out the door. When we got to the pizza place, we saw a few of our shipmates sitting at a large table in the back dining room. As our pizza arrived at the table, my division officer, Mr. Southern showed up, so we invited him to join us.

After a while, Chief Reynolds, the Leading Supply Chief, asked me if I wanted to go over some of the boats systems to help me review for my upcoming makeup board. I told him I thought that sounded like a good idea, since I needed all the help I could get.

After an hour or so of me reviewing everything I knew, Mr. Southern stood up and said "Everyone, raise your glasses." As I raised my glass he continued by saying "Westfall, I just wanted to let you know that you have just passed your submarine qualification board. Congratulations!" Wow! I couldn't believe it… They had tricked me into sitting a board, and since we were just some buddies having a slice, it took off all the pressure. What a great bunch of guys! Life was good.

Now that the Salt Lake City was a ship of the line, it was time for her to move to her new home on the West Coast. We had been told that the entire crew was to ride through the Panama Canal all the way to Point Loma off the coast of California. It sounded exciting, but I specifically chose to be on the East Coast so I could go home and see the folks every now and then. After talking to my Chain of Command, they allowed me to do what was called a split tour to an East Coast boat. That simply meant that I could cut my four year assignment with the Salt Lake City in half, and serve the remainder of my tour on a boat staying on the East Coast

I did have a unique opportunity to make a few bucks while the boat was preparing for the move. Many of the guys aboard had cars that were what we called beaters. These were mostly older, used cars that they would never ship to the West Coast. It would cost lots more than the cars were worth, so the owners were looking for anything they could get for them. If they could not sell the cars to someone, they would be forced to simply leave them parked on the pier, to be towed away later. On the last day, the day the boat was due to leave, I had about a hundred dollars in my wallet. At the end of the day, I had no money, but I did have the keys and titles to a 1962 Nova, a 1979 Nova, and a 1976 Volkswagen Bug.

I remember my first day when I reported to the USS Baton Rouge (SSN-689). It was undergoing overhaul in the Norfolk Naval Shipyard in Portsmouth, Virginia. I had never been to Portsmouth before, so I left early that morning, around four o'clock. Being a cook, I figured I would show up early and give whoever was on duty a hand. As I was driving down the deserted highway, I passed over a bridge into a residential area. I was driving the speed limit, 45 miles an hour. The last thing I needed was a ticket in a strange town, so I was trying to be careful. What I didn't know is that I was entering a highly congested residential area, and that the speed limit changed just over that bridge, from 45 miles per hour to 25 miles an hour. As luck would have it, right on the other side of the bridge was a police car, just waiting for some dummy to speed across the bridge. Welcome to Portsmouth!

Since the Police Officer had ticketed me for twenty miles over the posted speed limit, I had to appear in traffic court. And since I was new to the Command, the Skipper insisted that my division Officer, Ensign Banks. Go to court with me. We both arrived an hour early, with our dress white uniforms on. After I checked in with the Bailiff, we were told to wait on a bench just inside the Portsmouth Courthouse.

As we sat there watching all the people come into the building, I couldn't help but notice that Mr. Banks and I were the only white people there. Normally, this would not be an issue, but since I was new in town, I was feeling a bit nervous.

Twenty minutes later, our court case was called, and we were escorted to a very large court room. I looked all around the room and once again, I saw that Mr. Banks and I were still the lonely minority. "Mr. Westfall, please step forward and state your case" the Bailiff called out. As I stepped forward, every eye in the room followed me. "Yes, your Honor" I answered. Then the Police Officer who ticketed me stepped forward and told the Judge what I was sighted for. The Judge then gave me a very disapproving look and shook her head. Just when I started to address the court, she slammed down her gavel and said "Mr. Westfall, you are found guilty. You will surrender your driver's license for one month. You will also enroll in a mandatory safe drivers course. You will further pay a fine of two hundred and fifty dollars. Case closed!"

As Mr. Banks and I walked back to the Shipyard, he asked me how I felt about my day in court. I just smiled and said "It's a bad day to be a white boy in Portsmouth Virginia.

Since the boat was being overhauled, the crew had moved aboard a large three story shipyard barge. It was a lot easier cooking on a barge because there was more room for better equipment. Large steam-jacketed kettles, big mixers and steam tables made life much easier. One of the bad parts about cooking on a submarine is the lack of storage space for groceries. Most of the dry food has to be put into an auxiliary water tank, which is very hard to work with. The opening is on the top of the tank, and measures about twenty four inches by twenty four inches. If you need a case of peas, and its buried somewhere in the middle of the tank, you must take out every box and put them in the berthing compartment above the tank, until you can find the peas. Another problem is that there are about forty men in the berthing compartment trying to sleep, so you have to be very quiet.

When I first arrived at the barge, the watch sitting on the barge quarterdeck asked me for my ID card. As I looked around I couldn't help but notice how un-military it looked. After signing me into the deck log, the watch pointed me down the hall to the Crews Mess area. I walked down the passageway and when I got to the dining area I saw several members of the duty section eating breakfast. The duty cook, MS2 Albright, asked me if I had eaten yet, and when I said I hadn't, he offered to make me an omelet. I sat down next to a couple of electricians and made some small talk until my Division Chief arrived.

Once the chief got there I was briefed and checked in. Even though I had recently qualified on 688 class submarines, I still had to re-qualify on the Baton Rouge. Since everything was still fresh in my mind and I didn't have to go to a board, life was good. After morning quarters, I was showed the way to the boat. I couldn't believe it! It looked just as bad and the Salt Lake City did when it was in the shipyard! Everywhere you looked, wires, ventilation ducts, water lines... it was a mess. The worst part was the yard birds. Once again, they were everywhere.

The shipyard was a bad place to be when it comes to getting Navy work done, but it does have its advantages. I became an expert at finding anything we needed. The barge needed an extra refrigerator for the ward room. I found one. The duty section needed a way to move a ton of stantions across the shipyard, I found a truck. We needed a welder to replace the one we burned out on the boat. I found one. Everything you could ever need was in the shipyard... it was just a matter of locating it and 'liberating' it. I really didn't consider it stealing, since it was all shipyard stuff. I was simply relocating it to another place in the shipyard.

I had one of the fastest records ever re-qualifying. That was the best part about being a cook. If I had duty one night and one of the watches missed chow, I would always take the extra effort to make something hot for them, no matter how late it was. They would always be very grateful and ask for my qual card so they could sign something. I was re-qualified Baton Rough in eight days. Life was good.

The Baton Rouges' overhaul was completed by the end of the summer, and we were out on sea trials before we know it. This time I was assigned as the storeroom custodian or the "Jack of the dust" as the Navy called it. My job was to keep all the storerooms and food storage tanks clean and organized, and to break out the dry and frozen stores needed for the next day's meals. The job was a relatively easy one, if you did it right. I always tried to be done by dinnertime, and then I could get a good seat for the movie.

At the end of the day, the crew members that were off duty could pick out one of the twelve movies we had for the 16mm movie projector. These movies were usually the newest selections available. During the cold war, the government tried to keep us as happy as they could. They contracted to get the latest movies possible, usually three months before they were hitting the theaters at home.

Another of my jobs was being the Damage Control Petty Officer. That meant I was assigned to the forward DC party, and it was my job to rig the compartment during a casualty or a drill. On a Navy ship, the crew is constantly performing training exercises, or drills, to prepare them for a casualty. Flooding, fire, nuclear containment failure... these are all things that can go wrong on a nuclear submarine. If a casualty is not contained quickly, the entire crew could die.

When rigging the compartment for a casualty, there are many specific tasks that must be performed. For example, if you were trying to isolate the engine room ventilation, you may have to shut the YK-7 damper. If you were ventilating the torpedo room, the YK-7 has to be opened. The same with switch board breakers and water valves. Every drill had its own set of instructions, and if they were not done correctly, men could die.

Sometimes the duty cook would call up to the control room and ask the Officer of the Deck if there was a real casualty or just a drill. If the crew was expecting an elaborate meal, we may not want to shut off the ovens or the meal will be late. The OOD would usually tell us that it was a drill and we could leave that one particular piece of equipment on.

There was one officer, Mr. Parker, who did not care very much for me. Once when we were pier side, he had rented a catamaran and tried to pull up next to the boat after dark. He was drunk and he didn't announce himself, so I challenged him with my shotgun and reported the incident to the Duty Officer, as was protocol. I apologized afterward, but he told me he did not like me, and warned me to stay out of his way. Now he would lash out at me any way he could, and usually it was from the control room.

Once the boat is finished with all of it re-construction, it goes through what is called a 'shake down' period. This time is specifically allocated for recalibrating all of the boats equipment, especially the reactor and power plant. All of the wires, tubes and contacts for the test equipment had to pass through the same door (hatch). On a 688 class submarine, there are only two compartments. The reason a Navy ship is divided into compartments is to isolate any flooding or fire aboard ship.

The reason the Titanic sank was because the water from the iceberg damage filled one compartment after the other, until the ship could no longer stay afloat. If they could have isolated that one section, it would have stopped the water and the ship could have limped into New York and most of the crew and passengers would have survived. On a 688 class submarine, it is a matter of life and death for that one water tight door to be shut. Since I was in charge of rigging the crews mess for any casualties, my first and most important job was to shut the water tight door, and shut it fast.

On the second day of our shakedown, we heard the general alarm followed by an urgent announcement on the 1MC "Flooding in the engine room, flooding in the engine room!" I quickly picked up the sound powered phone and called the control room. Just as luck would have it, the Officer of the Deck was Mr. Parker. I asked the control phone talker if this was an actual casualty or just a drill. Then I heard the OOD yelling "Is that Westfall? You tell him there is flooding in the engine room, and just shut up and do his damn job!"

Angrily, I slammed down the phone and ran to the amidships passageway, where the water tight door was. The door could not be shut due to millions of dollars worth of testing equipment running through it. Since I was told that this was actual flooding, I grabbed the ax hanging on the wall and drew back to start chopping the equipment and clearing the hatch so it could be shut.

As I was just about to swing, someone grabbed the end of the ax and stopped me. I looked back and saw the Skipper. He started yelling "What the hell are you doing?" "Captain, I was told this was not a drill. I have to shut this hatch!" The Skipper started shaking his head and said "No, there is no real flooding. What idiot told you that there was actual flooding?" "The OOD did, Sir. Mr. Parker." The Skipper stormed out of the passageway and headed back to control. I was pretty sure this wasn't going to help my relationship with Mr. Parker.

Chapter Five

One of my favorite times aboard the sub was the maneuvering watch. A submarine cannot safely dive until it passes the hundred fathom curve. This is a line of soundings used on nautical charts to mark the limits of the continental shelf and the beginning of the abyssal descent. When the sub is transiting to and from the hundred fathom curve, the boat is on a high alert status called the maneuvering watch. During the maneuvering watch, the forward and after damage control parties have to stay assembled and alert for hours, in case there is a casualty.

Our DC party consisted on about twenty five men from all over the ship. Some of these men were 'Nukes' from the engine room. A Nuke, like previously stated, is generally a person with a very high IQ, who has been to several years of technical school and works with the nuclear power plant. As a rule, Nukes marched to the beat of a different drummer, and many of them were kind of, well, weird. Some of them really shouldn't be around other people. Also on the mess decks were Machinist Mates, Torpedo Men, Sonar Techs, and several Deck Seamen. Deck Seamen are usually younger men who have not yet been rated into a specialty. Until they are rated, they do all the deck and shipboard maintenance, painting, and basic grunt work.

I have seen and heard some of the most interesting things on the maneuvering watch. I once watched Archie Sanders slide seventeen plastic coffee stir sticks through his nose and into his sinuses. That record stood for seven months, until Joe Harrick slid twenty into his. Jerry Ore once stapled his clothes to his skin with over a hundred staples. Then there was the incredible needlework performed by Ted Shockley. He had sewed his left hand to the leg of the dungarees he was wearing. He started at his wrist, and then went around each finger until he came to the wrist again. I was quite impressed.

Another ceremony that takes place on the mess decks during the Maneuvering Watch is the grossing out of the nubs. Usually, the new guys on board get seasick on the first couple of underway periods. It was the sacred duty of the forward and after DC parties to see who can make the nubs puke first. I have seen some grisly sights in my day, but I have never seen sicker things than on a submarine mess deck during the maneuvering watch. The Nukes spend hours on watch with nothing to do but look at the gauges and discuss what they can do to gross out the nubs on the Maneuvering Watch. I still remember my first Maneuvering Watch aboard the USS Buffalo. The Chief Cook and a Radio Man each had gargled a cupful of raw eggs. Then they spit the eggs back into the cups, and the exchanged cups with each other. Then, after speaking some immortal words of wisdom, drank each other's cup full of spit and eggs. That image will be with me forever.

A time honored custom aboard the boats was the Mail Buoy Watch. The mail buoy doesn't actually exist, but most nubs don't know this until they have been properly chastised. When a submarine is under water out on operations, there is obviously no mail. We like to tell the nubs that there are floating buoys out in the ocean that have arms with hooks on them. We further tell them that helicopters come by and hang mail satchels on them with our mail inside.

If the Officer of the Deck is a good sport, and usually they were, we will get an unknowing nub to dress up in a foul weather suit with KAPOK (life jacket) and stand by in the control room. His mission: Stand on top of the boat in the middle of the night with a boathook (a long pole with a hook on the end) looking for the mail buoy. If and when he sees it, he is to use the boathook and retrieve the mail satchel. Now, if he is not the smartest of fellows, he might just stand there all night waiting for someone to spot the mail buoy. We realize this is a bit of a mean practice, so it is usually reserved for the nubs with the biggest mouth.

Sometimes during the Maneuvering Watch, we will assign a task to a nub, just to watch him run in circles. My favorite task was to find a squeaking door and have a nub fill out the proper forms to request a small can of relative bearing grease. Now, as most military warriors would know, relative bearing is the clockwise angle in degrees from the heading of the vessel to a straight line drawn from the observation station on the vessel to the object. In other words, there is no such thing as relative bearing grease; relative bearing is a position or direction. When the nub shows up to the supply cage to submit his request, the Supply Chief will initial the documents and say "We need the

Engineering Officer of the Watch's initials." After that, the nub is sent somewhere else. After he spends the next two hours running back and forth, proving to the crew that he is not very smart, he finally figures out that we are just messing with him and he will return to the Crews Mess.

One of the most celebrated times on a nuclear submarine is the commissioning of the cups ceremony. Every watch stander on board had his own personal, spill proof coffee cup. One of the first things I was taught as a nub was to never forget your coffee cup in the engine room. Whoever sees a nubs cup sitting unattended usually takes it and prepares it for commissioning. My personal cup commissioning ceremony took place about ten days after my cup disappeared.

Just after quarters on the pier one day, the Nukes called everyone together. The leading Electrician, Jack Mondale, held up a very nice looking model of a submarine. It was about three feet long, and perfectly proportioned. On the side of the sale were the words "USS Westfall" written in gold. Jack said "Will Petty Officer Westfall please come forward?" I nervously walked to the platform where Jack was standing, and then he handed me the model. Then he said "I am returning your cup to you. As is the tradition on all nuclear submarines, you are not allowed to throw your cup away. You must retrieve it from this model, and bring it back to work with you tomorrow." I was touched by his words, although I had no idea what he was talking about.

When I got home I decided to un-wrap the model and find my cup. It was at that time I found out just how dedicated these guys really were. First, I took off the tin foil hull. Under it was what I think was fly paper soaked in some kind of cooking lard. This is when I decided it might be better to do this outside.

Once I was outside, I got all the flypaper off to find a layer of wax paper. Under the wax paper was a layer of chicken wire and a wax coating of some sort. When I finally broke off all the wax, I found my cup wrapped in many layers of duct tape. Once the tape was all cut off, I was able to open my cup and find it full of dog poop and sour milk. I almost threw up from the horrible smell. After regaining my composure, I washed it, sterilized it, and took it to work the next day. I never drank out of it again, but I did take it to work.

One of my buddies, James Olin, came to us with some wonderful news one day. "Hey guys" he said during lunch one day "Guess what? I am getting married!" Now, normally this would have been good news, but Jimmy is new on the boat, and he has only been in Norfolk for a couple days now. He doesn't know the local people like we did. "Her name is Sophia, and she lives in town with her brother. He owns a club in town called 'The Kings Head.' She is perfect!"

The King's Head was a local bar just outside the front gate in the early eighties. It catered mostly to druggies and prostitutes, and the owner also ran a dating service out of there. Jimmy's perfect woman, Sophia, was actually Sophie Almond, one of the call girls. Jimmy had no idea that his perfect woman was well known by most of the Second Fleet. I knew her personally from a ships party we had the year before, but I decided to keep that to myself. She had been looking to marry a Navy man for quite a while now, to escape Norfolk. She always said she would take his money and benefits, and then dump him.

Ok, there was no way we were going to let a sweet young farm boy like Jimmy be swindled into marrying a local lady of the night. We had to think of something. "So, when are you getting married?" I asked Jimmy. He smiled and said "Friday afternoon. I am going today to buy two bus tickets to Indianapolis so we can go home on leave after the wedding on Friday night."

That Friday, about three hours before Jimmy and Sophie were due at the Court House, we decided to have a beer with Jimmy. He was so excited! We started spiking his beers early, and since he was an innocent, sweet farm boy, he was not a very heavy drinker. With a bit of help from a prescription sleeping aid, Jimmy was down for the count. Thirty minutes later, he was on the early Greyhound to Indiana. Pinned to his sleeve was a note explaining what we had done, and who Sophia really was. We figured by the time he woke up, he would be at least six hours down the road.

A couple months later, Jimmy finally forgave us. He cut things off with Sophie, and stopped seeing her. Jimmy will probably do something stupid eventually, but it would not be on our watch.

The Baton Rouge had an extended underway period that was scheduled for later in the year, but now, due to another boat colliding with a Japanese fishing trawler, it had been moved up to next week. Normally, this wouldn't have been that bad of a problem, but our Chief's back blew out on the pier, and two day later my First Class had a heart attack. All of the sudden, I was in charge. Normally, this wouldn't have been so bad, but since we were getting underway in a couple days, it was bad.

The first thing I needed to do was make sure we had enough food. We did. Next, I needed to make sure we had enough consumables, things like napkins, paper plates, forks and spoons, terry cloth for cleaning... the list goes on and on. We were short on many things, but there was no time to order supplies. I had to figure out how to get the supplies we needed without going through the supply system. I had an idea.

I borrowed a government truck and got two of the cranks to come with me, and then we headed out to the Aircraft Carrier piers. There were four carriers in, so I focused on the USS George Washington (CVN-73) and the USS Abraham Lincoln (CVN-72), on pier four.

The first thing I did was to walk up to the Lincoln and ask to purchase a ships hat. Once I purchased it, I went back to the truck, and then drove it over to the Washington. After I had saluted and asked to come aboard, I asked for the CPO Mess Leading Supply Petty Officer. About fifteen minutes later he showed up. I pulled him aside and said "Hi, I'm Petty Officer Arlington from the CPO mess on the Lincoln. We just had a small fire aboard and one of our storerooms was burned out. My Master Chief had told me to empty the room over a week ago, but I forgot to do it. Now, I have to cover my ass before I get hanged. Can you help me out with a few things?" I handed him a short list of supplies, and he looked at it carefully. "Well, I guess I can help you out with some of this." Then he called down to his shop and gave some instructions. "Ok, park your truck over there" he said pointing, "and we will load it up." I shook his hand and thanked him. A few minutes later we were heading back to the sub. We had everything we needed, and it didn't cost us a dime. Life was good.

My last underway with the Baton Rouge was in December of 1986. While we were underway the Skipper received the boats orders for the upcoming Mediterranean deployment. That was excellent news for me; because I was due to get out of the Navy in February so I couldn't go. I was so happy I volunteered for duty the first night when we pulled in. What I didn't know was that Mr. Parker had duty too.

That night I had finished cleaning up from chow in record time, and we were just about to leave the boat when the duty section leader called a repel boarders drill. Repel boarders was what we would do if the boat was under attack while tied to the pier. The most important thing was to shut the hatches quickly, because once the hatches were shut, no one could get aboard the ship without a really big can opener. When the drill commenced, I ran to the hatch and started to shut it, when I noticed the potable water hose was fouling the hatch.

The only way to bring on power and water is through the opened hatches. There are suppose to be quick disconnects right by the hatch in case the hatch has to be shut in a hurry. After looking toward the pier, I saw that there were no quick disconnects anywhere. I dropped back down the hatch and called control. As luck would have it, Mr. Parker answered the sound powered phone. "Control, Crews Mess." "Control" Mr. Parker answered. "Control, Crews Mess... I am unable to shut the forward escape trunk hatch due to..." Then, I was cut off before I could finish my sentence. I could hear swearing in the back ground. "IS THIS

WESTFALL? WHY THE HELL ARE YOU CALLING ME?" he yelled. "YES, THIS IS AN ACTUAL CASUALTY... DO YOUR JOB AND RIGG THE BOAT!" I was so angry, I could spit. Fine. I would follow the Duty Officers orders. I quickly ran into the galley and grabbed a large chef's knife. Then, with the knife in my teeth, I quickly climbed the ladder up the hatch, cut the potable water line in half, and dropped it three decks below into the machinery room. Then, as the hatch was no longer fouled, I shut and secured the hatch.

After I reported back to control that the forward hatch was secured, I heard a loud voice from down the passageway. Then the Executive Officer and the leading machinist mate came into the crews mess with the Mr. Parker right behind them. "Who cut the potty water hose?" the XO asked. "I did, Sir" I answered. Before he could ask me why I did it, I explained what had happened. The XO turned red. He looked at Mr. Parker and said "Mr. Parker, did Petty Officer Westfall call control to report that he couldn't shut the hatch?" "Yes Sir." Mr. Parker answered. "And what did you tell him?" "Uh, Sir, I told him, a, that it was an actual casualty and to do his job." The XO immediately started walking toward his office and said "Parker, I want to talk to you in my stateroom!" I was pretty sure I would not be getting a Christmas card from the Parker family that year.

A couple days later, I was detached from the ship and sent to the tender. The rest of my time in the Navy would be spent working for COMSUBLANT (Commander, Submarine Force, Atlantic.)

My duties consisted of making and drinking the coffee, sitting at a desk and not falling asleep. They called me the "Desk Watch", but it was just so I could feel useful. I was also used for special assignments, like posing as a Zulu Five Oscar. COMSUBLANT was constantly testing the security of the subs tied up at pier twenty-three. The Zulu Five Oscar was assigned to breech the security of any submarine at any time. Now, all of the submarines Topside Watches on pier twenty-three were armed with a .45 caliber hand gun and a 12 gauge shotgun. Needless to say, getting shot would not be a good thing, so caution was the most important thing to keep in mind.

That morning I purchased a ships ball cap from the USS Cincinnati (SSN-693) so I could better mingle with the crewmen topside. Since they often sold ships ball caps to people on the pier, I didn't draw much attention. Now all I had to do was to come up with a plan to sneak aboard without getting shot.

As I was coming back from the Navy Exchange that afternoon, I noticed the Cincinnati was having a stores load. That's where a Navy semi truck full of groceries parks on the pier and the crew form a long line, passing the food down to the proper storage room. It makes for a long, miserable day, and the crew usually doesn't care what they drop. This was my chance.

I quickly ran to the tender and grabbed my dirtiest dungaree shirt and my newly purchased ball cap that I had smeared with engine grease, and mingled with the guys on the pier. As soon as I saw a break in the line, I grabbed a case of oven roast, ducked my head down low and boarded the boat. The Topside watch was shooting the bull with some of his buddies, so he didn't give me a second look.

Once I was below decks, I quickly dropped the case off in the crews mess and made my way to the

Ward Room. The Skipper and the XO were just sitting down to lunch when I removed my hat, knocked on the door and requested to come in. "Enter" the Skipper said. I took a couple steps in and handed him a small black box with a sign on it that read "I am a Zulu Five Oscar. Bang... your dead!" The XO stood and looked at me, and said "What's your name, Sailor?" I said "MS3(SS) Westfall, Sir." "Well, Petty Officer Westfall, you have about 30 seconds to get your ass off this boat before I rip your head off!" I took the XO's advice and quickly ran back to the tender. After reporting my success in breaching the Cincinnati, I begged my boss not to ever make me do it again.

I was very excited about the New Year arriving. Only thirty-eight more days and a wake-up, and I would be out of the Navy! Just as I was sitting at my desk dreaming of my next career move, in walked Ensign Banks, the Supply Officer of the Baton Rouge. I really didn't care much for him because he always looked down his nose at the enlisted guys. As my boss, he would always wait until the last minute to order the supplies, and then ask me to fix his mess. Now that I was no longer working for him, he seemed a lot nicer.

He started out by asking me how I liked working on the tender, then before I could even answer, he said "Westfall, I'm in trouble." Then he looked at me like he was going to cry and said "Remember how you told me to order TDU weights a few months ago? Well, I never did, and now we leaving for the Mediterranean in three days and I am going to be fired!" This was a big deal. There are only a few things that can keep a boat from going on deployment, and TDU weights are one of them. Now, this wasn't a small thing. He needed three pallets of TDU weights. That's thousands of dollars worth of weights in three days, when it usually takes two months. I told him I would see what I could do, but I wasn't making any promises.

Every boat in Squadron Eight gets its consumable supplies through CEP-204. This is like a staging and holding area for all the boats while they are at sea, or just until they have time to pick them up. Each Navy command has a Unit Identification Code (UIC), kind of like a zip code. It doesn't matter whether you are receiving a can opener or a pick-up truck, each one comes with the same receipt printed with the commands UIC on it, and that's all they look at. I figured CEP-204 was where I needed to start, so I went to talk to the Petty Officer in charge.

CEP-204 has pretty tight security, and there are always people walking around everywhere. When I finally found the Leading Petty Officer, he was really no help at all. He told me if I forgot to order my TDU weighs, I must be an idiot. With that helpful thought in mind, I decided to hang around for the day and see what I could find out about what happens when ships order the weights. As I was walking around, I noticed several deployed boats had TDU weights in their locked storage areas. That gave me an idea.

I quickly ran over to the Baton Rouges storage area and started looking for receipts with the boats name and UIC on them. I found some on some on boxes of plastic forks and spoons, and carefully folded them so that you could see the boats information, but not the description of the contents. Once that was done, I went over to the USS Cincinnati's storage area and removed the screws from the hinges on the door. At that point, I left the area to go and see where security was. When I found the security guards, I asked them if they could help me sign my receipts and fix my paperwork. When they laughed at me, I tried my best to look disappointed and embarrassed, and then walked away. I knew they would laugh at me, but I wanted them to think I was hopeless so they would disregard my being there, and not see me as a threat.

With the guards out of the way, I returned to the Cincinnati's storage area. I quietly slipped through the door where I had removed the hinge screws and removed the packing lists from the display pouches on three pallets of TDU weights that were there, waiting for the boat to return. I knew that the Cincinnati was heading to the shipyard for a refit soon, so they would have lots of time to get more weights. Once I had removed the packing lists, I carefully put the receipts from the Baton Rouge in the display pouches, and carefully taped them back down. This way, when someone looked at the weights and checked the receipts, they would assume the weights were meant for the Baton Rough. When all of that was done, I replaced the hinge screws and headed back toward pier twenty three. As I was passing by the security office, the guards were still laughing and making fun of me.

The next day I went over to CEP-204 early, just as they had finished quarters. I made sure lots of people saw me walking around, looking in all the areas for some 'missing' item. Then, after a few seconds of mental preparation, I stormed over to where the Senior Chief was drinking his coffee. "You have got to be kidding me!" I yelled. "I am going to be sent to Captains Mast because you people screwed up!" The Senior Chief looked up from his coffee and yelled "Calm down before I have you hauled off!" Then he lowered his voice and said "What's the problem son?" I quickly worked up some tears and said "Senior, I have been waiting for the TDU weights I ordered two months ago to arrive, but they never did. Now the boat is deploying in two days, and we don't have our weights. This morning my boss, Mr. Banks, said he was going to write me up for dereliction of duty. And now I find my missing weights in the Cincinnati's storage area!" At that point, I dropped my arms and turned to walk away, still talking "Great. Now my career is over because you people can't do your jobs." That's when the magic happened. As expected, the Senior Chief started ripping a hole in me "SAILOR! Stand at attention!" I quickly turned and popped to attention. "You will not talk like that to me again or I will have your stripes! Now, shut your mouth and come with me!"

When we arrive at the Cincinnati's storage area, the Senior Chief used his master keys to unlock the door. He quickly walked up to the three pallets of weights and looked at the receipts through the plastic pouches. As I had hoped, he was so mad at this point he didn't pull out the receipts, he just walked back out the door and yelled toward his First Class Petty Officer. "Jones, get a fork lift and the big truck and take these three pallets of weights over to the Baton Rouge on Pier twenty-three, NOW." Then he looked at me and said "Are you happy now? Get the hell out of my area before I call your Commanding Officer!"

As I walked back to where the Baton Rouge was moored, I saw that the truck had beaten me to the pier. A TDU weight loading party was already assembled, and the weights were being loaded onto the boat. Mr. Banks was standing topside talking to the XO. When they saw me walking up, Mr. Banks said "Westfall, how in the world did you do that?" I just smiled and said "it was pure freaking magic."

The next morning my Chief told me that I was requested to report to the Captain of the Baton Rouge. When I got to the mess decks, there were several people sitting there waiting for me. The Captain and Mr. Banks were standing in front, and the Captain said "Attention." When everyone was standing, the Captain continued "Petty Officer Westfall has once again saved the day, and saved Mr. Banks career. I would like to present him with this special plaque to show our deep and sincere gratitude." Then he handed me a small plaque with a large set of submarine dolphins on it. Under the dolphins was an inscription that read "MS3(SS) Westfall, Squadron Eight PFM Coordinator." I accepted the plaque with great pride, and saluted the Skipper, and thanked him. As I was walking back to the tender, I proudly looked down at the plaque, and read it again. "Pure Freaking Magic."

February 8, 1987. Exactly four years after I had joined the Navy, I was a free man once again. No more working parties. No more after hours field day. No more Navy.

I remember that final drive back down to Alabama. It was kind of weird, not having to be anywhere except for where I wanted to be. Finally... I was a civilian! The twelve hour drive home seemed to fly by, and when I finally got there, all I wanted to do was see my folks and sleep. It was good to see mom and dad. I missed sitting in the kitchen talking to mom at six thirty in the morning.

The next day, I had a problem. What was I going to do with my life? I knew mom and dad would let me stay at home, but I needed to pay my way. It was time to find a job.

Since I was a trained cook, I was sure that was the ticket to my financial future. I decided to start filling out applications in Opelika, about fifteen miles from my house. There were literally hundreds of possibilities, but I wanted something that I could make a career out of. After filling out about fifty applications, I started missing the Navy. This is the first time in four years that I didn't know what I was going to do for money. If it wasn't for Mom and Dad, I would be out on the street. How could I work for four years and not save any money? What an idiot I was. Ok, now it was time for a do over. It was time to start my life over again.

About a week later, I got a call from Sammy's restaurant in Opelika. The position was for a manager trainee, who would eventually work his way up to manager. That sounded like the job for me, so I called and made an appointment for an interview.

The following Monday I dressed in my best (and only) suit and drove to Opelika. The interview went well, and I was soon hired as the manager trainee for the Opelika store. I was to start working the following day. Life was good.

My job with Sammy's was going really well. I was promoted to kitchen manager and moved to a bigger restaurant in Columbus, Georgia. One of the things I loved about working there was how you were always encouraged to use your imagination and try out new ideas. One of the ideas I had was how to save money by using things you would normally throw away. For example, the soup bar. Sammy's always had two soups available, and they changed them daily. When I was in training, I learned that when preparing the salad bar, the prep girls would take fresh broccoli, cut off the sprigs and throw the stalk away. They would also grind the cheese and throw away the end pieces that were too small to hold. These were the things I decided that I could use to save the company money, so I started making soup. I decided I would experiment the next day.

As soon as I arrived at work the next morning, I gathered the broccoli stalks and cheese that I had saved and made a big pot of cheese and broccoli soup. The menu for the day called for beef vegetable and minestrone soups, so I decided to put my soup in the place of the minestrone, and see what happened.

Usually, the soups would have to be replenished about one time each diner service. The Cheese and broccoli soup ran out in the first hour! I had to make three more batches to get through the dinner service. Using my soup made with leftovers had saved the restaurant about seventeen dollars that evening. Now, with a successful test under my belt, I was ready to pitch my idea to corporate.

The next day the corporate training manager, Betty Grey, was making her rounds through Columbus, so I asked for some time with her to show her my new money saving idea. Once she had tasted my soup, she was a believer. She said she would pitch the idea to corporate, and see what they said.

A couple days later, I got a phone call from Ms. Grey. She told me they looked at my recipe, and decided that it wasn't going in the direction they wanted to go, but thanks for trying. Oh well, nothing ventured, nothing gained.

A couple weeks later, we were having a meeting of all the city managers. The district manger liked to give the corporate highlights, and announce some of the goings on in the Sammy's corporation. About halfway through the meeting, he held up a picture of Betty Grey, our corporate training manager. He told us how she had been awarded a check for five thousand dollars for saving the company money. It seems that she had a wonderful idea that saved waste from the salad bar and made a wonderful cheese and broccoli soup. Corporate just couldn't say enough about Betty Grey... but I sure could.

As angry as I was about her stealing my idea, I decided that I wouldn't let one evil person ruin my brand new career. This never would have happened in the Navy. Hmm... the Navy...

Chapter Six

The next couple weeks were busy, but productive. I had been able to bring in more customers by beefing up the wait staff. Our best night was Wednesday, and I was expecting a full house that week. Wednesday was Sammy's new "all you can eat shrimp night." I had been advertising all week for this night, and I was ready to break the record for the most money brought in. This was going to be my night!

Earlier Wednesday afternoon, I brought out ten cases of frozen shrimp from the freezer, in preparation for the evening, and put them on the counter in the back of the kitchen. Just as I was coming out of the freezer, the City Manager, Mr. Roberts, walked into the kitchen. "Hello, Mr. Westfall. Are you getting ready for the dinner rush tonight?" 'Yes, Sir. I have ten cases of shrimp sitting in the back." He looked to the rear of the kitchen and said "Ten cases? That's too much. You only need five cases." "But Sir" I said "Last week we used eight cases, and I almost ran out. I am sure I will need at least ten this week." I knew that if the shrimp was still in the freezer, it would be too late to use it. If I didn't break out the shrimp now, I would run out. Mr. Roberts looked at me and shook his head. "Mr. Westfall, put five cases back. I will stay and help you through dinner so all will be well." I finally bowed to his experience, and did as he told me too. I guess five cases would be enough.

Later that evening, with a full dining room, we started running low on shrimp. I told Mr. Roberts that we were running low, and I asked him what we should do about it. He said "Just keep sending bread and salad out. They can eat that." "But Sir, they didn't come here this evening for bread and salad. They came here for shrimp!" The customers were starting to get angry. Almost every table was asking to speak to the manager.

I went back into the freezer to pull out the frozen boxes of shrimp, hoping to figure out a way to defrost them. When I came back out, I asked my Kitchen Manager where Mr. Roberts was. "He left out the back door about ten minutes ago." I couldn't believe my ears. The only reason I had run out of shrimp was because he had made me put five cases back, and now the coward runs out the back and leaves me with a store full of angry customers.

That was the final straw. This would be my last night working for Sammy's. I did find a way to satisfy the customers in the store, though. Since this was one of Mr. Robert's stores, I decided I should start refunding everyone's money. About ninety percent of the meals served in that restaurant that night were free. That should send a message,

The next day I located Mr. Roberts in one of the stores across town. As I walked into the restaurant, he said "Mr. Westfall... Aren't you supposed to be in your store right about now?" I just smiled at him, slammed my keys down on the table and said "You screwed me last night. Now, I am paying you back. Here are your keys. Have a great day!" And that was my last day with Sammy's restaurants.

The next day I found myself back at Mom and Dad's, sitting on the back steps. I enjoyed sitting there, looking out over the field at sunset, wondering, what are those guys on the submarines doing right now? Some are on the mess decks eating dinner; some are in the engine room trying to get their qualifications done. I found myself longing to be with them. Home was a wonderful place, and Mom and Dad were so good to me, but it was like I really didn't belong there right now. I knew that I was supposed to be somewhere else.

One thing I did do was to enlist in the Navy Reserves. It wasn't the same as the Navy, but it did get me a couple hundred dollars a month, and I really needed that. I would drive down to Montgomery one weekend a month, and do whatever they wanted me to do. They would put me up in a motel above one of the hottest nightclubs in town. Actually, I had so much fun on those weekends I would have drilled for free!

One weekend I was assigned to work in the main galley on Gunter Air Force base. Since I was in the habit of always reporting early, I found myself standing outside the galley's locked doors at four thirty that Saturday morning. As I was looking out over the parade field, I started smoking a cigarette. I noticed that the Air Force had moved about thirty old planes out onto the field. There was a man with a clipboard walking around checking off things on the planes. Since I had nothing else to do, I walked out to see what he was doing.

As I walked over to where he was standing, I started looking at the plane he was inspecting. Now, I know nothing about planes, period. I never had that childhood desire to be a pilot, or to jump out of any kind of flying vehicle. But I would have to admit, this plane looked cool. It had a caged canopy and twin engines. There was a picture of a ghost with a machine gun just under the canopy. I thought it looked really cool!

The man walked up to me and said "What do you think?" I said "It's really cool. If this was my plane, I would park it on the side of the road in Beulah and putt a mail box out in front of it." He smiled and looked down at a base access list he was holding and said "You must be Westfall, one of the new reserve cooks." I looked at him kind of surprised and said "Yes, that's me. What kind of plane is this?" He looked at it fondly and said "This is a World War II B-25 Mitchell medium range bomber. They were use in the Doolittle raid over Tokyo. It's been totally stripped, and it hasn't left the ground since 1959. Since then, it's been displayed on a parade field on a small reserve base in Georgia. How much would you give me for something like this?" I could just imagine living in this thing. It would be cool. Stupid, but cool. "Ok, I'll give you a hundred dollars for the plane" I said laughing "but that's all, unless you put the guns back on it!" Just then, I noticed the lights in the galley coming on, so I wished the man a good day and went off to work.

A couple weeks later, I was sitting on the front porch with my dad when the mail man came by. I had received a letter from the Gunter Air Force Base salvage department. I opened it and started reading it to my dad "Dear Mr. Westfall, We have received your bid of one hundred dollars for the 1942 B-25 Mitchell hull. The salvage specs are as follows: Weight – twenty thousand pounds. Length – fifty three feet. Wing Span – sixty eight feet. Please make arrangements for shipping your lot by calling the number listed below. Thank you for your interest in the Gunter Air Force base salvage program." I thought my dad was going to laugh himself off the porch. It looked like I was the proud owner of a World War II United States Army Bomber.

The next day I called Gunter and spoke with the salvage team leader, Major Somers. I explained the misunderstanding and asked him what I could do about it. He said "Petty Officer Westfall, it was understood that you made a bid in good faith. If you renege on that bid, your Command will get a nasty gram. I do have an idea though. Let me call you back in a few minutes." A few minutes later, Major Somers called back. "Good news! I talked one of our biggest scrap metal customers into paying the hundred bucks for the B-25. With your OK, you will be off the hook." I quickly agreed and thanked the Major for his help. I managed to dodge that bullet, and life was good again.

While I did have the Reserves, I still needed a real job. One evening my brother Toby had called and asked me if I wanted to do some construction work with a friend of his who owned a small constriction company. Anxious to make some money, I agreed and he picked me up and drove me over to meet my new boss.

A few miles down the road we came to a large white house. As we stepped onto the front porch, a stocky man in over-alls stepped out the front door. "Hi, I'm Mack Mitchell" He said in a friendly voice. I quickly shook his hand and introduced myself. After Mack talked to Toby for a couple minutes, he asked me "So, can you roof?" I said "Uh, no." Then he asked "Can you frame?" "Uh, no" I said reluctantly. He shook his head and smiled, then said "Hell, what can you do?" I quickly answered "I can out work anyone on your crew, and I am a fast learner. After one week, if I haven't proved myself, you don't have to pay me." Mack looked at me and said "Well, you served your country, so I guess I can give you a try. I will pick you up at seven sharp tomorrow morning."

The next day Mack showed up promptly at seven. He was driving an old powder blue Ford flatbed with dual wheels. It felt good to be part of something, even if I didn't quite know what that something was. Mack told me we would be putting on a new roof that morning, and our first stop would be Baker and Sons Lumber Company. He told me what I would need as far as tools go, and said he would advance the money for them from my first weeks pay check. I picked out a tape measure, a hammer, and a modest tool belt to hold it all.

Once we arrived at the job site, my training started. I learned how to properly remove the old roof, cut and replace the plywood decking, and lay down the felt paper. Mack taught me how to measure and mark the felt paper so the roof would be straight. Then, he showed me how to nail the shingles properly. I was impressed with just how talented Mack was. He seemed to know everything there was about building and roofing houses. I knew I would learn a lot from Mack, and it would serve me well over my life.

Soon, that job was over and we were off to the next job. Mack was excellent when it came to home repair, but bookkeeping was not a strong point for him. My third week of work was coming to an end, and Mack was dropping me off at home. He pulled out his wallet and said "I am sorry Clay. I owe you two hundred and ten dollars, but all I have right now is a hundred and eighty. Can I give you the rest next week?" I just smiled and said "Sure, Mack. Have a nice weekend." If I said I wasn't disappointed, I would be lying. I needed that money, but my parents had raised me to be patient and think before acting. Something told me that everything would be alright.

The summer was strewn with roofing jobs, big and small. I became quite the expert at roofing, decking and estimating the cost of a job. As we grew in experience, we started much bigger jobs, like building garages and later, building complex houses. When we would build complete houses from the ground up, we had to subcontract the plumbing, electrical, heating and cooling, etc. After working together on several jobs, Mack offered to take on a contract plumber named Andrew Simms. With Andy on the crew, we could complete the houses about two weeks faster.

I remember the first job that Andy worked with us. We had already set the walls of the house, and now we setting the trusses on the walls. Most houses today are built using trusses for the roof framing. Trusses are pre-fabricated, triangulated wooden structures used to support the roof. The alternative is to frame the roof with 2x8s and 2x10s.

As the trusses were being set on the walls, I would stand in them and hold them up so they could be nailed in place. In order to do this, I had to stand with one hand and one foot on one truss, and one hand and foot on a second trusses, holding them upright. As I was waiting for them to be nailed, they started to slide on the wall. If I was to let go, they would fall and possible hurt one of the electricians working in the house below us. As it turned out, it was a very hot day, and all of us were sweating so much our clothes were soaked. As the trusses spread farther and farther apart, my soaking wet pants started to split, and there was nothing I could do about it.

One of the electricians brought his sixteen year old daughter, Lisa, with him as an apprentice. It just so happened that Lisa was standing right under where I was holding the trusses. As she looked up to see what was happening, my pants tore completely and everything I had just kind of fell out for the world to see. As Lisa stood there staring up in disbelief, Big Mack pointed at me and yelled as loud as he could "Clay... rod... Clayrod!" I pretty much just wanted to die. After that day, I was known as Clayrod.

From day one, I knew that I would be going back into the Navy one day. I just missed the sea something awful. It was like there was always something going on that I was missing. I told Big Mack that one day, I would join the Navy again. It might be tomorrow, or it could be three years from then, but I knew that I was going back to sea someday.

Mack and I became good friends. I also knew his wife, Sherry Leigh, pretty well. She was very pretty, and used to go to school with Mack. Mack was the star running back on the football team, and Sherry Leigh was the leading cheerleader. There was one thing about Big Mack that I did not like at all... he would run around on his wife. I did not agree with anyone cheating on their spouse, no matter what reason they gave for it. Andy was also married, and he too was always chasing one skirt or another.

Every Friday evening after work was over, we would head off to Spuds. Spuds was the name of a club in Opelika where there was live music and cheap pitchers of beer. There were lots of ladies there and on occasion I would flirt with some of them or maybe take off with them. Being the only single guy on the crew at the time, it was kind of expected. But when Mack and Andy started trying to pick up girls, I had to make a new rule. I knew both of their wives, and considered them friends of mine. I was not going to be any part of Mack and Andy cheating on them. One evening I told them if they wanted to cheat on their wives, they had better not tell me about it, or let me know what was going on. I would not lie for them, or help them in any way, so if they were planning on cheating, they had better not invite me that evening. And that's the way it was.

One of the biggest problems Mitchell Construction had was bad tempers. Mack and Andy would get into big arguments at least once a week, and if I wasn't there they would have come to blows. Usually, it was over a business transaction or something that took both of them to agree on. Most of the time everyone got along pretty well, and we enjoyed working together.

I remember once Andy and his wife went on vacation, so I suggested that Mack and I break into his house and rearrange all of his furniture. We changed his master bedroom with his guest room, including the rugs, drapes and the clothes lying around on the floor. We also switched around the living room and the den, and rearranged the kitchen by moving the refrigerator and the dining room table.

Two days later, Andy showed up to work early, and since I was always early, I was already there. He came up to me and anxiously asked "Clay, did you guys change around my furniture?" I laughed and told him we did, and how it all happened. With a sigh of relief, Andy said "Thank goodness. My wife and I were worried about who might have done it. She actually likes the way it is now, so we will leave it all the way you moved it."

As I was drinking my coffee, I said "Andy... would you like to have some fun with Big Mack today?" I told Andy what I had in mind, and then he started laughing, got into his truck and drove off.

A few minutes later, Big Mack drove up. Like always, he would get out of his truck and yell "Clayrod!" As he walked over to where I was sitting, Andy drove up. Looking very angry, he climbed out of his truck and slammed the door. He walked over and said "You will not believe what happened. While we were on vacation, someone broke into our house and rearranged all of our furniture!" Mack quietly looked over at me and started smiling. Then Andy continued, saying "Then they stole our big screen TV and three VCR's! The Police were at our house late last night getting fingerprints, and they found some good ones. We are going to get those bastards!" The look on Big Mack's face was priceless! He looked terrified and slowly shook his head. "Clayrod, it looks like you and I are in big trouble." We let it sink in for a few minutes for effect, and then Andy and I started laughing. As the color returned to Mack's face, Andy and I told him what we did. I knew then that I was going to have to sleep with one eye opened.

The following day was a very busy one. All of the sub-contractors were there, about forty people in all. When lunch time finally arrived, I was starving! I walked out to get the lunch sack I had left by the truck, and saw that it was missing. I looked around for it, but it was nowhere to be found. Never, in four years of being in the Navy had this ever happened to me. Someone had stolen my lunch.

About twenty minutes later, Big Mack and Andy came out to join me, but I was just sitting there, staring at the spot where my lunch had been sitting. Mack said "Clayrod, are you alright?" I looked up at Mack and said "It's time. I'm going to join the Navy tomorrow, and I'm going back to sea."

The next day I was in the recruiting office in Opelika, sitting in the same chair I sat in almost six years ago. As a rule, the Navy was not taking any Navets, which is, prior service Navy Veterans. But there had been a shortage of cooks in the fleet, so the window for getting back into the Navy was opened for me. When I was asked when I wanted to go, I said "Now is good for me." We finally agreed that I would go back into the Navy a couple days later.

The following day I went over to Mack's house to tell him that I was back in the Navy. I really couldn't believe what happened next. Mack started crying and hugged me. He said "Clayrod, I love you like a brother. I am really going to miss you." I was going to miss Mack and Andy, but that part of my life was over. Now it's Haze Gray and underway again!

I found out later that when I left, the friction started. Mack and Andy got into a huge fight about a week later, and that was the end of the Mitchell construction.

Orlando Florida was absolutely beautiful. The Navy had three boot camps at that time, and one of them was in Orlando. A large section of this base was set aside for what the Navy called "Navet University." At any one time, there are about a hundred Navets there, in various stages of reintegration into the active duty Navy. Usually, the process takes about two months. In this time, the records are processed and brought back from the archives in New Orleans and brought up to date. A complete physical has to be done, as well as a full dental screening and a job placement in the fleet.

There couldn't be a better place for the Navy to have Navet U. The weather was perfect, the women were absolutely gorgeous, and all we had was time and money. Life was good. The only bad thing about Orlando was the lightning. Orlando Florida is the lightning capitol of the United States. Every day at four o'clock you could hear sirens go off throughout the town, warning people to head for shelter. After the lightning had passed, the sirens would sound again giving the all clear to come out again. I paid close attention to those sirens. I already had one bout with lightning a few years before. My brother and I were trying to repair the chicken pen back home one evening before a storm hit. While we were tacking the wire down, a bolt of lightning hit the roof of the chicken coup and knocked us flat. That was a very frightening experience that I did not want to repeat.

Every morning revile sounded at six o'clock. After getting up and hitting the shower, shaving and put on the dungarees, it was off to the chow hall. The food in the Navy was still excellent, no matter what anyone says. The Orlando chow hall was no exception. The whole time I was there I never missed a meal. Anything you ever wanted was there, and you could have as much as you wanted.

After breakfast every day during the week we had quarters. That's where everyone showed up to be counted and the Chief read the plan of the day. After quarters, usually around nine o'clock in the morning, we were done with all the Navy stuff for the day.

Once we were on our own time, we would usually gather on the patio to decide what we were going to do for the day. Most of the time we would head to the beach and play volley ball, or buy a bushel of oysters and a few cases of beer and sit around the barracks all day and watch movies.

There were a couple guys there that I met on the first day, and we became pretty good friends. Glen Colson was an Electrician, awaiting orders to a West coast aircraft carrier. Glen was happily married and basically liked to have fun without getting into too much trouble. My other friend was Mark Hudson, a Boatswains Mate looking to get stationed on any ship overseas. The three of us would usually meet for a cigarette on the patio every morning and then decide what it was we wanted to do with the day. No matter what we decided, we always did it together.

One of the things that seemed to take the longest was waiting for your orders to come in. Being the only submariner there, my orders took a bit longer than everyone else's. I had to reestablish my Top Secret security clearance, and that took time.

Anyone who worked on a submarine during the cold war had to have a Top Secret security clearance. This was a lengthy process that involved lots of paperwork. The government would go back into your past and investigate every job and every person you have ever known. Twenty years after, I was still discovering people that the Government spoke with.

Most of the sailors at Navet U were there for only a few weeks, but for me it would be a bit longer. The guys got a good laugh when my orders did come through. The USS Monongahela (AO-178) – a surface ship! That last thing I wanted at that time was to go to a surface ship, or 'target' as we called them in the sub fleet. I quickly protested the orders and prayed that I could get them changed in time.

The following day Glen, Mark and I went out into town early. We hit a couple bars, and pretty much took it easy. We got back to the base around four that afternoon, and decided to walk to the chow hall and have a nice dinner. As we were walking towards the mess hall, we noticed a huge cloud looming overhead.

Glen and I were walking side by side, with Mark following closely behind. I remember we were talking about Glen's two year old son Seth, and then all of a sudden there was a brilliant flash of light. There was the sound of a deafening thunder clap accompanied by a light that was so bright, I couldn't see anything.

The next thing I knew, I was standing under the roof of a small storage shed, and the sirens were sounding. I had a hard time seeing; my vision was so blurry, I couldn't make anything out. Next, I heard the voices of two women shouting "Are you alright? My God, call an ambulance!" I could feel someone pulling me down into a sitting position on the sidewalk, and then one of the women said "Wait. Your contacts have popped out and are stuck to your cheeks." I looked and I could see the rank insignia of a Senior Chief. "Senior, what happened?" The Senior Chief told me that her and her friend had been walking back from their duty shift when they heard the lightning. "We looked and saw a huge bolt of lightning strike right where you and your friends were standing. Don't move... we called an ambulance and we are going to take you to the base hospital to get checked out." I looked and saw Glen and Mark sitting with another Chief not too far away.

At the hospital, the three of us were all sitting on gurneys in the emergency room, and I noticed that I couldn't taste anything but ozone, kind of like when you touch a battery to your tongue. Glen couldn't feel anything in his legs, and neither of us could stop shaking. Mark didn't suffer any effects of the strike whatsoever, and was asking when we could leave. The Doctor insisted on keeping us there for at least one night of observation. He said many times when people are hit with large charges of electricity, they can suffer a heart attack an hour or so later. They wanted to play it safe, so we were stuck there until the following morning. That was the second and hopefully the last time I would get struck by lightning.

The next week, Glen and Mark received their orders, and were both scheduled to fly out that Friday around noon. When military personnel are transferred, their records are sent with them. Medical, dental, pay and service records are placed in a large manila envelope and taped shut. Everyone knows that you must take very good care of this envelope, and it is not to be opened until you arrive at your new command. As you are reporting in, the duty officer opens this package in front of you and dumps the records on the desk, then stamps your service record.

Since there were still a couple hours left before Glen and Mark were to depart, they decided it would be a great time for them to go and get haircuts, so they would look sharp as they reported to their new commands. Since I didn't need a haircut, I volunteered to watch their packages while they were gone, and they agreed. As soon as they walked away, I had an idea.

Earlier that morning, they had taken my boots and filled them with liquid laundry detergent. I was annoyed, but it was kind of funny. Now, it was my turn. I quickly locked the records in my locker so they would be safe, and then ran over to the exchange to buy a large box of condoms. When I got back, I opened Glen and Marks packages very carefully with a knife, making sure my cut would not be detected. Then, I divided the condoms into two equal piles, and carefully slipped them into the packages, and then I taped the package back exactly like they were. There was no trace that the packages had been tampered with.

A couple hours later a taxi pulled up to the front of the barracks. Glen and Mark were wearing their dress uniforms, looking very sharp for their journey. As I shook their hands and wished them well, I could not help but to smile. My only wish was to be a fly on the wall when the Officer in Charge of their new command dumps their records and all of those condoms on his desk. The look on their faces would be priceless!

About two weeks later, my orders finally came through. The USS Norfolk (SSN-714), stationed in Norfolk Virginia, back on pier twenty three.

When I first arrived aboard the USS Norfolk, it was tied up outboard of the Emory S. Land (AS-39), the tender for Squadron Eight. I arrived late on a Thursday night, and the duty cook, Billy Dorn, was just getting cleaned up from dinner. He offered me some leftovers and poured himself a cup of coffee. We sat for a while and talked about the boat, and what was in store for me. Could you believe it? The Norfolk was due to pull into the shipyard in Portsmouth, New Hampshire early next year. They were also due to go to sea the following week, so I needed to get all my stuff ready to go.

After leaving the boat, I went to the other side of the base to Groshong Hall, the barracks that the Norfolk was assigned to. The USS Norfolk Sailors had the entire fifth floor, so that is where my room assignment was. When I got to the fifth floor, I noticed lots of guys running around doing their laundry, watching TV in the TV lounge, and some just talking in their rooms. All the doors were opened, and everyone just kind of went wherever they wanted. After a while, I had met several of the guys, so life was good. As I made up my bed and lay down for the night, I couldn't help but to wonder what the future had in store for me. I guess I would soon find out...

I went in to work the following day, and was told to report to the Chief of the boat. I walked to the forward part of the sub and knocked on the door to the Goat Locker. "Come in" came the reply, so I entered and stood at attention. "MS3(SS) Westfall, reporting for duty!" I looked down as I was reporting, and I recognized the COB from my days on the Baton Rouge. "Senior Chief Zubowitz... it's good to see you." He just stared at me, then after a couple minutes he said "Westfall, we were told that you were dead!" He motioned for me to sit down, and started explaining his comments.

"When you got out of the Navy, all was well. Then one day a couple months later, NCIS came to the boat and started asking questions about you. Apparently, a badly decomposed body was found out in a desert in Nevada. There was no head on the body and no identification at all, but he was wearing a USS Baton Rouge cook's tee shirt with your name inside of it. Your death was even recorded in the ship's log."

I started thinking back, and remembered one of the cranks at the time, a Seaman Becket. "Cobber, do you remember SN Becket? He went UA a few months before the Med run. He had stolen all of my mess tee shirts... I'll bet that was him." The COB nodded his head. "Ok, the mystery of the headless dead body is solved, welcome aboard and get to work!"

The next week we were heading out to sea. There was a lot of secrecy about where we were going and when we would be getting back to port. This was one of those missions no one would talk about, so the best thing to do was to just get to work and not ask questions. I was assigned as the Galley Watch Captain, in charge of cooking lunch and dinner for the entire crew every day, nonstop. Since I had been cooking on a submarine for some time now, I easily stepped up to my tasks.

The only problem I had at the time was the drills. Constantly, day in and day out, fire drills, flooding drills, toxic leak drills, reactor scram drills... you name it, we drilled it. Cooking dinner for a crew who expected to eat on time was difficult enough without all the problems drills caused. For example, if I was baking sheet cakes for desert and the ship pulled a hard turn to starboard, my cakes dumped into the bottom of the oven. If there was a major steam leak drill, my electric kettles wouldn't work. Every drill affected something, and that made it harder for me to do my job.

Once everyone had eaten dinner, and all the watches were relieved, it was time to clean up. By this time, we were all exhausted. It took about an hour to clean up the galley, and when it was finally clean the Night Baker would take over and start his shift. Then, it was off to the showers and finally to bed. If you were a nub, you would have to do your qualifications for the next four hours. Thank God that was over. Now, I could actually sleep for eight hours if I wanted to. As a rule, the Captain wouldn't run drills at night, so we could actually rest.

I really enjoyed being back at sea. There was nothing quite like it. I would often think about what all my friends back home were doing while I was cruising the sea lanes in a state of the art nuclear submarine. It was just so cool. This time, it was different... I wanted to be there. Almost everyone in the military hates the first enlistment. They think they made a mistake and wish they could have a do over. Well, I had my do over, and this is where I wanted to be. Now, I wanted to do the best job I possibly could.

Chapter Seven

That year we were scheduled for a Northern run. For the first time in my life, I was going to the North Pole! The South Pole, as most people know, is on an actual land mass. The North Pole, on the other hand, is nothing but huge, floating ice masses.

On August 3, 1958, the USS Nautilus (SSN-571) became the first submarine to reach and cross under the North Pole. Since then, submarines from all countries routinely cross under the North Pole. Some of the actually surface and break through the ice, if it's thin enough.

When the USS Norfolk crossed the Arctic Circle, we were initiated into the "Blue Nose" fraternity. For all of you "old Salts" who are familiar with the shellback celebration, the "blue nose" is very similar. It can be traced back to the days of sailing ships. When ships crossed the equator, it was considered a rite of passage for a new sailor and it was signified by a ceremony that was pretty brutal by today's standards. Our "blue nose" initiation was fairly mild, but still had its challenges.

The first thing that happened is we were told to strip down to our underwear and then were sent to the Torpedo Room bilge, where cold water from the ships potable water talks was sprayed upon us. The temperature of the water was pretty cold (just above freezing) and very uncomfortable. I never knew that your entire body could actually turn blue. After that, we crawled through the passageway on our knees to the Crew's Mess, where we were treated to a very stylish haircut by the Royal Barber and made to eat some of the royal grog that had been made for us ahead of time. I am not sure what was in it, but it was absolutely horrible.

After that, we were all made to crawl through a trough of ships garbage. As best I can tell, most of it was edible but it sure did not smell like it. Upon exiting the chute, we had to take a seat on a huge block of ice as we were addressed by the Royal Court. I also recall having to drink more grog as I awaited my opportunity to address the "baby".

The "baby" is the heaviest guy on board and we had a very large man as the baby. Inside the baby's belly button was a cherry and it was your job to get it out. If that is not bad enough, the baby's belly was covered with more disgusting, but edible, materials. I think the prime ingredients were molasses and peanut butter. As my face was pressed against the belly, I remember being told "Don't use your tongue, just suck the cherry out." I was able to extract the cherry a lot quicker than most of the guys.

With the most disgusting part complete, the Skipper then painted my nose blue and I was sent to the showers. As one last cruel twist, the electricians had removed all the hot water heater fuses. The showers used to clean up had only cold water! As a consolation,

I was awarded a bluenose certificate in my service record, and a great big one to hang on my "I love me" wall. Thank God, I will never have to go through that ceremony again!

Since we were in the neighborhood, we pulled into Halifax, Canada for a few days. It didn't take us long to find the watering hole, and that's pretty much where I spent all three days. I did have Wardroom duty on the third day, and I was in charge of setting up for captain's mast. In naval tradition, a mast is a non-judicial punishment (NJP) disciplinary hearing in which a commanding officer studies and disposes of cases involving those in his command. If the officer is a captain, as in most cases, it is referred to as a captain's mast.

This particular mast was in honor of two of our shipmates who had lost their way home on the first night of liberty. TM3 Cramer and TMSN Ames were due back on the boat on the second morning, but did not show up until almost lunch on the third day. The Skipper called for an immediate captain's mast, so he could deal with the punishment before the ship pulled into home port.

Both Cramer and Ames were good workers, but this was not the first time they were late reporting in from liberty. They both had a tendency to drink too much, and both of them were plastered when they finally showed up. My duties as the Wardroom mess specialist was to set up the room, then stand as a witness to the proceedings. Today, the Skipper was seeing Cramer first, then Ames.

The Skipper called the mast to order, and then he addressed Cramer. "Petty Officer Cramer, you reported to duty a day and a half late in a liberty port, knowing that it was a mast offense. What do you have to say for yourself?"

Petty Officer Cramer popped to attention and started telling his story. "Well, Sir, Ames and I were heading off to see Canada. We wanted to take pictures and see how the local culture lived. We met up with some local girls, and had a few drinks. Then we had a few more drinks, and the next thing I knew, it was the next day. I am sorry Sir, and it will never happen again."

The Skipper said "Petty officer Cramer, I am going to take into account that you are an excellent Torpedo man, and have not been in trouble lately. Two weeks restriction once we get into home port. That is all. Send in the next case."

TMSN Ames was led in by the Master at Arms, and he stood at attention and saluted "Sir, TMSN Ames reporting as ordered." The Skipper saluted him back and said "Very well. Seaman Ames, you reported to duty a day and a half late in a liberty port, knowing that it was a mast offense. What do you have to say for yourself?"

Seaman Ames started stuttering, which usually meant he was trying to think of something good to say. "Sir, it happened like this. Cramer and I wanted to see Canada, and we went out to take a few pictures and see how the local people lived their lives. Cramer started drinking a lot, so I told him that he should slow down a bit because we wanted to see Nova Scotia. We had purchased two tickets to Amherst, but the train wasn't leaving for a couple more hours. By the time we were leaving, Cramer was passed out drunk. That's when we saw the two men in the dark glasses and black suits."

The Skipper looked up from his notes. "Did you say two men in dark glasses and black suits?" "Yes, Sir, I did. Cramer was so drunk, I am sure he wouldn't remember it." Ames replied. The Skipper was looking a bit skeptical, but said "Please, go on."

"Well, I was trying to drag Cramer onto the train, but I was having an awful time of it. The men in the dark glasses and black suits asked if they could help, so I said they could. As we were sitting on the train waiting for it to leave, they introduced themselves as Mr. Brown and Mr. Gray. That was when I started getting suspicious!" Ames looked at the floor, trying to think of what he was going to say next. "I knew then that they wanted to get top secret submarine intelligence from me! I kept changing the subject, but when I told them about my Aunt Helens wooden leg, they started to get angry with me."

The Skipper was quite intrigued with the story now, and was giving Ames one hundred percent of his attention. "I can't wait to hear what comes next!" He said. Then Ames continued.

"That's when they pulled out their guns, and told us we were getting off at the next station. Cramer was still passed out, so I am sure he wouldn't remember any of this. We got off at the next stop and were met by two more men with dark glasses and black suits." Ames was on a roll now. He was barely stopping for air. "They put us in a dark car and blindfolded us, and then we drove for about an hour. When we finally stopped, we were taken into a house. Cramer was still passed out, but they started asking me questions. I was careful not to tell them any top secret submarine stuff, but then I saw them forcing Cramer to drink some kind of liquid. After that, they split us up. I was so scared, Skipper. I didn't know what to do!"

The Wardroom was silent. The Skipper was listening very intently to everything Ames was saying. Ames reached down to take a sip of water from the glass in front of him, and then he started talking again. "That's when they put me into a room with the girl." The Skipper narrowed his eyes and asked "What girl?" "The girl that they had taken from her home Sir, and were holding hostage." Ames continued. "She told us she had been kidnapped a couple days earlier, and they told her they were going to shoot her if we didn't tell them about our submarine. As much as I didn't want her to die, I still didn't give them any secrets." Ames carefully looked around the Wardroom. I think he was evaluating how well his story was going. Then he started speaking again.

"That was a long night. All I could think about was getting back to the boat so I wouldn't be late for muster. But what could I do? I have to think about Cramer, and I needed to save the girl. That's when I realized that she must be a spy for them. She kept trying to seduce me, and said she wanted to be my girlfriend, but I am a family man with good upbringing, so I ignored her. All I had to do was to tell them my submarine secrets, and they would let us all go. But I would NEVER betray my country!" Seaman Ames stood to attention again, showing that he was really not a drunken loser, but an American hero!

Now the Skipper was starting to smile, and tried to cover it with his notes. "So, Cramer is drugged and passed out, and now this agent woman is attempting to seduce you to get top secret submarine information. How is it that you escaped?" "Well Sir" Ames started "I told them that I had to use the head, so they allowed me to go to the bathroom. As I was pretending to use it, I quietly found the room where Cramer was hiding, and dragged him into the head with me. Then I quietly broke the window and pushed him out. The men in dark glasses and black suits started to get suspicious, but I was talking to them through the bathroom door, so they assumed I was still going to the bathroom. When they noticed Cramer was missing, three of the men went out to look for him. I quickly overpowered the last man, and took his gun away. Then I ran out the door and picked up Cramer from outside the bathroom. He was still drunk and passed out, so I am sure he would not remember any of this."

Ames took another sip of water, and then he finished his story. "After dragging Cramer back to the road, I flagged down a car and got us a ride to the train station. I begged the Conductor for two tickets to Halifax, so we could get back here to the boat. I threw the gun in the water before coming aboard, because I knew bringing a gun onto the ship was wrong. I am just so glad, Sir, that I could live through this, save Cramer, and still not give away any submarine secrets. I do have one request, Sir. After this is all over, could you give me special liberty so I can run to the station and give the Conductor his money back? I am a man of honor, Sir, and I promised I would repay him. That's all I have to say about that, Sir.

The Skipper just looked at him. After a couple minutes, he said "Seaman Ames that was the biggest pile of bullshit that I have ever heard. That being said, I do love a good sea story, so I have taken that into consideration. Two weeks restriction once we get into home port. That is all.

Whenever you are underway on a submarine, the world disappears. There are no phone calls, the mail only goes out when you are in port, and you obviously can't run on home for dinner. The crews' morale can go down pretty fast, and the best way to improve the morale is with the best food possible. Steak, crab legs, lobster, shrimp... the list goes on and on. The Navy goes to great lengths and expense to keep the crew of a submarine happy. Sometimes, I would think of something silly to do to get everyone's mind off of the duties at hand. That's when Bob showed up.

Our next mission was somewhere in the southern Atlantic. When I was cleaning the Wardroom one day, I found Bob. Bob was a six inch stuffed man with long red hair. He had brown pants, a striped shirt and little black shoes. Bob was very cool. He fit perfectly into my breast pocket, and would stick out half way so everyone could see him. As I would stand watch in the galley every day, various members of the crew would stop by the serving window and say "Hi Clay, hi Bob!" Everyone loved Bob; well, almost everybody. After a month or so, Bob disappeared from my rack while I was taking a shower. You see, Bob didn't really like to take showers, so he would lie in my rack while I was in the head. I knew that foul play was involved, and Bob's safety was my chief concern. Life was not good.

I did what any submarine cook would do. I put up posters all over the boat 'Missing: Bob. If found please return him, unmolested, to the galley. No questions asked.' I had sketched a picture of Bob on the poster, and hoped for the best.

A 688 class nuclear submarine is designed with the galley and crew's mess on the middle level. Just above the galley is the radio shack. In the galley ceiling just above the dishwasher, there is an escape hatch designed for the Radiomen to escape radio in the event of a fire. Do to the top secret nature of the radio shack, the hatch can only be opened from the top. When I walked into the galley the next day, there was a sign hanging from the hatch that read: 'Bob is ok for now, but I wouldn't want to be in his shoes if there is not a plate of chocolate chip cookies delivered to Radio by the end on the duty shift.'

A few hours later, a mysterious picture showed up in the passageway. It was a photocopy of Bob with a noose around his neck. Under the pictures was one sentence made up of letters cut from different magazines and pasted to the paper. It said 'give me cookies or give me death.' I knew that they meant business now. I quickly threw together a batch of chocolate chip cookies and delivered them to the radio shack. A mysterious man (RM2 Collins) answered the door with a mask on. He took the cookies and slammed the door while yelling "You will receive further instructions!"

When I returned to the galley, there was yet another sign. It read "The cookies are great, but we will also need some spice cake, delivered to the shack by midnight." That was the final straw! I quickly scribbled my own note and delivered it to radio. It simply said "If you do not want spit in everything you eat for the rest of the voyage, you will return Bob to the galley by morning!" The next morning when I arrived at the galley, there was Bob on the grill, and in the kettles, and in the steamer, and in the dishwasher. Bob had been returned, but he was in a million or so pieces. Perhaps the next time my note will be more specific and say something like "Return him in one piece."

Towards the end of the cruise things started to settle down. The drills came to an end, and the workload slowed down. All the nubs were making good use of the time by get their qualifications done. Every now and then, the boat would take on some Midshipmen, or as I liked to call them, 'baby officers.' These are students of the Naval Academy in Annapolis, Maryland, and they sometimes ride on boats to get a look at how the real Navy works. They are not officers yet, and they are not enlisted. The ward room would like for us to treat them like officers, salute them and call them Sir, but that's just not what happens. If the Midshipmen are smart, they will treat everyone with respect and do as they are told to do. If a Midshipman is arrogant and condescending, he usually finds himself in trouble with the crew.

On this particular run, we had four Midshipmen. Three of them were easy to get along with, and they were learning a lot from the crew. The last one, Midshipman Howard, was not the sharpest pencil in the box. On his very first day onboard he walked into the galley and said "Attention on deck, Midshipman Howard coming through! Feed me now or you will be put on report." I knew then that this was going to be a long trip for Howard. As he was trying to get some signatures back by the propulsion plant, he insulted the whole duty section by telling the Skipper they were not knowledgeable enough. Not too smart at all.

Before pulling into port, the Skipper liked to do a cleanliness inspection of the ship. He was scheduled to walk through the engine room at noon, so we decided to make his inspection a bit more enjoyable. The Nukes called up and asked me if I could lure Howard back to the engine room, between the main engines. I agreed and went to find Midshipman Howard. When I located him in the wardroom, I said "Midshipman Howard, I am having a hard time understanding where the main engines are. Can you help me find them?" He looked at me and said "Wow. How long have you been on submarines? You cooks don't know anything. Come on, follow me." Oh yes. This was going to be fun!

As we neared the main engines, I saw a couple of the Nuke Machinists slowly following us. The main engines were very big, and took up a lot of room. There was a walkway running between the main engines, and the rear throttles were located there. The throttles looked like two big wheels, one just inside the other. These wheels are similar to a huge steering wheel. As we neared the throttles, Howard realized something was up. I smiled at him and said "Don't worry, SIR, I'm just one of those stupid cooks!" I grabbed him and spun him around just as five Nukes grabbed him and started tying him up. Just then I had an idea, and said "Hang on guys... I know what we can do."

About a half an hour later, the Skipper came through the engine room. As he entered the area between the main engines, there was Midshipman Howard, totally naked, tied up hand and foot to the throttles. We had also taken the liberty of spray painting his genitals battleship gray, just for effect. As the Skipper looked at the cleanliness of the area, he didn't really pay any attention to Howard. When the walk thru was finished, he looked in Howards direction and said "The throttles are a mess... please clean them up ASAP." And that was the end of Midshipman Howards arrogance problem.

The final night underway was a fun night. As a reward for a job well done, the Skipper called for a pizza and casino night for the crew. We used real money, but the house had a twenty dollar limit and used twenty five cent chips. We had a blast, and the crew was able to let off some steam. Midshipman Howard was the big winner that night. The cruise was over, and we were heading home. Life, once again, was good.

When we arrived back at pier twenty three, it was cold and there was snow on the pier. Since we had been at sea for so long, we had the next five days off. I did nothing but eat and sleep, and it seemed like the time passed instantly. The following Monday we had quarters on the pier, and the Skipper wanted to address the crew. After a few minutes, he called everyone to attention, and then he said "MS3 Westfall, front and center." I had no idea what was going on, so I quickly marched to the front and made a snappy salute. "For outstanding service to the crew of the USS Norfolk on our recent underway operation, I am proud to name you as the USS Norfolk Sailor of the Quarter." After shaking my hand and handing me my certificate he continued "Petty Officer Westfall has been nominated by this command for duty at the White House cooking for the President of the United States. Congratulations!"

Actually, as good as it was to be nominated for the position, it was a long way to the White House. There were actually 154 sailors nominated for that one position, and they were all going to have to be weeded out through a comprehensive interview process. After a few weeks, it was down to only four. Then the White House staff sent down its own people to interview the ones of us who where left. After a week of interviews, there were only two of us left.

Katie Sonnet was an MSSN who worked on the tender in the Jack of the dust office. She was an excellent MS, and she was my competition. I had known Katie and worked with her a couple times before, and she was pretty knowledgeable. But, when you put my career next to hers, she didn't stand a chance. The next day I almost ran to the boat. I was so excited! The White House! I was going to cook for the President!

As I got to the Captains stateroom, he looked at me and said quickly "They chose Sonnet." I couldn't believe my ears. There were four criteria for the position. First, the candidate had to be the rank of at least an E-4. Sonnet was an E-3. Second, you had to be well rounded and knowledgeable in all areas of the rate. Sonnet had done nothing but records her whole time in the Navy. Third, you had to have at least four years of active duty service. Sonnet had only been in for two years. And fourth, the candidate must have at least a 3.8 evaluation. Sonnet had a 3.4 evaluation. She missed all four criteria, and I hit all four criteria. The only thing she had going for her was the fact that she was very pretty.

The Skipper asked me what I wanted to do about it, and I said I wanted to file a grievance against the White House for discrimination. He agreed with me, and we headed off to the tender to talk to the Commodore.

A week or so later we got a call from the White House Staffing Officer, a Senior Chief Yancy. The Captain put him on speaker phone so we could all hear him. He said "Petty Officer Westfall, I hear that you have a problem with our selection process." That's when I politely told him I thought I was discriminated against. He said "Well, it's just a matter of preference, that's all." I replied "Oh, so if I prefer a white man to a black man, that's alright?" He paused a minute and said "Petty Officer Westfall, you are fighting City Hall. You need to let it go." After a couple words with the Skipper, the Senior Chief hung up. I knew right then that it was over. It wasn't fair, but it was over anyway.

The following week, we set sail for the Virgin Islands once again. We needed to run a couple of sound tests, and since we would be in the neighborhood, Squadron let us spend a couple days in St. Croix. I hadn't been there since the infamous USS Salt Lake City island take-over, so it would be good to get back to the rum and sunshine.

Since I had the galley watch every day underway, I was allowed to go on liberty as soon as we pulled in. I changed into my beach bum clothes and hit the pier as fast as I could. There was old Sadie one leg, sitting there with her truck load of beer. I handed her three dollars and sat down on the pier with my three beers and waited for my buddies. A short while later my friends came topside and we headed down the pier into Fredricksted.

Just at the head of the pier was a brand new liquor store, so we decided we should stop in. The owner of the store had set up a long table just inside the doorway, so I asked what it was for. He said that they were expecting a cruise ship early the next day, and the table was set so visitors could taste all the different types of rum. Just then we realized our goal for that day; to drink as much free rum as possible!

After tasting about thirty types of rum, we decided to buy six bottles, each one a different flavor. We also purchased some ice, cups and three large bottles of soda, and then headed out to the beach.

The beach was very close to the pier, and we could see the submarine from there. This beach was perfect! There were very few people there, and the wind was blowing cool salt air off the water. There were several coconut trees along the beach, and several large cabanas with barbeque grills. The best part was the rum store was just a five minute walk! Life was awesome!

As the morning went by, several guys from the crew came to the beach, and we were all feeling no pain at all. It was the perfect day! As we were basking in the sun, and old Rastafarian man walked into our area of the beach. He looked at me and said "Have you ever tasted grilled shark, man?" I looked back at him and said "No, I can't say I ever have. I sure would like to, though!" He pointed out into the water and said "Look. There is an injured sand shark. If you can bring him closer to the shore, I will kill him for you. Then we will have a beach feast!" Right then I caught myself saying something I never thought I would have said. "Hey guys, let's get in the water and catch the shark!"

Lucky for me, drunken sailors are easy to motivate when it comes to adventure. We decide the best way to herd the shark was to go about half way down the pier and then get into the water. We went in one at a time, and made a line between the ocean and the shark. It slowly swam back and forth each time turning toward the beach.

As I swam closer to the shark, I saw that it was about six feet long, and looked to weigh about four hundred pounds. I knew from watching a TV special the sand sharks don't normally attack people, and will usually do everything they can to get away. Oh, just so you know, I agree. This is the stupidest thing I had ever done.

Once we were fairly close to the beach, the Rastafarian man waded out into the water and speared the shark with a long pole he had been sharpening. Once he pinned the shark to the ocean floor, he just stood there, holding the spear until the shark stopped thrashing about. He then asked for some help to pull him out of the water and started skinning the shark. About an hour later, we were eating the best seafood I had ever tasted. Life was good.

The next morning we were due to leave St. Croix and head home. As the Maneuvering Watch was being set, a very large cruise ship pulled into the port and was mooring just across the pier from us. The deck was full of people, all getting ready to go ashore. Just forward of the fantail was about ten beautiful college girls all looking and waving to the submarine.

As the Norfolk started to pull out, Billy Waters was standing on the forward deck. He really wasn't supposed to be topside, but he had been flirting with one of the girls in the group and pretended he had business with the topside line handlers. Just as the sub started pulling away from the pier, the girl that he had been flirting with disappeared from sight. A moment later she yelled "Take these to remember me by" and threw a pair of yellow panties into the water. Without thinking at all, Billy dove into the water after the panties.

"MAN OVERBOARD!" the COB yelled. Whenever someone has gone into the water by an operational submarine or ship, everything has to stop. A nuclear submarine is constantly drawing in cooling water, using its active sonar, and turning its screw. Any one of these will kill a swimmer instantly. By going into the water, Billy caused a lot of problems.

The Skipper went ballistic. He ordered the screw to stop turning, and secured all underwater operations. I knew that Billy had just made a big career mistake over some girl. But, I had to admit, she was a very nice looking girl...

The cruise back toward Norfolk was quiet and uneventful. One thing worth mentioning was Billy Waters new watch station. The Skipper had station Billy under the main seawater pump with one mission: Make the bilge clean enough to eat out of. I remember bringing Billy a snack and a soda the next day. I looked at his sparkling bilge asked him if it was worth it. He just smiled and waved those yellow panties at me.

The day before we were to pull back into Norfolk, life aboard the boat was quiet. We were scheduled to perform a few more sound tests, but other than that the day was uneventful. Sitting on the mess decks was one of the crew's most seasoned members, Master Chief Everett. Master Chief Everett had been in the Navy since Noah was a mess crank, and he was older than dirt. This was going to be his last cruise with us, and he was due to retire in a couple weeks.

One of the Master Chiefs passions was going through the service records of the new sailors, and memorizing certain bits of information, and then he uses the information against them later. This morning I noticed him looking down at his note pad, so I knew something was up.

Just before the boat left port, a new sailor, Seaman Barret checked aboard. He had been assigned to the Crew's Mess as a mess crank, and was getting along well with the others. As SN Barret walked through the mess deck, the Master Chief looked at me and winked, then said "SN Barret, could you please bring me a cup of coffee?" Barret smiled and said "Sure thing Master Chief" and rushed a cup of coffee right over. As Barret was setting the cup on the table, Master Chief asked him what state he was from. "I am from Nebraska, Master Chief." Barret was so excited that someone as senior as the Master Chief was interested in him. 'Nebraska, huh? I have only been in Nebraska one time in my life. It was back in the summer of 1970." Now, the Master Chief knew full well where Barret was from and exactly when he was born. "I was taking a train to Las Angeles, passing through Southern Nebraska. We stopped at a small town called, what was it now... oh yes, Pickrell. It's about thirty five miles South of Lincoln." After hearing this, I saw Barrets' eyes light up. Just as he was about to say something, the Master Chief continued. "I only stayed one night in Pickrell, but it was a night I will always remember. I met a saucy young lady named... now what was it... Meryl Bowline, I think."

Now, this was probably the funniest thing I had ever witnessed. As the Master Chief well knew, Barrets mother's maiden name was Bowline. Her first name was actually Sheryl, so you could imagine the look on Barrets face. To top it all off, the Master Chief said "Wow. I later found out that she was engaged to be married, but that night she was mine. Yes, I will never forget that July in 1970." A quick look at Barret found him doing math in his head. Barret was actually born in April of 1971, so you could imagine what was going on in his mind. As the Master Chief stood up to leave the mess decks, he looked at me and smiled. His work there was done.

Once we pulled back into port and were settled back into our daily routine, I received a call from Medical on the tender. They asked for me to come there immediately. During the last underway period, I had gone to the Corpsman twice because of weird chest pains, especially in my lungs. He was concern about the pains, so he sent me to see a specialist on the tender. After the specialist ordered chest x-rays, they saw some suspicious looking shadows in my lungs, so they decided to send me to the main naval hospital in Bethesda, Maryland.

After a week in Bethesda, the experts decided my lungs were at risk from the pressures of the ocean, and it would be unsafe for me to continue undergoing the changes in pressure experienced on a submarine. Their final recommendation was total disqualification from the submarine community. I would now go back to the boat and wait for my orders. And that was that.

Chapter Eight

A few months later, the USS Norfolk cruised up the East coast to Kittery, Maine. As we were pulling into the Portsmouth Naval Shipyard, I glanced up at the huge, gloomy building that has stood looking over this harbor for about a century now, the Portsmouth Naval Prison.

No matter where you were in the Navy, you could hear stories about the prison. The history of the fortress is a long and Nobel one...

The island site was first used in 1775 during the Revolution when the New Hampshire militia constructed an earthwork defense called Fort Sullivan atop the bluff. In 1901, the site became available for a naval prison. Constructed between 1905–1908, the brig was modeled after Alcatraz, set on an island with tidal currents to deter escape. Colonel Kelton of the Marine Corps was in command when the first Navy prisoners arrived in 1908. It would eventually house Marine inmates as well. During World War I, the prison housed wartime convicts, reaching a maximum of 2,295 in 1918. Two wings were added—in 1942 the northeast wing, and in 1943 the unornamented southwest wing, dubbed "the Fortress," which rises sheer beside the rocky shore.

Maximum occupancy reached 3,088 in 1945. After World War II ended in Europe on May 5, 1945, several German U-boats in the area surrendered and were towed to the Portsmouth Naval Shipyard, the nearest submarine base. Arrival of the U-boats created a stir, so one was put on display and opened to visitors. After Marine guards stole various crew belongings as souvenirs, the Germans were confined at the naval prison. The brig was used throughout the Korean War and almost to the end of the Vietnam War. During warmer months, it was not uncommon for boats navigating the river to hear shouts and whistles coming from within barred windows of "the Fortress."

No one had ever escaped from the prison, and credit for that is given to the Marine guards. Back when the Marines were put into place in 1908, they were told that if they were to allow anyone to escape, that guard would have to complete the escapees' sentence, no matter how long it was. That incentive was all it took to keep the guards motivated.

In 1974 the Department of Defense developed a three-tiered, regional correctional facility plan. Inmates would be placed depending on the service, sentence length, geographical location, and treatment programs. First-tier offenders are those with sentences less than a year, and second-tier up to 7 years. Male convicts from all the services sentenced to punitive discharge and incarceration longer than 7 years are confined at the third-tier — the maximum-security U. S. Disciplinary Barracks located at Fort Leavenworth, Kansas. The Portsmouth Naval Prison, built to be a modern correctional facility for a navy which had once disciplined by flogging and capital punishment, was rendered obsolete. After containing about 86,000 military inmates over its 66 year operation, the brig closed in 1974. Now it is maintained by the shipyard, and its future is anyone's guess. What I would give to walk those halls...

Being a submariner who was not supposed to be on submarines was a bit of a challenge. After a couple days in the shipyard, I received orders to the Groton Naval Submarine Base in New London, Connecticut. I had not been there in just over eight years, but I remembered liking it very much. There was a lot to do in the area, and the base had everything you could ever want on it.

My orders called for me to join the staff at the Combined Bachelor Quarters. Most of the sailors in the Navy were single, and not given an allowance to live out in town. On most naval bases, there are 'hotels' that are operated by Navy cooks.

When I checked in to the Combined Bachelor Quarters or the CBQ as most people called it, I met the Leading Chief, David Alcon. I was relieved to see how laid back he was, as he poured me a cup of coffee and started to tell me about the chain of command and explain how things worked there. The CBQ consisted of fourteen enlisted barracks, one bachelor officers barracks, one maintenance service center and three warehouses. It was a pretty big operation, and cooks ran all of it.

After talking with me for an hour or so, Chief Alcon asked me if I was mechanically inclined. When I told him I thought I was, he said he had the perfect job for me. Then he asked me if I wanted to be a Locksmith. The CBQ Locksmith, Petty Officer Roper, was going to be transferring soon, and they needed a replacement for him. I had no idea what the job entailed, but I liked the idea of being my own boss, so I accepted the offer. Besides, who wouldn't want to know how to crack a safe?

The CBQ Locksmith was in charge of everything that had a door. Fire exits, alarm boxes, resident rooms, safes and room lockboxes. I also had to make sure that every morning there were keys available for the residents checking into the barracks. In case of emergencies, I had to carry a pager so I could be reached twenty four hours a day. With over four thousand doors, there was always one that some drunk kicked in, or the lock failed and the resident was locked out of his or her room. The good part was that I had keys to more doors than the Skipper did. There was no door or safe on that base that I couldn't get into.

While I was stationed on the Submarine base, I decided to get a second job. I was used to being at sea, and working sixteen hour days. Since I had left sea duty, I was home every day by four thirty, and bored out of my mind most of the time. Since I was a professional cook, I applied for a job at the base enlisted club.

The base club was a pretty busy place. It had a nice country bar with a few pool tables, a karaoke bar with a large dance floor, and the main club 'Night Winds' where all the action was on the weekends. As far a base clubs goes, the sub base enlisted club was a pretty nice one.

My job was to cook all the fast food, things like burgers, personal pizza's, hot wings... the list goes on and on. When I wasn't cooking, I was asked to play backup bouncer. That job was pretty easy, since most of the time the patrons were too drunk to cause much trouble. It was a pretty cool job, but the fringe benefits were the best reason to work there. Things like no cover charges for events and being able to take home the leftovers. Oh, I don't mean the food... I mean the drinks.

Every Friday night, there would be a theme drink on special, so they would make three gallons at a time. At the end of the night, there might be a couple gallons of Sex on the Beach or Kamikazes left over, so they gave them to me. I don't think I spent any money on liquor that whole summer.

The best reason for working there was being buddies with all the waitresses. Whenever I would have an off night and come to the club, they would bring me anything and everything, usually at cost. When you are paying thirty cents for a four dollar drink, your money tends to go a lot farther. That was a fun summer.

There was one not so good thing that came with the BQ Locksmith position. Whoever filled the position of Locksmith also was the Leading Petty Officer for the military funeral detail. Every veteran who has ever served honorably in the United States military has the right to a military funeral with all of its honors. That consists of a Chaplain, if requested, a firing squad, honor guards, pallbearers and me. If the veteran died on active duty, they were entitled to a seven man, twenty one gun salute. If the veteran was separated honorably, then they were entitled to a three man, nine gun salute. Being the man in charge, I was responsible for arranging everything.

One of the biggest problems we would have was transporting everyone to the cemetery, church or wherever the funeral was to be held. The base motor pool had several eighteen passenger vans that could be checked out, and they usually fit everyone in just fine. The problem was the distances we would have to drive. We were based in Groton, but sometimes, we had to drive down past New Haven which took about two hours, or up to Providence, Rhode Island which was always a pain.

The way the service usually goes is the military Chaplain, or the civilian clergyman that officiates, performs the service and then gives me a nod, signaling me that it is time to start. After that, I give a sign to the leader of the firing squad. He then gives the order to his squad to fire three volleys into the air. As soon as the last shots are fired, the bugler plays taps. When taps is over, I smartly march over to the leader of the firing squad and he salutes me, then hands me three shells from the volleys that were just fired. I march back to the head of the casket and the honor guards fold the flag. Once the flag is folded in the proper triangle, the leader of the honor guard marches over to where I am standing and salutes me. At that time I put the three shells into the final fold of the flag and tuck the last flap, holding it all together.

With the flag held firmly in my hands, I solemnly march over to the family member, hand them the flag and say "On behalf of a grateful nation and the United States Armed Forces, I present you with this flag and these shells for the honorable services rendered by your beloved." Then I hand the flag to the family member and stand at attention, saluting very slowly. Then, I do a snappy about face and march back to the head of the casket. I then dismiss the detail, and we walk back to the van.

I remember the first funeral that I participated in. The deceased was a very young veteran. He had died in a car wreck, and I think he was about thirty or so. The service was going pretty well until the end. I slowly marched over to the wife and presented her with the flag, and then I looked into her eyes. I will never forget her face. She was about thirty years old, and her blonde hair was wrapped in a black silk scarf. She was so broken down, and I just felt so sorry for her. I didn't get half way through my line before I started to lose it. While I was saying "for the honorable service rendered by your husband" tears were streaming down my face. I felt so unprofessional, like an amateur.

While we were loading up in the van, the funeral director came over and asked to speak to me. He said "Petty Officer Westfall, Ms. Romans, the widow, asked me to give you this" he handed me a hundred dollar bill and said "She was deeply touched by your services. She wanted me to tell you she would be in touch with your Commanding Officer." I wasn't quite sure how to take that, but it sounded like good news. Besides, she gave us a hundred dollar tip! That said something.

According to the Uniform Code of Military Justice, we could not legally accept money for something that falls under our duty as members of the Armed Forces. Our Skipper told us that if we ever received a gratuity, we had to use it for lunch, and leave whatever was left as a tip. In other words, we had to spend all of it on lunch. Sometimes we would go to the steak house, if there was enough money. On this day, since there were so many of us, we went to McDonalds and put what was left, about thirty dollars, in the box for the McDonalds house. All in all, it was a good day. Not all days were good days.

One bad thing about doing funerals in New England is the snow. The Navy dress uniform looks very nice, but when the designers added the dress shoes with the leather soles, they forgot about snow. I remember once I did a funeral in New Haven in February. The cemetery was very old, and had headstones dated back to the late seventeen hundreds. It was a large cemetery located in the center of town and covered several city blocks. There were lots of steep hills, and as luck would have it, we had to carry the casket up a steep embankment.

The casket was slowly brought out of the hearse by our honor guards acting as the pallbearers. Every step is carefully coordinated between the honor guards as the attendees watch them take the casket out and slowly start up the hill. As the Petty Officer in Charge, I was following closely, about one yard behind the casket. This way, if anyone were to lose their footing or if the body was a heavy one, I could help carry it.

While the detail was slowly carrying the casket up the hill, I noticed that everyone was slipping and sliding. As I was reaching to hold the foot of the casket and help the detail, everyone slipped at once, and the casket dropped to the ground. The deceased weighed about three hundred pounds, and all that dead weight started sliding down the hill towards the hearse. I tried to stop it, but my shoes slipped and I fell onto the casket. I quickly rolled off and dug my heals into the snow, holding on the sidebar. After only sliding a few feet, I was able to stop the casket. Once the team recovered, I gave a special order to forget about protocol and carefully sidestep the casket up to the site.

The rest of the service went well. Once the service was concluded, I went back to talk to the funeral director and see just how angry the family was. He pulled me aside and started laughing. When he finally took a breath he said "You have no idea how funny all of that looked! But the family knew you were doing your best, and that the conditions were very bad." He went on to say "The daughter said her father, the deceased, had a wonderful sense of humor and probably loved every minute of it!" Then he handed me an envelope with two hundred dollar bills in it. We hit the Sizzler for lunch that day. Life was good.

The most memorable funeral I ever did was for a Revolutionary War veteran. There was a young man in Danbury who was trying to get extra credit in his biology class. He had recently found the unearthed remains of what he thought at the time were of a cow. Thinking that this would be an awesome project, he picked up the bones and brought them to school. As he started assembling the skeleton in the classroom, the teacher realized these were the bones of a human being, so he called the police. They went to the grave site and found the unmarked grave of a man named Arthur Bickle, later identified as a foot soldier in the revolution Army.

Since Mr. Bickle died in the line of duty, the city of Danbury wanted to rebury him with full honors in a proper revolutionary war cemetery. The ceremony was very cool. There was a large wagon pulled by four horses. Mr. Bickle's casket was the only thing on the wagon, and it was covered by a replica of a period flag. I was asked to guide the lead horse slowly down the road toward the cemetery. The Honor Guards stood side by side following the wagon, with the firing squad right behind them.

Then there was a mile long parade and everyone in the world was in it. There was the AMVETS, the American Legion, the Rotary Club and the Women of World War II. It was quite the show, and all of it was on the local news.

There was one more funeral that I will remember forever. The deceased was one of the only ten survivors of the USS Juneau (CL-52) that was sunk off the coast of Guadalcanal in November of 1942. This was the same ship where the five Sullivan brothers were killed. This man had the most impressive career that I had ever encountered. He had saved the lives of seven men, and lost his arm to a shark while waiting for rescue. As I stood at attention, listening to the awards and qualifications that this man had achieved, I couldn't help but be moved by the honor and tradition represented at the service. The following day my picture was in the New London paper. I was saluting the Chaplain as a tear was streaming down my face. My boss was so impressed that she gave me the next day off.

Altogether I lead just over a thousand funerals in four years. It was one of the proudest times in my naval career. Towards the end of my time, my boss recommended me for the Law Enforcement Academy at Lackland Air Force base in San Antonio, Texas.

San Antonio is always beautiful, especially in the fall. Lackland Air Force Base is not only the home of the Law Enforcement Academy, but it is also where the Air Force has its boot camp. Like the Navy, the Air Force has state of the art facilities, including the barracks. The rooms were only a couple years old, and they were situated in a semi-circle around the parking lot and the laundry room. The chow hall was only a couple of minutes from the barracks, and the Law Enforcement training center was just a five minute march from there.

One thing about San Antonio that bothered me was the jack rabbits. I have never seen anything like it. The rabbits were everywhere, and some walk around on all fours like a dog. To this day, they are one of the strangest things I have ever seen.

Every job in the Navy has a Navy Enlisted Classification (NEC). The job of Law Enforcement usually fell under the Master at Arms (MAA) rating, but there was a shortage of MAA's, so they had to be supplemented by other rates. This new supplemental force was classified as 9545. In the eyes of the Navy I was no longer a cook; I was a 9545, or in civilian terms, a Navy Police Officer.

Our class started the following Monday. One thing I really liked about it was that all the people in the class were from the fleet, with the exception of two girls, Candy and Edith. I could never figure out why the Navy sent Candy to Lackland. She was a sweet enough girl, but really had no common sense at all. She had just come from boot camp in San Diego, and other than that, she had never been anywhere outside of Houston, Texas, where she was from.

The first week of training was classroom scenarios. I had never really give much thought to being a Police Officer professionally, but as the days went on I really started to get into it. In the afternoon, we would go to the gym and learn hand to hand combat. It was just like you see on television. We all stood in a circle and just waited for our turn to get our butts kicked by the instructor. Since I was a bit bigger than most of the class, they seemed to want to make a point out of beating me up in front of everyone else. But every time I got thrown to the ground or flipped over on my head, I learned. Soon I became good enough to help out with the training. It was nice to be able to beat up on someone else.

The second week of training was all hands on. There was a big building next to the training center that was once used as a barracks, but had since then been refurbished as a training facility. It was set up with bedrooms, living rooms, kitchens... just about any scenario you could imagine. This is where we took all the things we learned in the classroom and put them into practice.

I was on the first team to search the building. We were supposed to find the 'drug dealers', arrest them, and search the 'house' for the drugs. It sounded easy. I was appointed as the senior officer on the call, so I gave the orders. There were three men on our team, and I led the way.

The idea was to advance only when someone else was covering you. In other words, there should always be another patrolman watching you, ready to protect you if someone should pop out of a closet or in from another room. The 'fatal funnel' is the term used for the area where you are most likely to get shot and killed. For example, when a patrolman is approaching a car, the fatal funnel would be in the window area where you are most likely to be shot. If you were to approach the car from the rear, staying behind the driver and against the car, you would avoid the fatal funnel. The main idea was to stay out of the fatal funnel, no matter what.

It seemed pretty easy to clear the hall way, then the front room, then the living room. We also knew that there might not be anyone there, so we had to react to whatever we found. As we were coming to the last room, we knew the house was empty. We quickly cleared the bedroom and started searching for the drugs and the drug money. Just as I was looking behind the bed "BANG BANG", I was dead. I was shot two times in the chest at close range. The 'perpetrator' had been hiding behind the bed, and I assumed the room was empty. The instructor quietly walked over to me and wrote DEAD across my forehead in permanent marker. Then he smiled and said "There. Now you can walk around like this for a few days and think about how your mother feels now that her baby is dead." The point was well taken. Being 'killed' there was much better than being killed out in the real world.

That wasn't the only time I screwed up. A couple days later my partner and I 'arrested' a 'druggie' who was disturbing the peace in a local park. He was very small and very doped up, so he was no problem at all. As I was putting him in the police car, he dropped something from his mouth. Ha! I knew that I was supposed to miss it, but I saw it! As I proudly bent over to see what it was, the 'perpetrator' kneed me in the face, kicked me in the stomach then stole my gun and shot me in the chest twice. As if that wasn't bad enough, he 'killed' my partner as well. Oh well, maybe there was still time for Clown College.

As the days went by, I started getting better and better, and made fewer mistakes. One thing I was really good at was the gun range. In the military, you don't shoot one shot. You don't shoot to wound someone. You shoot to null the threat. You always shoot twice, or "double tap" when you shoot your weapon. Now, everyone in the military, aside from the Chaplains, qualifies on the use of a weapon. I had been qualified on the .45 caliber pistol for years, as well as the M-14 rifle. But the police force was now using 9mm Berettas and they were a lot lighter and easier to shoot. I had never shot one, so I was a bit worried about how well I would do. The secret for me to shoot well was to do exactly as they told me to. I held the gun in my right hand, and pushed forward, while pulling back with my left hand. When doing this, I found that I have total control over the weapon, and I can shoot pretty well.

The targets we used were just standard silhouettes. The idea was to hit the target as many times as you can in the center, or 'center mass' as they called it. The better you shoot, the higher your score. On my very first try I shot almost every round into the center of the target, earning the Expert Pistol medal. Life was good.

As we were getting closer to graduating, we started venturing out into the town more. Anyone who has ever been to San Antonio will tell you about the river walk and the Alamo. The river runs through the town and there are shops and parks on either side. As you work your way down the river, you will soon come to the Alamo. A couple of my buddies asked me if I wanted to go down to the river on Saturday, so we decided to make a day of it. We decided to get a drink at the first bar we came to, and just see what happened from there.

The area surrounding the river walk is very nice. There are tourist boats that run up and down the river, allowing people to take pictures, or just have a relaxing drink while taking in the scenery. This time of year people were wearing bathing suits, shorts or whatever clothing they could stay cool in. My buddies and I were enjoying just sitting there watching the girls go by. We decided to have a drink in every bar we came to, until we ran out of bars, or we ran out of time, whichever came first.

After nine hours and about thirty bars, we decided we were done for the day. None of us were sober enough to drive, so we started looking for a way to get home. Since we were just waiting around anyway, we decided to have one more drink. As I was getting up on the bar stool of the next pub, I noticed a wallet lying under the stool, just next to the bar. I picked it up, looked in it and found a couple hundred dollars in cash and several credit cards.

As I was looking through the wallet I found an address book, so I decided I would try to find out whose wallet it was and see if I could return it. The only address and phone number in it was "Mom", with an address for Akron, Ohio. After getting some change for the pay phone, I gave the number a call and found out that her son was on vacation with his wife, Donna, in San Antonio, and he had recently called her and said they were going on the river ride. I asked her for a description of her son, in case we saw him. As we were finishing our drinks, I suggested we go and try to find him.

As soon as we left the bar and started walking toward the river, I recognized the owner of the wallet and his wife walking back toward us. I called out "Hector? Donna?" They looked at me puzzled and he said "Yes?" I walked up to him and said "I can't believe it is you! I haven't seen you in years!" I gave him a quick hug and said "It's me, Reggie, your old friend from Ohio." Just as he started scratching his head I told him who I really was and returned the wallet. After taking a quick inventory, he said "Thank you so much. I don't know what I would have done if I hadn't found it. Can I offer you a reward?" I thought a minute and pointed toward our car and said "Uh, we drank a bit too much to drive. Can you help us get back to Lackland?" He smiled and said "Here, give me your keys and get in. Donna can follow us in our car." After getting safely back to the base, I smiled and remembered what my dad used to tell me. If you do the right things in life, you will always come out ahead.

The next day was a Sunday. I went to early Mass so I could be back for the big game. Our class was taking on our sister class on the football field. According to base regulations, we could only play flag football. That was usually alright, but there are times when the flag was soaked in blood. As long as it wasn't my blood, life was good.

The ladies from our class set up all kinds of food, from hotdogs and hamburgers to steak and chicken. We had everything! I was in charge of the 'fruit' course, and I had started preparing the fruit the morning before. First, I filled my bathtub with ice. Then, I put in four watermelons. The watermelons were special watermelons. First, they had to be set up on one end. After that I carefully cut a plug about two inches in diameter in the end sticking up. Then, I took a long blade knife and sticking it into the hole, I carefully cut about twenty slits through the meat of the watermelon, careful not to cut any holes through to the outside. Once the slits were in, I took four bottles of vodka and up-ended one of them in each of the watermelons, allowing them to slowly fill the watermelon with the vodka. This process usually took an hour or two, so it's best to start the day before. This procedure is called "juicing a watermelon". I only needed two melons, but I made four just in case.

It was a beautiful day! There was not a cloud in the sky, and there was a cool breeze blowing across the playing field. Our team, "the pistol whippers," won the toss, so we kicked off. It took about fifteen minutes for them to score, and then they scored again a few minutes later. At the end of the first quarter, we were down fourteen to nothing. The other team was much faster and bigger than we were, and it just seemed unfair. The second quarter was just as bad, and at the half they were beating the crap out of us, twenty eight to nothing.

When the halftime alarm went off, everyone went to their side of the field to eat lunch. We took an hour off for lunch, so everyone would have plenty of time to enjoy themselves

While we were sitting back, enjoying the only good part of the game, Candy showed up in her truck. Then, I had an idea. Now Candy wasn't the sharpest knife in the drawer, but she was very pretty. I decided to use her powers for evil, so I gave her an assignment. We quickly loaded two of the juiced melons into her truck, and she was off to the other side of the field. The other team, "the J-walkers," didn't know that Candy was with us, and a couple of their classmates had been giving her the eye over the past month. When they saw her, they quickly invited her over to eat with them during half time. When she offered to share the two watermelons she just happened to have with her, they quickly agreed.

Over the next hour, the J-walkers ate both of those watermelons. We also had two melons, but we were saving them for after the game.

When both teams showed up for the beginning of the second half, the J-walkers didn't seem as anxious to play football. It took them four tries to kick the ball to us, and it was pretty obvious that my plan was working. Over the next two hours, we scored seven times, winning the game forty nine to twenty eight. Candy was unanimously chosen as the team's most valuable player.

After the game the girls decided to go out dancing. Of course, I didn't dance, so I suggested that we go to the base club instead. Since they had a dance floor, that's where we all went.

The base in San Antonio was divided up into the training base and the boot camp, on both sides of the main highway. In order to walk to the club, you had to walk across a huge parade field, lined with museum fighter jets and ancient aircrafts. The walk to the club was not really a problem, but when you were walking back to the barracks, there was a shortage of bathrooms.

That night after we left the club, we were walking back through the parade field. Since there was plenty of beer that night, I was in need of a restroom. I asked the guys to keep walking as I borrowed a nearby F-104 to relieve myself. Just as I started to go, a large spotlight lit up the plane. A deep voice broke the silence "Why are you disrespecting my aircraft?" As I squared myself away, I quickly walked toward the light and tried to explain my actions. The First Sergeant in the MP patrol car laughed and said "Get in before I arrest you. We will take you home." I was home and in bed before my buddies could figure out what happened to me.

The following week went by very quickly. The whole week was dedicated to qualifying with the PR-24, gun quals, and hand to hand combat certifications. There was also the high crawl, low crawl, which was probably the hardest thing physically that we had to do.

It was basically a long obstacle course filled with barbed wire, walls to climb, mud holes to crawl through and ropes to swing on. It was tough, but once it was over, we knew we were almost finished. All that was left was the graduation.

That Friday was the graduation ceremony. Everyone had passed the class with flying colors. Four of us received medals for qualifying expert on the 9mm pistol. Then, they awarded me an unexpected certificate, the 'Top Gun" award for the highest score out of anyone who had graduated that year. Yep. I also cook.

Chapter Nine

Bahrain is known as the pearl of the gulf. It's a small island just off the coast of Saudi Arabia. It's the home of the United States Naval Forces Central Command (NAVCENT), and the United States Fifth Fleet. It also houses the Administrative Support Unit, Southwest Asia, or ASU as we fondly called it. ASU was the main base in the Persian Gulf, and NAVCENT was located on the base.

As soon as I stepped off the plane in Bahrain, I knew I had entered another world. Everywhere I looked I saw Bahraini police officers with automatic weapons. There were lots of women in the airport, and all of them were wearing some type of head coverings. One of the first things I was told by my sponsor was to not stare at the women, or they may be offended.

My sponsor met me at customs, and made sure I got through the tight security with no problems. I had to totally unpack my entire luggage twice before they would let me leave the airport. They were all very friendly, but it was obvious they wanted to find something illegal on me. It seemed like forever, but I finally got out of there.

After what seemed like forever, I was outside and heading away from the airport. The air outside was very hot and musty. The cars all looked odd, much different from the cars and trucks I saw every day in the States. They all drove fast, and it seemed like none of them could really stay on the road without swerving and hitting their breaks every thirty seconds. Just when I was getting used to the air and the swerving, I heard something odd. A man was signing in Arabic, and it was being amplified from speakers all over the place. My sponsor told me that this happened several times a day, all over the Persian Gulf. This was going to take getting used to.

I was dropped off at a very nice hotel slash apartment building just across from the biggest mosque that I had ever seen. I later found out it was actually called the Grand Mosque. The hotel had a very large tile swimming pool, and was located right off of a popular shopping area called 'Shawarma Alley'. A shawarma is kind of like a small burrito, but it's filled with shaved lamb and spices. There were at least twenty of the roadside shawarma stands all up and down the road, thus, it is called Shawarma Alley.

Since it was still light out and I was extremely jet lagged, I decided to go for a walk. As I was walking toward shawarma alley I noticed the houses were all located in private compounds, usually guarded by armed Bahraini guards. I wondered who lived in them that they needed to be so heavily guarded, but the guards didn't look too friendly, so I stayed away from them.

As I was walking down the road, looking into the shops at all the many interesting things, I came across one of the oddest things I had ever seen. Now the average Bahraini did not have very much money. They lived humble lives and worked very hard for the little bit they did have. Keeping that in mind, there was a Ferrari dealership right in the middle of the town, and directly across the street from it was a Lamborghini dealership. It was so strange seeing these hundred thousand dollar cars along the street, when most people couldn't even afford a bicycle.

The shops along the street had so many curious items, the likes of which I had never seen before. There were many Indian women walking around from shop to shop. They were all dressed so beautifully! The vibrant colors and decorations that they used in their everyday lives were amazing.

Another thing I noticed was the cats. Everywhere I looked there were cats. I did ask the man at my hotel why there were so many cats, and this is what he told me. Bahrain is a small island. Many years ago, they started landfills off the coast in many areas. As they fill up, they cover them with dirt and would build on top of them. I was told that about five percent of Bahrain was built on top of landfill. Anyway, all the garbage bred lots of rats. In fact there were so many rats the island was getting overrun by them. To solve this problem, I was told the king at the time, or Amir as the Arabs called him, decided to import cats from Europe to help get rid of the rats. So, they brought in a couple thousand cats and turned them loose in the streets of Manama, and that solved the problem. Now, I can attest to the fact that there are practically no rats at all in Bahrain now. But, there are many, many cats.

As I walked farther down the road, I smelled something wonderful. It smelled like steak, but with lots of spices. I had been craving a good steak for weeks now, and the steaks I had in Texas were a bit disappointing. I realized I hadn't eaten in several hours, so I followed the smell to an Indian restaurant. The restaurant was pretty full, and the host led me to a small table in the middle of the room. The waiter showed me a menu written in an odd looking language, so I just pointed to a picture of something that looked like the steak I smelled.

While I was waiting for my steak, the waiter brought me a loaf of fresh bread and some cucumber and sour cream dip. It looked a little odd at first, but it was wonderful! A few minutes later the waiter set this huge piece of meat in front of me. It looked a little strange, but I figured it was just because of the spices. I cut off a small bite, and the meat seemed to just fall off the bone. It tasted absolutely perfect! Never in all my life had I tasted a better, more tender steak! I guess the cows in Bahrain were just juicier. About twenty minutes later I had finished my steak, and took my bill up to the counter. I smiled at the waiter and said "That was the best meal I have had in a long time!" The little man smiled and me and said in broken English "Thank you, Sir. The camels we cook in Bahrain are better than anywhere else in the Gulf." Camel? Just then I felt my stomach cringe a little bit. With that wonderful thought in my mind, I headed back to the room. I think that was just about enough local culture for one day.

The following day my sponsor picked me up in front of the hotel and took me to ASU. As we neared the base, I noticed that the area surrounding the base was all desert, and there were no buildings close by. In the distance you could see some large apartment buildings scattered about. I later found out that many of the sailors that worked on the base lived in them. As we approached the front gate, I noticed that there were two guard houses, one manned by American servicemen and the second manned by Bahraini Public Security (BPS).

The base was very small, in comparison to other bases I had been to. It was too small for any real traffic, but there was a central parking lot just inside the front gate where everyone parked. Off to the right was a small mall like area where I could see a couple of families walking around. In the middle of the compound I saw a large fenced in area with several trailers and other structures all around it. It had its own guard shack, so I guessed it was a high security area. Looking to the left side of the base, I saw a huge "golf ball" looking dome. I knew it must have some kind of satellite dish or radar in it. All in all, it looked like a very busy base.

My first stop was the security building, where I would be spending the next few years of my life. It was located inside the security complex, where the security detachment held its training and did its processing and briefing. Right inside the door was the weapons cage where the officers going out on patrol were issued their weapons and radios. That's where I met the Chief of Police, Chief Allen. "Welcome to the Arabian Gulf." He said, as he led me down the hall to his office. He motioned me to have a seat on a couch next to his desk. He proceeded to ask me about myself and my career, and then he started telling me about the police force.

The police force on ASU was broken down into four watch sections. The senior members of the security force, usually the rank of E-6 or E-7, were the Watch Commanders over the individual sections. Each section consisted of twenty five to thirty patrolmen. Of those patrolmen there was an Assistant Watch Commander, a Dispatcher, Weapons Petty Officer and a Training Petty Officer. The Chief of Police was over the Watch Commanders, and the Security Officer was overall in command.

The daily function of the Police Force was to man the gates of the base and provide security to the base and the surrounding area. Also falling under the ASU area of responsibility was the Mannia Plaza, a hotel where all the transient Americans and servicemen stayed when passing through Bahrain. There were often SEAL teams staying there temporarily, and that was an experience in itself. There was one other apartment building out in town called the Dima Complex, where many of our troops lived.

A few miles away was our Aviation unit, or the Av unit as we called it. This was our part of the airport where all of the military flights were coordinated. We also had a Harbor Patrol Unit that was located about two miles from ASU. They patrolled the harbor around the pier where there was usually one or two US ships moored.

The United States Embassy was located just outside of Manama, and the Ambassador lived a mile or so from ASU. His house was also a security interest that we protected. All of these places were not only protected by the ASU Security Force, but the local Bahraini Military Guard as well.

Whenever new Service members arrived in Bahrain they had to go through an indoctrination process. There was much to learn about the new environment, and the United States Government does not want its people running around insulting the native culture of the countries it is hosted by. My indoctrination started with a man called Mr. Hamza. Mr. Hamza was a Bahraini citizen who served as the Military Liaison to ASU. Anything that had to go through the Bahraini Government was handled by Mr. Hamza. I needed a Bahraini driver's license and a Bahraini identification card. These were processed through Mr. Hamza and were necessary to do anything out in the local community. Once the paperwork was finished, Mr. Hamza started briefing me on the interaction between Americans and Bahrainis, and the things I would have to know before being turned loose on the local population.

The biggest thing that Americans need to remember is that we are guests in these Arab Nations. We must respect their culture, and that includes the way we dress. We were required to always wear a shirt with a collar. We were not allowed to wear shorts or shirts with logos on them. The females were not allowed to wear short sleeves at all, and could not wear excessive makeup. I was instructed never to make eye contact with an Arabs wife, or engage them in conversation, unless they engaged me first. It was very obvious to me that we were no longer in Kansas.

One of the biggest things to get used to in Bahrain was the weekends. Unlike the rest of the world, Bahrain, Saudi Arabia, Yemen and Qatar all had Thursday and Friday weekends. Friday is considered the Sabbath, or basic prayer day. So, I had to get used to going to Mass on Friday, and considering Sunday the second day of the work week. Work, business, and school days run usually Saturdays through

Wednesdays, with Wednesday night being the big night to go out and party.

Saudi Arabia was looking into changing its weekend to Friday and Saturday, because when it does business with the rest of the world, it loses two work days. As of the year 2000, most Arabic cultures did change the weekends to Friday – Saturday, just to recapture one more international workday.

Along with my briefing on the local population, Mr. Hamza explained how life works on ASU. Everyone attached to ASU gets supplemental allowances from the United States Government. The cost of living allowance, or COLA, was very good at the time, so everyone who owed money in the United States before being stationed in Bahrain was debt free and had money in the bank when they went back home. In fact, I had to get used to carrying a couple thousand dollars on me most of the time, just because that's what you would need to get around.

Everyone was paid through the Navy Federal Credit Union on base. On payday, or whenever anyone needed money, they would go to the credit union and make a withdrawal. The credit union did not have any money anywhere in the branch, so they would give you a slip of paper that had your transaction numbers. Then, you would walk across the compound and visit the 'Dinar man', who ran the on base money exchange. In Bahrain, Americans had to get used to carrying two types of currency, the American dollars and the Bahraini Dinars. Normally if you were changing five thousand dollars, which was pretty common, you would ask for one thousand American for on base transactions and four thousand Bahraini for your rent, utilities and off base needs.

Almost everyone on ASU lived off base. The living conditions were nothing like I expected them to be when I first heard of Bahrain. Since the COLA we received was so lavish, we could afford the best of conditions out in town. Every apartment or house that any of the ASU personnel lived in had several rooms and bathrooms, all with side by side bidets. Every apartment had access to a pool and weight room. The furnishings were state of the art and the kitchens and fixtures were the best money could buy. After looking at several houses and apartments, I decided on a very large duplex home about two miles from ASU. The house was three stories with a full size, heated, indoor swimming pool. The pool room was the only common access point between my home and the adjacent home, occupied by another American family. I also had a maid from the Philippians named Mening, who lived on the premises with her husband, Cardine. Bahrain is a very dusty country, so I also had a car wash boy who washed my car every morning before I went to work. All in all, it was not so bad of a set up.

My first day of actual work started about a week after arriving at ASU. I had been issued several sets of desert camouflage uniforms, although they looked pretty rough on me. I found out that there are certain places around the base where you can take your uniforms and have them tailored to make maintaining them much easier. One of the biggest problems was the cargo pockets. The new uniforms had large, baggy cargo pockets that were impossible to iron down. Also, these uniforms were supposed to have military creases in them. Those are the sharp looking creases that run down the breast on both sides as well as the back of the uniform shirt. When getting them tailored they would sew down the cargo pockets and sew in the creases, making them always look perfect.

The gulf is a pretty warm place, and the uniforms that are worn on post can really get sweaty and stained. But, since money was not an issue, most people had a boy come to the house and pick up the laundry. The next day he would come back with freshly laundered and pressed uniforms. Life was good.

One of the first assignments I had when I arrived in Bahrain was to fly to Djibouti, Africa. In the early 1990's, Djibouti played a significant role in support of the Gulf War. From time to time, assets were stored in Djibouti on a makeshift Navy Base that not too many people knew about. Sometimes, the security detachment there would suffer from a lack of personnel, mostly due to changes in logistical staging in the theater. The ASU Security detachment was asked at that time to supply armed guards to assist with security until the permanent guards could arrive in a few days. It was early in November, and I remember the temperature was around 120 degrees Fahrenheit. My assignment: to augment the security force in guarding three spy planes. That was seventy two hours I will never get back.

Djibouti is not the nicest place I had ever been assigned to. It was very hot and strewn with open sewers. There were rats everywhere, and dirty bugs... big bugs. Huge bugs. I should have known what kind of assignment it was when they insisted that I get a new yellow fever vaccination. I have read stories about people who have gone on safaris through Africa, and have pictures of lions, tigers and giraffes... I have fond memories of six inch stink bugs that would walk off with my lunchbox.

Three days later, I was back in sunny Bahrain. Chief Allen thanked me for my misery, and promised I would never have to go back to Djibouti.

I had been placed in watch section four, under MA1 James, the Watch Commander. MA1 James was a very smart man, whom I learned a great deal from. My job was to learn how to be an ASU Police Officer. There were several steps in the qualification process. First, you had to qualify Patrolman. Then you had to qualify Weapons Petty Officer, Dispatcher, Field Training Officer and Investigator. All of these positions had a qualification card with necessary signatures in order to complete the qualification. Once the card was complete, there was a board formed to question you and see if you know enough to be qualified. All of these qualifications took time to achieve, usually a couple months.

The first step on my long climb to being a Patrolman was to qualify with the 9mm pistol and the M-16 rifle. Now I had qualified weapons many times before, but not these newer weapons. On the submarines, we used the .45 caliber pistol, the M-14 rifle and the 12 gauge pump shotgun. The only time I had ever shot the 9mm hand gun was at the Police Academy, and that may have been just pure luck.

First, as always, was the classroom part of the course. Now I knew how to shoot, but now I had to learn how to break down each weapon, clean it and maintain it. Here I was going to be issued my own weapon, the same weapon every day for my entire stay in Bahrain. Since the Marines know more about conventional weapons than anyone else, our weapons compound was run by Marines. My classroom qualifications went very well, and soon I was tearing down the 9mm and the M-16 and reassembling them like a pro.

The next step was the actual firing of the weapons. On the average military base, the firing range is usually located somewhere on the back of the base where the weapons fire is safe and not too noisy. Since space was not a luxury that the Navy had in Bahrain, our shooting range was a portable shooting range located in the back of a semi trailer. There were several different types of weapons that we had to qualify with. Being a bigger guy, I really liked the way the Beretta 9mm handled. The grip is big, and fits very comfortably in my hand. An expert shot shoots a 228 or higher. At the Police Academy, I shot a 231. This time I was a bit more comfortable with the 9mm, and I shot a 237. I wasn't quite as lucky with the M-16 though. I couldn't qualify higher than Marksman. The gun is just too light for me to handle comfortably. I did shoot Expert with the M-14, an older, heavier qualifying weapon. The M-14 just seemed like a better fit for me, and since it was heavier, it was easier to hold on to.

Once the weapons qualification was over, it was time for me to stand a post. There were four posts on base that had to be manned at all times. These posts are the main gate, the back gate, NAVCENT, and the compound rover. The other posts that are manned by the watch sections are the AV unit, the Dima Complex, and the Mania Plaza. Each of these posts, with the exception of the compound rover, required two patrolmen.

The watch sections worked in twelve hour shifts. Section one would work from six o'clock in the morning to six o'clock at night, three days in a row. Section two would work six o'clock at night to six o'clock in the morning on the same days. At the end of the third day, section three would relieve at six o'clock in the morning, and section four would relieve at six o'clock at night. Three days on, three days off. When the off sections came back to work, the section that worked days before would work nights the next time. This watch rotation was awesome! The first day off you would sleep all day long. The second day off would be spent having cook outs, pool side parties, and lots of drinking. The third day was usually spent with the family or running around doing errands. By this time, most of the off duty Patrolmen were bored and ready to go back to work.

The off duty watch sections would arrive at work half an hour before the watch started. They would report to the weapons cage so they could be issued their authorized 9mm and forty five rounds of ammunition. After signing for the weapon, they would approach the clearing barrel. The clearing barrel is a red barrel that is half full of sand, mounted in a predesigned location where weapons can be uploaded and downloaded safely. If there should be an accidental discharge of the weapon, the round will go harmlessly into the sand or the buffered area behind it. The Watch Commander or a qualified Weapons Petty Officer will stand by the barrel as the oncoming watch section prepares to upload. As the Patrolmen are summoned one at a time, they will show the weapon as safe, insert the magazine full of bullets, and release the slide. At that time the weapon is fully loaded and ready to shoot. The Patrolman inserts the weapon in their holster and they are now ready for watch.

Next was Guard Mount. Guard Mount is an Air Force term that is used to call the oncoming section to quarters. At that time, the oncoming watch section would form up and receive the orders of the day from the Watch Commander. This time would also be used to inspect the troops and insure they were in good physical condition. At this time, I was formally introduced as the newest member of watch section four. I was also introduced to my Field Training Officer, MA2 Phillips.

My first post was a six o'clock to ten o'clock at the main gate. On the post with me was ET2 Anders, who had been assigned to ASU for a couple years now. He introduced me to the Bahraini guards, big Mo and little Mo. When I asked him why they called them big Mo and little Mo, he just looked at me and said "Well, the big one's name is Mohammed and the little one's name is Mohammed." That cleared it up for me.

Anders showed me the proper way to approach a vehicle and told me what to look for as far as security concerns go. It seemed pretty easy, and I caught on fast. The rest of the watch was spent going over my patrolman qualification.

The next watch I had was with Petty Officer Phillips, my Field Training Officer. The post was the compound rover, so we just walked from place to place checking in with all the other posts. A couple of new ships pulled in, so there was a good crowd at the Enlisted Club, or the EM club as it was called. The EM club was actually located right next to the security compound. The side door to the club opened into the security training area, which made it very convenient at lunch time. It also came in handy when there was a fight at the club. Coming through the side door gave a bit of an advantage to the security force, because we could get into the building and be on the fight before anyone knew what happened.

There were four groups of people who came into the EM club. The United States Navy, the United States Marine Corps, the foreign services and the Merchant Marines. The Navy consisted of hundreds of ships passing through the Persian Gulf every year. It also consisted of four teams of Navy Seals who were constantly deploying to all parts of the theater. These Seals were usually returning from a mission, and blow off a lot of steam while they are here. The Marines were always in the area, and usually there were a hundred or so on base for R&R. The foreign services mostly consist of allied ships from the UK, France, Saudi Arabia, Canada, and Australia.

The Merchant Marines were the most fun. These were civilian sailors that came through the gulf on merchant ships. These sailors were sometimes a bit hard to manage because of the problems they would bring with them. The Navy has a weeding out process for problem people. The Merchant Marines were not quite as picky. This particular afternoon the club was full of French Sailors and Merchant Marines.

Later in the afternoon I had a second Compound Rover watch with MA2 Webster. Webster was his own favorite person. He had a loud mouth and pretended to know everything. Our assignment was to take one of the security vehicles, or 'Vic's' as we called them, around Manama checking on all of our interests out in town. As we were driving out to the Aviation Unit, Webster told me a tall tale about him being attacked by seven Bahraini police officers over a misunderstanding. Of course, he beat them all up and still made it home for dinner. I honestly could not believe his arrogance. I later found out that arrogance was something that could get a cop killed.

One thing that I couldn't get used to was the speed that some of the cars would travel. The King Fahd Causeway is a super fast highway/bridge connecting Saudi Arabia and Bahrain. The idea of constructing the causeway was based on improving the links and bonds between Saudi Arabia and Bahrain. Construction began in 1981 and continued until 1986, when it was officially opened to the public. The causeway ran from Saudi Arabia all the way through Bahrain.

The rich young Arabs would come screaming through Manama in their shinny Lamborghini's doing well over a hundred miles an hour. Sometimes a slower car would pull onto the causeway from one of the side streets, and not be going fast enough to merge with the oncoming traffic. By the time the speeding cars would see them, it was too late to avoid a collision. The wrecks they would get into were horrible. There would be nothing left but tiny pieces all over the road, and there were never any survivors. We usually had to cover at least a mile before we could find all the pieces of the people who were in the vehicles.

That first week the AV unit was hosting three air wings from one of the carrier groups, so there were aircraft everywhere. As Webster and I were circling one of the hangers, I noticed approximately five figures ducking behind some of the supply pallets. Webster stopped the Vic and asked me if I saw anything. I said "Yeah, over there. There are five kids hiding behind that pallet of supplies" I said pointing. Webster said "No, those were not kids. I think I saw one of them carrying a gun." Ok, that was just stupid. I clearly saw all of them, and the oldest one couldn't have been older than twelve.

I suggested that we just carefully walk up behind them and ask them how they got in. Then we could put a little fear in them and fix the hole in the fence. Webster said "You know that's why I am the professional and you are just a trainee!" At that time, Webster ordered me to take cover behind a utility building and not make any noise. As I was getting out of the Vic, I heard him calling the Watch Commander "Petty Officer James, we need immediate back up at the AV unit. There are at least five armed men taking up an observation position among the F-15 fighters. I recommend that you also alert the Bahraini Airport Police and ask for assistance."

The officers in the field were, as they say, the men on the ground. That means they are the ones who have firsthand knowledge of what is going on, and they are the ones who make the initial response decisions. If you ask for an army, you will get an army. When Webster said there were five armed gunmen among the F-15's, he called down the thunder.

Within about five minutes the Bahraini Airport Police arrived with about ten vehicles and about thirty men. As they were circling around us, the ASU security Force showed up with four of our own Vic's. There were guns everywhere.

When Petty Officer James came up to where I was standing, I said "They are just kids! I told that dumb ass that they were just kids, but he told me to shut up and do as he said." After calling off the dogs, Petty Officer James and I drew our weapons and slowly walked over to the spot where the 'gunmen' were hiding.

As we stood ready, He said "Ok, this is the United States Navy Police. Come out slowly, or we will open fire!" I was pretty nervous, but I was ready to back him up if necessary.

As soon as he had said it, a tarp that was covering the pallets started to move, and one by one, five young boys came out. It was obvious they were terrified. We called a nearby Bahraini Police Officer over to translate for us, and after a couple minutes he laughed. The boys lived nearby and when they saw the jets coming in, they were so curious they just had to see them up close. We decided to leave our dangerous gunmen in the able hands of the Bahraini Police, and headed back to the house.

The drive back to ASU was a long and quiet one. Webster didn't say a word until we approached the base. He looked at me and said "You probably wouldn't want to back me up on that decision to call in for support at the AV unit, would you?" I just looked at him and said "Hey, you are the professional... I am just a stupid trainee. What the hell do I know?" That was the last time I ever stood a watch with the man, nay, the legend, called Webster.

Chapter Ten

Once I qualified as a Patrolman, I started working on my Weapons Petty Officer qualifications. The WPO usually came into work a bit early so he/she could open up the weapons locker and inventory all the weapons and ammunition in it. Every watch section had its own WPO, and you always had to make absolutely sure which weapons were in your weapons locker.

The basic weapons were the 9mm Beretta handgun, the .45 caliber handgun, the M-16 assault rifle, the AR-15 assault rifle, the 12 gauge shotgun, the M-79 grenade launcher, the Uzi submachine gun, the Uzi machine pistol, and the Browning 50 caliber machine gun. The weapons can only be issued to Patrolmen who are qualified on that weapon. The bigger weapons, machine guns and grenade launchers, were for base protection and were not issued out on a regular basis.

Every round of ammunition had to be accounted for. Sometimes, the only way the command finds out there was an incident is if ammunition is missing. When the handguns are issued before a shift, they are issued with 45 rounds of ammunition. As the weapon is handed to the Patrolman, three empty magazines are also given out, along with a block of wood that has 45 holes drilled in it. In those holes are 45, 9mm bullets, so it's pretty easy to see if they are all there. If one of the bullets seems shorter than the rest, that's because the round has been fired and what you are looking at is an empty shell. If there is ammunition missing and you don't catch it when you sign that weapon back in, you will be the one who will hang for it.

As a rule, we did not fire our weapons very often. There is an escalation of force rule that must be followed. If you are holding a stick, I would pull out my PR-24, a club like weapon that can result in deadly force if it is used in that manner. If you pull out a knife, I will draw my 9mm. If you must fire your weapon, the military standard is to shoot two times center mass, or 'double tap'. You have to remember that if you are firing your weapon, you obviously need to null the threat. A double tap to the chest will null most situations. If you were ever in a police situation where weapons might be needed, you have to watch your fellow officers. If one Patrolman draws a weapon, everyone draws a weapon. You never draw your weapon unless you are ready to use it.

There is one building in particular where we would often draw our weapons, and that was the NCIS building. That was the only restricted access building outside of the NAVCENT compound, and it was secured by alarms. Whenever the alarms went off, we had to assume it was breached and secure the area. Once we arrived and secured the area, we had to form a security perimeter until the proper building authorities arrived and performed a sweep of the building. All in all, it was a big pain in the backside, and it happened way too often.

After a couple weeks, I qualified as Weapons Officer, and I moved on to my Dispatcher qualifications. Every watch section has at least one Dispatcher that acts as the nervous system for the watch section. The Dispatcher has to know everything from the watch rotation to the location of the senior staff. Every member of the watch section has his own call sign. The senior members have their own call signs. The Watch Commander is 1-7, the Assistant Watch Commander is 1-8, and the Dispatcher is 1-2. Every hour, or whenever the Watch Commander asked for it, the Dispatcher did a Situation Report (Sit rep) to make sure everyone was awake and all was well.

Everything was good with my qualifications and my life in general, until Petty Officer Steinway showed up. Like I explained a couple chapters ago, I was a cook in a security billet, or a 9545 as the Navy calls it. The Master at Arms are the ones who actually have the job as Navy Police Officers. 9545's do the same job, but since we are not actual MA's, sometimes the MA's look down their noses at us. MA2 Steinway was one of those MA's. As soon as she got there, she started spending lots of face time with the new Security Master Chief, MACM Fisher. Master Chief Fisher had been in the Navy for over twenty five years. She had seen lots of women treated unfairly in her time and liked the fact that Steinway was a hard charger. Since Steinway was also an MA, the Master Chief took her under her wing.

I had been doing very well in the Security Force. There were lots of good Patrolmen at ASU, and they did their qualifications adequately. Since I was a cook, not too many people took me seriously as a Police Officer. The first day I was there the Chief of Police, Chief Allen, told me if I worked hard, I could qualify as Weapons Officer or Dispatcher while I was at ASU. Right then and there I decided that I was going to be the next Watch Commander and have my own watch section. I would show him just how fast I could pass up his precious Master at Arms.

MA2 Steinway chose me as her competition as soon as she noticed me. By the time she had qualified Patrolman, she had already started on her Weapons qualifications. I really didn't pay too much attention to her because I was too busy with my Investigations qualifications.

At ASU we had two investigators. They were both senior Master at Arms who had been to special schools so they could do more in depth investigations at crime scenes. They didn't wear uniforms like the rest of us did, and usually ran around in civilian dress clothes. Not very many people had ever showed interest in qualifying Investigations, and since it was not required, hardly anyone ever did it. I decided to do it because I wanted to be the best Watch Commander I could possibly be, and learning everyone else's job was the best way to do that.

I remember one of the cases these guys had worked on. There was a sailor who lived on the twenty eighth floor of the Dima Complex, and he had invited some buddies up for a few beers. As they were partying, the noise level was getting too high for the neighbors, so they called security. When security knocked on his door, the sailor decided that he would avoid them by hanging by his hands from the balcony. When he tried to climb back in, he slipped and fell to his death. I can still see those gruesome pictures in my head. It always amazed me how one stupid decision can bring such tragedy into the lives of everyday people.

A few weeks later I started working on my Watch Commander qualification. There had been a change in many of the personnel, and they had two Assistant Watch Commander positions they needed to fill. Chief Allen came to me at Guard Mount and said "Petty Officer Westfall, you are now ASU's newest Assistant

Watch Commander. Not too bad for a cook." I smiled at him and quoted one of my favorite Navy movie lines "Well, I also cook."

The Watch Commander for section four at that time was MA1 Brooks. He was a nice enough guy, but he was more interested in covering his butt that taking a risk. I understood that to a point, but when you're a Police Officer, sometimes you have to stick your neck out. MA1 Brooks was not the bravest of Patrolmen either. Our first night on watch together we received a call that there was a fight at the bus stop on base involving several drunken sailors. He and I set out together, but just before we got there he stopped short and grabbed his radio mic and pretended to answer a call. I didn't think much of it at first, but I noticed that he always seemed to get a radio call just when we were about to confront trouble.

I had one advantage over Petty Officer Brooks. I was six foot four inches tall at that time, and weighed about 275 pounds, so I was bigger than most of the people I needed to take into custody. When I tackled someone, they went down. But I never did it without backup. That was the most important thing I had ever learned as far as police work went. You never know what to expect from anyone, so if at all possible, never confront anyone without backup. I tried not to do anything by myself, because things could go south in a hurry.

We had one Patrolman who was a very good Christian man, and one night he found himself alone in a room with a female suspect. When she was being charged, she claimed he had fondled her while she was cuffed and helpless. Luckily, she later admitted she was lying, so all was well. I never forgot about that incident, and always made sure I didn't put myself in that situation.

My time as Assistant Watch Commander of section four was mostly filled with paperwork. Whenever there is a call for security, there is usually an Incident/Complaint Report or ICR as it was called. Petty Officer Brooks quickly taught me how to fill out the ICR's so I would go blind with hours of paperwork instead of him. Under Brooks I learned all of the administrative working of the security detachment. Just when I thought I would never see the outside of the office, the CIA came to town.

The CIA went all through Southwest Asia in the nineties teaching military personnel how to clear out buildings and ships of bad guys. We formed four man teams armed with paint ball guns. The idea was to get in, clear the room and get out without any friendly casualties.

The first time we went into the 'house', I was in the lead position. My job was to shoot anyone directly in front of the door. The second guy was to shoot right, the third guy was to shoot left and the last guy was to fire for effect, or shoot at whatever presents itself after the initial attack.

We stood by the door and waited for the sign, adrenalin pumping. As soon as we heard 'go', we entered the building. I remember taking two steps when all of the sudden I felt this sharp pain in my chest, then another and another. When we were done the bad guys were 'dead', but so was I… six shots to the chest. Every other member of my team was unscathed, so I decided that the next time I would be the last one in the door instead of the first. This time someone else can die!

The second breach started without a hitch, but as soon as I got into the main room "pop, pop, pop..." four shots to the chest, one shot in the head (goggles). Dead again. Ok, maybe I should be in the second position. Nope, they killed me again. Well, my many faces of death did teach us one thing. When breaching and clearing a room, everyone in the room will shoot at the biggest target. The CIA was very successful in teaching me that I should never breach any buildings or ships.

After a couple months, a Watch Commander spot opened up, and I was the next in line for the position. I went to talk to Chief Allen and asked him about the position. He looked at me and smiled "There is no opening. Petty Officer Steinway was promoted to Watch Commander." "But Chief" I said "I have seniority. That was supposed to be my promotion." Chief further explained to me that his boss, Master Chief Fisher, thought a Master at Arms would make a better Watch Commander that a cook would. I complained and protested, but it didn't do any good. As luck would have it, MA1 Brooks was transferring later that month, and I was moved up as Watch Commander of section four. Finally, I could show all those Master at Arms that a cook can do this job as good as or better than they could!

My first day as Watch Commander was not as quiet as I would have liked it to be. Ten minutes after our shift started I was told I had some new Patrolmen, right out of BUDS (Seal school). Navy Seal training is extremely tough, and there are always guys who drop out for one reason or another. When that happens, they sometimes request duty as 9545's, and come to Bahrain. The only problem is that most of the time they are very arrogant and think they are bullet proof. Chief

Allen brought Petty Officer Attwood, our newest BUDS dropout, into the Watch Commanders office and introduced him to me. He seemed like a nice enough fellow, but I soon saw that he had an attitude of superiority. I could see that this was not going to be easy. I assigned him a Field Training Officer and went on about my business.

A couple hours later, just as I was about to head out to walk my rounds, I heard a commotion in front of the Security Compound. One of our newest Patrolmen, MA2 Harris, had accidentally backed the Vic he was driving over a new air conditioning unit. The Chief of Police, Chief Allen, was already out there, and he wasn't happy. He looked at me and yelled "You get your Patrolman and bring him into my office RIGHT NOW!"

I went out and told Harris to come with me and we went to the Chief's office. When we knocked at the door he answered with a yell "COME IN!" We entered the room and stood at attention in front of the Chiefs desk. He looked directly at me and said "Petty Officer Westfall, I would like for you to take Petty Officer Harris and put him on report for dereliction of duty." After hearing this, I asked the Chief is I could speak to him privately, so he dismissed Harris. When we were alone I said "Chief, with all due respect, don't you think that is a bit extreme? I know he screwed up, but I don't think he should be written up the first time he has an incident." Chief Allen frowned at me and rubbed his chin. "I am tired of wasting money on things like this. Someone needs to pay for this!" I thought about it for a moment and said "Chief, I am his Watch Commander, and I accept full responsibility for the accident. I should have trained him better." Since I had accepted responsibility, the Chief couldn't put Harris on report for the incident. I could see by the expression on his face that the Chief was not happy with me. He proceeded to chew me out and then threw me out of his office. Well, so much for my first day as Watch Commander.

The next couple weeks were quiet, and I settled into my position without incident. On one particular evening, the base was loud and busy due to four small ships being in port. We had the night shift, and it looked like the evening would pass without incident, when just before midnight we received a call from out in town. A young lady said she had been raped and her rapist was off one of the ships. I left my assistant, Petty Officer Oswald, in charge and then departed with three of my Patrolmen for the crime scene.

When we arrived the victim was hysterical, and wanted to take a shower. Knowing that this would contaminate any evidence the attacker left on her, I quickly started to interview her. She described her attacker as a large, black American, and said he was transferring off of one of the ships that were in port. She said he was due to leave that night but she didn't know his name. All she knew is that he was called "Geo", and he was a sailor about thirty years old. According to ASU procedure, we were to notify NCIS and they would assume jurisdiction over the crime scene. We called them immediately after receiving the call and we were told they would be there as soon as they could be. After two hours, they had still not arrived and the victim was getting hysterical. I decide that I was not going to wait any longer, and transported the victim to ASU medical so they could process a rape kit.

I assembled my four senior officers in the briefing room, and we went over the details of the incident. We knew that this guy was transferring, but we didn't know where. Since there were no ships leaving, he had to be flying out. We didn't know his name, but we had a very basic description of him. He went by the name "Geo", and all I could think about was the name George. I asked the Dispatcher, Petty Officer Weldon, to call the AV unit and get the passenger manifest for any outgoing flights. A few minutes later, she told me there was only one flight that left the Island, and it went to Spain. The manifest had seven Americans leaving the island, and while there was no George, one of them was named 'Washington". That was my "Geo."

After calling the embassy in Spain, I was connected to the airport authorities. I asked them to take Petty Officer Washington into custody as soon as the flight arrived, and give us a call. The flight would not land for another half hour, so we had to wait.

A few minutes later, NCIS arrived at Security. The agent in charge, Special Agent Alexander, asked me for a sit rep. I told him that the victim was at medical, and a rape kit was done and is being held for them. I further explained that we tracked down the suspect, and he was due to arrive and be detained by the Spanish Airport Authorities. Then I handed over the photographs, finger prints and evidence we had collected from the crime scene three hours prior to NCIS's arrival. When Special Agent Alexander asked me why we went ahead and processed the crime scene, I said "We waited for you for well over an hour, and decided if you weren't going to catch the bad guy, we would." It was very obvious to us that he was quite angry, and wanted credit for the case work.

Just then Weldon patched through a call from the Spanish Airport Authorities. I was told Petty Officer Washington was in custody, and they were awaiting further orders. It seems that once he was apprehended, he confessed to the rape and tried to make a deal. I asked them to document everything, and wait for transport from the American embassy. Bad guy caught, life is good.

Special Agent Alexander was pissed. He said "I will report this breach of protocol to your Commanding Officer. This isn't over." Then he and his lackey stormed out the door. My people looked a little nervous, so I reassured them "Look, we caught the bad guy. If there is any flack, I will take it. Great job team!" I just wish I felt as reassured as I sounded.

The next day Master Chief Fisher called me and the Chief of Police into her office. As Chief Allen and I stood at attention, she started reading off a sheet of paper on her desk. "... Furthermore, we would like to see the Watch Commander and his team punished for this obvious breach of procedure." Then she threw the paper in the trash as said "Petty Officer Westfall, you and your team did an excellent job. To hell with the NCIS!" And that was that.

A few nights later we were working the night shift. The base was hopping mainly because there was a large Merchant Marine ship in, and it had been at sea for a long time. I was in the office doing an ICR for a traffic accident earlier that night. All of the sudden I heard a call on the radio from Attwood, our new BUDS drop out. "1-7 Attwood." I answered "Go for 1-7." "I am in the club and I have a drunken female holding a broken bottle toward me." I started for the door and answered "1-7 heading your way" Then I heard a strange response. "That alright... I can handle this by myself."

I quickly made my way into the club and found Attwood in the Chiefs room. He was facing a woman in a corner of the bar, and she was holding a broken bottle towards him in a threatening manner. Attwood, bare handed, was walking toward her saying "Just hand me the bottle lady, and everything will be alright." I walked toward him and said "Back off Attwood!" Then I pulled out my 9mm and pointed it at her face and said "Drop the bottle or I WILL shoot you!" That was all it took, and she dropped the bottle. I quickly put her on the floor and handcuffed her, then lead her to the security building. Attwood said "Petty Officer Westfall, I had it under control!" I replied "Download your weapon, turn it in and stand by in the training yard. I will be there in a few minutes." I put my detainee in the holding cell until she calmed down. Then I asked my Dispatcher, Petty Officer Weldon to get relieved and report to the training yard.

Petty Officer Darlene Weldon was very pretty. She had been a Patrolman for about a year, and she excelled in everything she did. She was very athletic, and modeled for a local company out in town on the weekends. She was about twenty years old, and knew how to handle herself. She and I had become pretty good friends over the past year, so I knew what she was capable of.

I had all of the Patrolmen who were not on duty muster in the training area. There was a sand pit where we sometimes held training on hand to hand combat. I had Attwood take off his gun belt and stand on one side, and then I had Weldon do the same and stand facing him. Then I asked him "Petty Officer Attwood, why did you go against that woman in the bar without pulling out a weapon?" He smiled and said "I could beat her. I didn't need a weapon." Then I asked him "What about Petty officer Weldon here. Would you use a weapon with her?" He looked at her and smiled. "No, she is just a cheerleader. I could take her down with one hand."

Weldon started smiling, and looked over at me. I smiled back and said "Ok Darlene... let him have it." Then I looked at him and said "Alright, Attwood. Let's see how fast you can beat the cheerleader. Ready... fight!"

Weldon tried her best to look like she didn't know anything. She stopped, looked up, like she was trying to remember something, and started whispering to herself. Attwood started laughing so hard, he bent over forward. Then it happened. Weldon kicked him right in the face! When he pulled back, she kicked him in the crotch and then pushed him to the ground. Before he knew it, she had her knee in his back and had cuffed him behind. Then she stood up with one foot on his back, like a hunter posing with his prey. Attwood was livid! I have never seen anyone so angry in my life, but there was nothing he could do. I bent over and looked at him. His face was covered with sand and there was a little bit of blood coming from his nose. I said "What's the matter Attwood... did the little cheerleader kick your ass?" Well, that was the last time Petty Officer Attwood underestimated anyone. Training was over.

One of the most important things I tried to relay to my Patrolmen was safety. For example, one evening there was disturbance out in town involving four female sailors who were drunk and disorderly. When my guys brought them in, they told me that one of them almost got away. When I asked how it happened, I was told that she said she needed to go to the bathroom. When the Patrolmen brought her to the bathroom, she said she needed to have the hand cuffs removed so she could use the bathroom. He then took the cuffs off of her and waited outside the door. After a few minutes, he heard something that sounded like breaking glass, so he announced himself and went into the bathroom. Just as he walked in, he saw her trying to climb out the window. He called for backup, pulled her down and put the handcuffs back on.

This brought out a question I needed to get an answer for. Can a female detainee go to the bathroom while handcuffed? It just so happens that my mother was visiting Bahrain when this question came up. That night I was talking to her and telling her how my day went. When she heard about the female detainee's and how we almost lost one, she came over to me and said "Ok, put the handcuffs on me." I thought she was kidding at first, but she said if I cuff her she will find out if a woman can reasonably go to the bathroom with handcuffs on. After placing the handcuffs on her, she went upstairs. About five minutes later she can back down stairs and said "No problem at all!" The next morning at Guard Mount I gave the order that at no time will any detainee, including female, be uncuffed at any time while in transit. Then I documented the "training" discovery in the Watch Commanders Log, and it became standard procedure.

Civil unrest was something that we all had to live with in the Persian Gulf. The people were never really hostile to Americans; they were out to kill each other. I used to sit on the top of my house and watch the helicopters a couple miles away dropping tear gas on the crowds of rioting people. Almost every night you could be sitting in your living room and feel the ground tremor from explosions. It took a while to get used to it, but soon we didn't pay any attention.

One quiet Sunday night when Section Four had the duty, there was a huge explosion just outside the back gate. When I ran out of the office and looked toward the back gate, there was debris falling all over the base. "All stations 1-7, emergency sit rep" I yelled into the radio. When all stations reported in, I assumed the worse. "Secure the back gate. I repeat, all guards take up station inside the compound and secure the back gate. All personnel not on watch, report to Security NOW!" By the time everyone arrived, I had the weapons locker opened. I passed out shotguns and rifles to all qualified personnel. "Ok, everyone pair up. You two, run the compound fence as quickly as you can and let me know if there is a breach. You two go the other way. I want sit reps every two minutes. GO!"

My job was the security of the base. Once the base was secure, I could go investigate the explosion. "Petty Officer Weldon, call the Security Officer and the Embassy. Once you brief them, call all of the off section Watch Commanders. Have them standing by with their section call lists."

A few moments later, the radio came to life "1-7 Attwood, initial perimeter sweep complete. All secure with no breaches. Please advise." I responded "Keep sweeping, until I tell you otherwise." Once the base was secured and we knew the attack was not meant for us, I stood the troops down. "1-8, 1-7. Bring a Vic around to the back gate. We need to see what's going on."

When we got back behind the base, we found the Bahraini Police had already found and secured the crime scene. The target was a car owned by a reporter who had given an unfavorable report about some local Sunni businessmen. Lucky for the reporter, he was not home at the time. That was the closest ASU ever came to being targeted while I was there.

Every year Navy Bases all over the world select a Sailor of the Year. This selection was made from the top performers in all areas including professional knowledge, conduct, community awareness and personnel grooming standards. Candidates would be nominated by their individual Chain of Command, or in some cases they could be nominated by various senior officers. That year I had been nominated by my Chain of Command and two senior officers. I was the only Second Class Petty Officer in selection, along with twenty one First Class Petty Officers.

The process went kind of like this: The Selectees service records would be reviewed by a panel of ten Chief Petty Officers. Once they did that, they would call you to stand in front of the board and answer various questions selected by the members.

For over a month, I had been studying for this board. I memorized the Navy Times as well as the local and national newspapers. I was up to date on all current events and anything that was happening in the Navy at that time. The CNO's dogs were named Brandy and Clementine. The Presidents favorite color was orange. If they had a question, I had an answer. I was ready for this.

When my day to sit before the board arrived, I was wearing the sharpest Cracker Jack's you had ever seen. I entered the room and addressed the members individually, since I knew most of them personally. I sat down and took a sip of water, and then I proceeded to dominate the board. I was on fire! There was not one question asked that I did not know the answer to. Forty minutes later, I was dismissed. Over the next week I had been congratulated by eight of the board members.

They all said the same thing: I was the best candidate, and no one even came close to me. Being selected as the ASU Sailor of the Year would be an awesome addition to my service record.

Late one evening, the day before they announced the winner, I was called to the personnel building. A door had been found opened, and since we were short of Patrolmen at that time, I was asked to clear the building with the Roving watch. As I was walking through the Personnel Chief's office, I noticed a stack of files on his desk. On the very top of the pile was a letter to the board stating the name of the First Class Petty Officer that had been selected. Angrily, I dug through the pile of records until I found mine. On the cover of the record was a sticky note that said "He is only an E-5. We need to give it to an E-6 – disregard Westfall." At that very moment, the First Class Petty Officer they had selected as Sailor of the Year was in jail in Dubai for public intoxication.

The next day I talked to the Command Master Chief about the selection they made for Sailor of the Year. He explained to me that sometimes this is how things work out. I asked him "Master Chief, if I didn't have a chance of winning this, why do you encourage me to study so hard?" He said "Westfall, studying is good for you. Maybe next time..." That was the last time I ever crammed for a selection board.

Chapter Eleven

One of the problems we sometimes had at ASU was the Seal teams. The United States Navy's Sea, Air and Land Teams, commonly known as Navy SEALs, are the U.S. Navy's principal special operations force and a part of the Naval Special Warfare Command as well as the maritime component of the United States Special Operations Command.

Everyone knows what these guys do all over the world, and usually when they come to Bahrain, they want to blow off steam. The problem is many of the Seals are very arrogant, and do not like to listen when some Navy cop tries to tell them what to do. Whenever the Seals were in town, I had to adjust the watch roster.

Our first call came on Saturday afternoon. The Mania Plaza is a pretty quiet place usually. The bottom floor has several shops in it, so it was not uncommon to see people who didn't live there going in and out of the building.

Just after lunch, Dispatch received a call from one of the Bahraini guards saying there was an

American man who was drunk and threatening the guards. When Petty Officer Weldon, the Dispatcher, asked for a description of the man, she was told he had a tattoo of a 'fork' on his arm. We knew then that he was a Seal.

Knowing what these guys are capable of, I sent my two most physically fit Patrolmen to handle the situation. One of them, MA1 McAlister, had just finished the Iron man marathon in Hawaii a month before. The other Patrolman, ET3 Miller, was an amateur power lifter. I instructed them to meet with the senior guard at Mania Plaza and give me a sit rep once they located the suspect.

About thirty minutes later I got a call from McAlister. He said they were approached by the suspect as soon as they got there, so they didn't have time to call in. He said they had apprehended the suspect and was bringing him in to ASU. When they arrived, they brought the suspect into the interrogation room and cuffed him to a chair. I had the compound rover stand by the suspect while I was being briefed by the arresting officers.

The detainee's name was HT1 Salyer, and he was a member of the SEAL team that had come in the night before. He started drinking when he woke up that morning, and decided since he didn't like being in Bahrain, he would just declare war on everyone. McAlister said he fought like a bull, but they caught him by surprise and had him in cuffs before he knew what was going on. Salyer fought them the whole way home, and broke both rear windows out of the Vic.

The first thing we needed to do was a breathalyzer test on the detainee. I went into the room introduced myself. "Petty Officer Salyer, my name is MS2 Westfall and I am the ASU Section Four Watch Commander. You have been apprehended and are being detained because you were disturbing the peace at the Mania Plaza." Salyer was listening intently, and then he smiled and started talking. (Now, my mother will be reading this book, so I am going to write the following conversation in a PG format, omitting the foul language that Petty officer Salyer was using.) "Who the heck do you think you are? I am a trained Navy Seal, and I will break these doggone handcuffs and rip out your fluffy wind pipe!"

One thing that I always told my troops was to remember that the servicemen and women at ASU are far from home. They are missing their spouses, their kids Birthdays, and most of them don't want to be here. I too had been in my share of drunken predicaments, and it is only by the grace of God that I didn't ruin my career in the Navy. We need to take care of these people, and try not to let today's lapse of judgment roll over to tomorrow.

"Petty Officer Salyer, I know what you guys do for a living, and I very much respect that. If you would cooperate with us, we can get this done as quietly as possible and get you back to your command." Salyer look at me and nodded his head. "Petty Officer Westfall, I have a better idea. Why don't you and all your little Policeman followers go and fluff yourselves. The only real people in the United States Navy are the Seals, and the rest of you are just here to serve us." Well, I could clearly see that diplomacy was not going to work here.

"Petty Officer Salyer, I need for you to submit a breath sample into this breathalyzer." "Petty Officer Westfall, I need for you to kiss my horse." Ok, now I was getting annoyed. "Petty Officer Salyer, if you will not submit to a voluntary breathalyzer test, we will be forced to take a blood sample." Salyer looked at me and smiled. "I would love to see you try." At that time I walked back to my office with McAlister and Miller, and called medical, requesting a Corpsman to take the blood sample. As we were waiting, I told the Patrolmen how we were going to do this. I called in Petty Officer Weldon and asked her to videotape the procedure for our protection.

A few minutes later an HM1 arrived from medical. I briefed him on how this was going to go down and told him what to watch out for. When we went back into the interrogation room, Salyer looked like he was asleep. His chair was sitting in the center of the room, sitting away from the table. His hands were cuffed behind his back. I asked him for cooperation one more time. "Petty Officer Salyer, you could make this so much easier on all of us if you would just volunteer a breath sample." This time he just ignored me.

I gave a nod to McAlister and Miller, and then I went behind Salyer and said "Now." McAlister and Miller each grabbed one of his shoulders while stepping on his shoes. As he yelled and stood up, I jerked his chair out from under him and pushed him forward. Since his feet were pinned down, he fell forward and was quickly guided down to the ground. At the same time I held his handcuffs and pulled his arms up while stepping on his back. As he lay there and screamed, I said "Ok, Doc. Get that sample." The Corpsman quickly swabbed the injection site and took a blood sample from Salyer's left arm, and that was that.

About an hour later, Salyer's Chief arrived. He stormed into the officer where McAlister and I were filling out the ICR and yelled "Where the hell is my man?" I stood up and said "Please follow me Chief." We walked to the interrogation room where Salyer was now sleeping. The Chief pointed his finger in Weldon's face and said "Uncuff him NOW!" I stood between the Chief and Weldon and said "Chief, with all due respect, you are not in charge here. Please come with me so we can discuss this in my office." After walking back into my office I shut the door and said "Chief, if you will calm down I think we can settle this." The Chief stood up and put his finger in my face saying "Oh, this is done. Let him go now or I swear there will be problems!" McAlister and I both stood up at the same time. I said "Chief, you need to listen to me. There are two ways we can do this. I can place you under arrest right now for threatening me, and send you and your man Salyer to a Courts Martial, or you can sit down, be quiet, and listen to me. It's your call!" The Chief saw that I was not kidding, so he sat down and said "Ok. I apologize for getting bent out of shape. I am listening."

Over the next fifteen minutes I explained how I wanted to handle the situation. I said "Chief, we know what you guys do for a living and the last thing I want to do is to cause a couple of America's Hero's a bunch of trouble. Right now we have Salyer for drunk and disorderly, resisting arrest, threatening bodily harm, destruction of Government property and assault. I have no desire to process this ICR and ruin his career." The Chief was listening intently. "Go on" he said. "Now, I would be willing to forget all of this if you take care of the windows on my Vic and promise me that I will never see Petty Officer Salyer again." The Chief looked at me and smiled. "Sounds like a deal to me." "Ok, let me call the Security Officer (SECO) and run it by her. She usually supports my decisions, so everything should ok." After a quick phone call, I took the Chief back to the Interrogation room where Salyer was awake and singing to himself. "Petty Officer Salyer, I would like to take the cuffs off of you and let you walk out of here with your Chief. If you do anything that suggests that you are anything less than a gentleman, I will put you under the brig. Do you understand me?" Salyer smiled and said "Yes, Petty Officer Westfall. I promise to be a good boy." I motioned for McAlister to take his cuffs off, and then they quietly walked out. Just another Saturday at ASU.

On way too many occasions we would receive the bodies of service members who had fallen in our Area of Responsibility (AOR). We would hold these bodies, usually over night, in one of our refrigerated units. Our job was to monitor the temperature of the storage caskets and make sure everything was optimal until they could be processed and transported back to the States.

We received one storage casket on a Thursday night, just before shift change. A helicopter had gone down during a mission, and everyone had survived except this one sailor. I started recording the information of the deceased in our body log, when I realized that I had known this person. "HT1 Edward N. Salyer, United States Navy Seal." This was the same man who had given us so much trouble just two weeks before. I told his Chief I never wanted to see him again. I really didn't want to see him dead.

A few months later, the USS New Orleans pulled into port. With it came yet another Seal team, looking for a little rest and relaxation. I had talked to a couple of them at the Exchange, and they seemed nice enough. Maybe this time we could get through the weekend without any problems. That was wishful thinking.

Later that night, at about ten o'clock, Dispatch received a call from the Mania Plaza. It seems that there were men climbing and repelling from the roof of the building. The local people around the Mania Plaza were scared, and had called the local Police. Well, there goes the weekend. Knowing that it was our beloved Navy Seal's, I assembled a team and headed out.

When we arrived at the Mania Plaza, I sent Petty Officer Miller to find the Seal Team Commanding Officer and have him meet me on the fourth floor, where the team was staying. There were two other Patrolmen with me when I got to the fourth floor.

My Assistant Watch Commander, MA2 Harris, and Petty Officer McAlister were standing behind me when I knocked on the door from where the most noise was coming. Finally, after several progressively louder knocks, a young sailor answered the door. He looked me up and down as said "Yeah, what do you want?" I introduced myself "My name is Petty Officer Westfall, from ASU security. I need to speak to the senior person in the room please." He just smiled at me then slammed the door shut.

I knocked again louder, and the same guy answered the door again. "Oh, it's still you. What do you want?" I put my foot in the doorway this time and said sternly "You, come out into the passage way right now." He looked at me and smiled, then yelling into the room "Hey guys, the cops want us out in the passageway!" He walked slowly out of the room followed by about twenty other men. As they walked out of the room, they lined up against the wall.

When the last one came out, I addressed the entire group. "Look guys, I know all you want to do is have some fun and blow off some steam, but you are scaring the locals. This is their country, and we need to respect them. If you will just stop repelling down the building and not get too loud, we can all have a good night." Usually, that would be good enough. But not with these boys... they were drunk, arrogant and looking for a fight. "Why don't you drop your gun belt and let's fight fair and square" the young sailor said to me. I replied "This isn't a game. All of you get back in the room now!" Then I pointed at the mouthy guy and said "You are coming with us."

Just then, Petty Officer Harris stepped forward to arrest him, when all of the sudden the SEAL reached out and grabbed Harris by the throat and said "I am about to kill you, punk." Now if anyone else would have said that, we would have taken it with a grain of salt. But when a SEAL who is trained in deadly hand to hand combat tells you that, it's a totally different matter. I quickly pushed myself between Harris and his attacker and drew my 9mm, and then I took a step back and pointed it right at his face and said "BACK OFF! If you take one more step towards him, I will use deadly force." If he took one more step, I was going to shoot. When I drew my weapon, the rest of my team drew their weapons as well. So, now we had three weapons drawn on twenty drunk Navy SEAL's. This was not a good place to be.

Right when I thought it couldn't get any worse, here comes another Seal up the stairs. "What the hell is going on here? My name is Senior Chief O'Neil and these are my guys. Put those guns down now!" I quickly addressed him "Senior Chief, My name is Petty Officer Westfall with ASU security. You are NOT in charge here, and you will do as I say. Now tell all of your team, with the exception of yourself and this man right here, to get back in that room right now!" Realizing how serious the situation was, the Senior

Chief did as I told him to. The men returned to the room, and we holstered our weapons. Thinking the situation was resolved, the Senior Chief said "Ok, Petty Officer Westfall, this is over. You guys go back to base and leave us the hell alone."

At that time, Petty Officer Miller arrived on scene with the Seal's Commanding Officer. He introduced himself as Lieutenant Commander Holmes, and asked me what it would take to make this all go away. I said "Sir, this man assaulted and threatened the life of a Police Officer. This is not going away. This man is under arrest, and you are accompanying us back to ASU security. There are no other options." At that time I cuffed the detainee and handed him over to McAlister. "Senior Chief, your men are on lockdown. You will send them to their rooms where they will spend the rest of the night. If I hear one more sound out of them, I will wake up the Security Officer and she will call the Admiral and ask the USS New Orleans to leave this island."

As we were en route to ASU, I called ahead and had Weldon contact the Security Officer to brief her on what happened. SECO decided to call the Admiral anyway and inform him that one of his Seals was being detained at ASU headquarters. Whenever one sailor draws a weapon against another sailor, it's a big deal. The next hour was spent processing the mouthy sailor, whose name was HM3 Nester. LCDR Holms was very polite, and made life much easier for us by volunteering all the information we needed.

A few minutes later, the Security Officer called and told me the Admiral was very angry at the Seal team. He said he would be holding Admirals Mast the next morning on the USS New Orleans, and asked if my men and I could be there. I told her we would wrap up things at security and be at the New Orleans at seven o'clock the next morning. Since we were finished processing Petty Officer Nester, I turned him over to LCDR Holmes. I instructed Mr. Holmes to place Nester on ships restriction for the remainder of his time in Bahrain. Then I asked Petty Officer McAlister to drive them to the ship.

Later that morning, at quarter to seven, we arrived at the docks and boarded the USS New Orleans. We were met on the Quarterdeck by the Chief Master at Arms, and led to the wardroom where the mast was taking place. There were already many people in the room, all standing by waiting for the mast to start. Sitting in the front was Petty Officer Nester and his Senior Chief.

After a few moments, the Chief Master at Arms came to me again and asked me to come with him. I followed him across the large room and was led to the Admirals stateroom next door. The Admiral answered the door and asked me to come in and have a seat. "Petty Officer Westfall, I want to apologize to you and your men for what happened last night. No man should ever be put into a situation where he has to decide whether or not to shoot a fellow warrior." Then he sat down and took a sip of his coffee. "Now, tell me, what do you think I should do to this young idiot?" "Sir" I said "I honestly don't think that a temporary lapse of judgment should cost a man his career. I agree what he did was stupid, but these men are under so much stress and pressure. I recommend that you be tough, but not career damaging." The Admiral looked at me and said "I agree with you. Let's keep this between us until I make my ruling. Get on back out there, and thank you. You're a good man."

Back out in the wardroom area, mast started a few minutes later. After hearing all the arguments, the Admiral gave his ruling. "Petty Officer Nester. I sentence you to thirty days in the brig, reduction in pay grade to E-3 and loss of half a month's pay for three months. Mast is secured."

When you spend enough time standing sentry duty in the Persian Gulf, you make friends. Khalid Ali was a low level supervisor in the BPS (Bahraini Public Security). He usually stood watch at the back gate, and after a year or so, he and I became great friends. Khalid, like most Bahraini Soldiers, had very little money. He lived in a two room house with his wife, his mother, his father, his uncle, and his three sons.

Khalid told me one day that his wife was expecting a child in the next month or so. When I was shaking his hand and congratulating him, he looked a bit worried. "Hey man, what's the matter? You look worried about something." He stopped smiling and said "My friend Westfall, I do love my family, but we do not have the money for the things we need for the new baby." I told him that I was sure everything would be alright, and he should not worry.

The next day at Guard Mount, I told my section about the conversation I had with Khalid. Everyone in the section knew him, and wanted to help out. I suggested that we show him a wonderful American tradition, and throw him a baby shower. Everyone seemed to like the idea, so we made up a list of things to buy for them.

The next week, I told Khalid that I needed his help translating a BPS document I received from out in town.

When it was time for his break, he followed me to the Watch Commanders Office where Darlene and a couple other Patrolmen were waiting to surprise him. He was so touched by our gesture, he just cried and cried. He asked me to tell his subordinates that he was sick so they wouldn't see him crying. Before leaving Bahrain, Khalid gave me a gift: Two handmade ceramic pitchers that Khalid made just for me. They may be warped and imperfect, but they will always be special to me.

One of the bad parts about security in Bahrain is the boredom. For every exciting day there are thirty boring days where time seemed to just stop. The night shift was the worst, and to make the time go faster, I decided we should have training drills throughout the week. Since Petty Officer Phillips was the section four training officer, I decided that he and I would set the ground rules.

Drills would only be performed after the club and the rest of the base was closed down, after two o'clock in the morning. All drill periods would be announced at Guard Mount and over the radio at the start of the drill period. If, during a drill, there is a need for the Patrolman to draw a weapon, it will be simulated. Lastly, the Dispatched had authority over all drill periods. The Dispatcher, usually Petty Officer Weldon, is the first to know about any calls or situations, so she would need the authority to call all the shots. Since she had long earned my trust and respect, I had no problem giving her that authority. All of the training drills were videotaped so we could replay them as desired for future training.

Our first training drill was designed to make the Patrolman think outside of the box. Many of our situations dealt with people being so drunk that they are irrational and unpredictable. I used a couple of the new Patrolmen as actors.

The first scenario had a young male sailor sitting in the club at the patio bar. I gave the training announcement, and then I called the scenario in to the Dispatcher, Petty Officer Weldon. "Hello... is this the Police? I am calling from the base club, and there is a guy sitting here at the patio bar and he keeps saying he is going to blow everyone up. The waitresses are starting to freak out and he is scaring the customers off." About a minute later, Darlene's voice rang out on the radio "This is a drill, this is a drill. All stations 1-2... any available personnel respond to a disturbance at the Oasis. See the bartender on the patio about a suspicious patron. Approach with caution. This is a drill." Within seconds there were three responses.

The first to arrive on the patio was the Assistant Watch Commander, Petty Officer Harris. Since there was only one person sitting at the bar, he knew where the threat was. He cautiously approached the suspect and announced himself. "Sir, I am Petty Officer Harris with ASU Security. May I see some identification please?" Now I have to give my Patrolman actor his due credit. He did exactly as I asked him to do, and did it perfectly. He looked at Harris and said is a sad, depressing voice "Why do you care who I am? You don't like me any more than she does." Harris was visibly confused by this, and was not sure how to respond.

As three more Patrolmen entered the patio to back him up, Harris said "Sir, I need to know who you are." The actor answered "Why do you care? I am nobody. I am just a dead guy, but you can call me Ernie." As Harris was briefing his backup team, Ernie stood up, threw a five dollar bill on the bar and started walking out. When Harris saw him leaving, he quickly caught up to him and said "Sir, you can't leave until we ask you a couple more questions." It was obvious that Harris had no idea what to do next. Ernie looked at him and said "Dude, it's my time. Please, let me leave so I can do what I have to do." Harris was out of answers. He finally said "Ok Ernie, who are you going to blow up?" Ernie looked at him and said "I would never hurt anyone. If I wanted to blow someone up, I would probably blow myself up!" Then he started laughing and asked if he could go. Harris saw no reason to hold him any longer, so he said "Ok, Ernie. Just be careful!" After that I approached Petty officer Harris and asked him if he was done, and he said he was. I picked up my radio and gave the all clear.

As the Patrolmen were walking back to their designated places, the Petty Officer Weldon's voice came over the radio "All units 1-2, this is a drill, this is a drill, be advised, there was an explosion in the parking lot. A man named Ernie Thompson committed suicide by blowing himself up. Any available units respond. This is a drill"

Every time we ran a drill, we would have an after action review to discuss the outcome of the drill. Our first after action review covered the mistakes that Petty Officer Harris made earlier that shift. The first thing he did wrong was not listening to the suspect. Ernie had said "Why do you care who I am? You don't like me any more than she does." That should have told him that Ernie was angry over a woman. The next thing he said was "I am nobody, I am just a dead guy, but you can call me Ernie." The reference to death should have been a red flag. So far that's one reference to a romance problem and one reference to death. The next thing he said was "Dude, it's my time. Please, let me leave so I can do what I have to do." This, along with the earlier references, was a clear sign of self destruction. At that time Harris should have taken the suspect into custody and called medical for a physiological evaluation. That man died because Harris didn't pick up all the signs. I believe the best drills are the ones that you fail. This way, you won't forget.

Drills weren't the only thing we did to kill the time. We also tried our hand at acting and making our own episodes of 'Cops'. Since Phillips had the most experience with the video camera, he was the director. We only did this when there were no ships in, so the base was dead quiet.

We would usually start out by downloading a few of the extra Patrolmen and using them as actors. Our first 'episode' had three of us trying to cut a hole in back of the Credit Union to steal the safe. Now, if you remember what I told you in the last chapter, the Credit Union didn't have any money. It might not even have had a safe, for all we knew. Who cares, as long as we get the ratings.

Just as we started breaking the wall, here came the cops! The fight scene was pretty cheesy to say the least. It's a wonder that we didn't have words like "Pow" and "Smash" on the screen, like the old Batman movies did. It was a lot of fun to film, and the watch section loved it! We would have been a much bigger success if Philips wouldn't have screwed it all up. You see, Master Chief liked the idea of us doing the drills, and she sometimes asked for the tapes so she could see what we were doing. Phillips screwed up and gave her the "Cops" tape we had been working on. Needless to say, she was less than thrilled at our movie making skills.

Luckily for me she liked me, and turned her head this once.

My favorite time of the week was our second day off. The first day was usually spent with the family, but the second day was a party day. Since we all had more money than we knew what to do with, there was always lots of food and beverages. Because everyone had a pool, we would take turn hosting the party.

My house was huge, and you could open the sliding doors from my living room to the indoor pool. The living room could hold about fifty people comfortably, so my house was a pretty popular party spot. If we ran out of anything, we would just send the house boy out to get it. If we ran low on food, we would ask the maid, Mening, to make some more. Life was always good on the second day.

Since we lived on an island, there was always the best seafood, and it was caught that morning so it was always fresh. Actually, we had to kill it most of the time, so it may have been a little too fresh. The favorite was crabs and shrimp by the bushel. Once they talked me into buying a shark tail. I ended up with about ten steaks, and they were incredible!

One thing that I like to use to stir up the party was a small urn I found at a yard sale one day. I think it was supposed to be a small lamp, but it didn't have any holes in it for the wires. It actually looked more like the kind of urn you would put cremated remains in. I kept it on a small table all by itself, and had it adorned with a special cloth. Every time I would walk past the urn, I would stop for a minute and reflect on it.

After a while, I noticed that my guests were also showing respect when they passed it. When they asked me who it was, I told them. "Here rests the remains of my Great Uncle Howard. Howard Westfall was a wonderful man. He was a World War II hero, and his name was known all over Europe and Asia back in the day. He led a militia against the opposing forces in France back in forty four. That was the year he lost his left leg saving two little girls from a fire." (This is the point when I would look off into the distance, reflecting on his greatness).

"When the war came to a close and the people returned to Paris, Uncle Howard led the people in rebuilding their home. After eight years in Europe, Uncle Howard came back home and spent most of his time researching ways to build inexpensive farm equipment using obsolete machinery from the war effort." (Here is where I would sniff, and take another dramatic pause).

"His final years were spent in the Peace Corps building schools and churches in the Congo. One day, as he was helping a busload of orphans to get home during a flood, Uncle Howard came under fire from rebel forces who thought he was a war criminal. He was shot once in the head, but it didn't slow him down. He fought through the blood and the tears until all the orphans were safely returned to their home. Then, just as he was walking out the door, he fell to one knee and said the house mother... 'If only I had the strength to repair the leaking roof...' then he lay down and breathed his last..." Then I would hold my glass high and look to the heavens. "Here is to Uncle Howard. You, Sir, were the man." Then I would sniff again and take a deep drink. The room was silent, as everyone paid their respects to my empty two dollar lamp urn.

The first time I did this, Darlene followed me into the kitchen and whispered "Clay, I just wanted to tell you that you and the urn in the other room have one thing in common... you are both full of crap!"

Chapter Twelve

One thing I did while I was stationed in Bahrain was travel to every desert known to man. One week I was at the Al Udeid Air Base in Qatar working security, and the next week I would be at the Prince Sultan US Air Base in Saudi Arabia escorting VIPs. Everywhere in the Persian Gulf looked the same to me, no matter how long I was there. I started to wonder if I would ever get back to the United States...

I remember One of the things I told my mom I wanted to do when I got to the gulf was to ride a camel. Now there were many opportunities for me to ride a camel, so I did it the first chance I had. The camel I rode was absolutely huge! It must have been ten feet tall. In Bahrain, all the camels have only one hump. The two hump camels live in Asia, and have much shorter legs. When one imagines himself riding a camel (like I did) he imagines the ease of sitting between the two humps and the ride is just grand. But, that is not the reality one will find in Bahrain. You have to hold on to the single hump and just kind of straddle its hind end. The first time I did this, let's just say it was less than graceful.

One thing people don't realize is just how nasty it is when a camel spits on you. They are actually very good at this, and look for opportunities to catch someone off guard. While I was getting up my courage to mount this huge beast, he showed his approval by spitting on my leg. At the end of the day I was happy that I had done something that I had always wanted to do. Now that it was over, I could tell folks I rode a camel and lived through it. Little did I know this was just the beginning of my camel experience.

As the time in Bahrain passed, I had a decision to make. I really liked being a Police Officer, and I loved leading my section. This is something that I might want to do with the rest of my Navy career. The main problem I had with Law Enforcement was the politics. I hate politics, and I do not care for people who have to shake with their left hand because they are holding a knife in their right hand.

A good example of this is when we were teaching our newest Patrolmen how to write tickets on base. I was showing the proper way to do this with cars that were driving too fast. I didn't realize that Master Chief was watching until she approached us. We had just stopped one car driven by a junior enlisted man and gave him a written warning. Then, we stopped a senior officer, and were writing him one when the Master Chief approached us and said "Petty Officer Westfall, can I speak to you a minute? Do me a favor and tear up that warning." When I asked why she said "We don't bite the hand that feeds us. Don't stop senior officers on base." I replied "Master Chief, what about the enlisted man we just warned?" "That's alright, just not the senior officers." At that time I apologized and dismissed the driver. Then I took the ticket book from the Patrolman and dismissed her. That was the last time me or any of my people wrote a ticket.

NAVCENT is a highly restricted area. All of the top brass in the AOR (Area of Responsibility) work out of NAVCENT in one way or another. The entire area is enclosed and surrounded with a high fence and rolls of barbed wire. Access was tightly restricted to one entrance guarded by two of our ASU Patrolmen. Every hour one of the Patrolmen would take a tour of the compound, turning knobs and checking windows to make sure the individual areas are secure.

On one particular night, I received a report from NAVCENT that there were a particularly large number of discrepancies, so I started writing down what we were finding. I would drop by late at night, just after everyone went home and check to see how good of a job people were doing. As time was going by, the security had gotten more lax and more mistakes were made. High security safes were left open in empty rooms, and level three doors were left unlocked. Just when I thought I had seen it all, something worse would happen.

One afternoon while briefing the security personnel, a first class Radioman walked out of NAVCENT carrying a piece of paper that had "TOP SECRET' stamped at the top and the bottom of it. I stopped him and said "Excuse me; you can't walk around with that document like that. You must have a cover sheet and a folder." The guy looked at me startled, and then he tried to hand me the paper. "You can't just give that to anyone! You need to take it back inside and prepare it the right way."

After seeing all these major discrepancies, I decided that I needed to write a detailed report and send it in to the NAVCENT Chief of Staff. Attached to the report was four pages of detailed examples, giving the time and date of each incident. Once the report was completed, I turned it in through my Chain of Command as proper protocol dictates.

When the report reached Master Chief Fisher, she called me into her office. "Petty Officer Westfall" she said "I don't think you really want to turn this report into the NAVCENT Chief of Staff." I was confused by this. "Master Chief, these are some very serious security violations. Someone has to know what is going on so these discrepancies can be corrected." Then she asked me to sit down, and started talking to me like I was an old friend. "Clay" she started. Now a Master Chief Petty Officer would never us the first name of a subordinate, unless there was a really good reason to do so. She went on "Sometimes you have to think carefully about the ramifications of something before you do it. How might this report you are filing be a bad thing?" Now I was starting to understand. This has got to be political... "If we turn in this report, it's like slapping the Admiral in the face. It would be like telling him that he is all screwed up."

I had really enjoyed being a Police Officer up until this point. But I had this sinking feeling in the pit of my stomach that all of that was about to change. I knew that I was about to see something ugly. The Master Chief continued "I think you should bury this report, and forget this ever happened. Lets spare the brass the embarrassment and just shred this thing right now." That was the moment I lost all respect for the Master Chief. I knew right then that I was going to leave my career as a Police Officer in her office that night. "Master Chief" I started "I have held a Top Secret clearance for the past ten years, and I am telling you that these offences are some of the worst I have ever seen. National Security demands that someone know about this before it's too late." The Master Chief looked at me and shook her head. "Petty Officer Westfall, I will not forward this report." I stood at attention before the Master Chief and said "Master Chief, with all due respect, I must forward this report with or without your endorsement. If that happens, the Command will know that you dropped the ball for political reasons." The Master Chief stood up and said "Alright. I see I have no choice. I am very disappointed with you Petty Officer Westfall. Now, get out of my office!" I was right. I knew then that I would never be a cop again.

Since my tour was quickly coming to an end, I only had a short time to do all the things I had planned to do while I was in Bahrain. I needed to get out of my housing contract, so I moved into the Adari Complex, just outside of the ASU gate. I had a great apartment on the seventh floor. It had three bedrooms and two bathrooms, a lot of space for one guy.

I needed to take more pictures of the Arabic way of life. I needed more... camels. That's it. I would take a trip across the island and look for camels. As I was making my way across the island, I decided to try the place where I had first ridden a camel here in Bahrain.

When I arrived at the small farm, I saw a cute baby camel standing out in front of the barn. He was about five feet tall, and didn't look older than a couple months. Just as I was reaching out to him, I saw an Arabic man coming from the barn door.

One thing you will notice about Arabic men is how proud they are when foreigners appreciate what they have. I asked him if I could take pictures of his baby camel, and he smiled and said "Yes, of course my friend."

As I was taking pictures from every angle, he asked me if I wanted to buy his camel. Now, this was a very odd request because Americans were really not supposed to buy livestock from Arabs. When I asked him why he wanted to sell his camel to me, he said "My friend, I am a simple man, a Shiite by birth. My family lives in Saudi Arabia, and I have to move back to there so I can take care of my mother." He started shifting on his feet, and it looked like he was embarrassed, then he said "I must sell all of my livestock, and the only person who wants to buy them is the Sunni who owns the big camel farm down the road. I will not sell him my baby camel. I would rather sell him to an American first!" I really am not sure how the next few minutes played out, but soon I found myself counting out two hundred dollars American for the baby camel. I figured I would buy the camel and take it to the other side of the island. Then, when I was done taking all of my pictures, I would just bring him back over to this side of the island and sell him to some other camel guy.

Here is something that I never thought I would write. Do you know how hard it is to get a camel into a 1993 Chevrolet Cavalier? If you ever find yourself in this situation, put the camel in backwards, letting his legs fold in last. It took me about an hour to figure out how to do that. Once he was in the car, I let him hold his head out of the passenger window. I have never gotten so many strange looks in my life.

When we got back to Manama, I drove over to the opened field that was next to my apartment building to take the pictures. The camel was a natural, and soon I had all the pictures I could want. When I finished with my photo shoot, I saw that it was too late to be driving across the island again. Now, what was I going to do with this camel? I quickly tied him to my bumper and went into the apartment building to talk to the ever helpful doorman, Yoshi. Yoshi taught me a little bit about camels.

It seems that young camels do not respond well to being left alone. They would much prefer to be with people, and if that isn't possible, a donkey is usually purchased to live in the stable with the young camel. Well, that narrowed it down. There was only one thing to do now, and that was to get him up to my apartment on the seventh floor. This might not be so easy.

The ground floor of the average apartment building in Bahrain was spectacular! They put so much money into the gold trim and the attention to every decorative detail was incredible. They would do everything they possible could to please any American guests that would walk through the door. When they saw me walking through the beautifully decorated lobby leading a camel, you would have thought it happened every day. They just smiled and pretended not to notice.

One thing that I found it very hard to get used to was the size of the elevators in Bahrain. They were about half the size of even the small ones here in the States, and maybe six people could ride on one, but it would be very tight. And there would always be a sign on the side that said "Twelve person maximum." If you have ever been on an elevator with a camel, then you know how smelly it can get. Those seven floors seemed like a hundred!

My apartment was pretty big for just one person. I decided that the camel would have the big spare room for the night. I spread a large sheet out on the floor where he would be standing, and brought up a large bundle of straw that I picked in the field next to the Adari Complex. I was afraid he wouldn't eat it at first, but soon he was chomping away. Camels are funny animals to watch while they eat. They chew for like thirty minutes, and then they swallow it. After about five minutes, they bring it back up and chew it again, and then they swallow it, again. Then, one more time, they bring it up to chew it again. It was kind of disgusting, but trust me... they chew their food well!

The biggest problem I thought I was going to have was when the camel went to the bathroom. Since I had no point of reference, I had no idea what to expect. Luckily, that camel only went to the bathroom once a day, and that was when I brought him back down to the field by the building. He was only supposed to be there for a day or so, but soon it turned into a week, then two. He was just so easy to take care of; I kind of enjoyed having him around. I even named him "Camelot."

I remember once some of the Patrolmen who lived in the building came up one Saturday to watch a ballgame. A couple of the girls asked if they could look around my apartment, so I told them to go ahead. When they opened the bedroom door and saw Camelot, they screamed so loud the manager came up. When I explained it was just Camelot, he laughed and didn't say another thing about him.

I finally had to sell Camelot to a Shiite who had a petting zoo just outside of Manama. He paid me the same two hundred dollars American that I had originally paid for Camelot.

The last three months in Bahrain went by pretty quickly. I had received orders to a Destroyer, the USS

Arthur W. Radford (DD-968) out of Norfolk. I had never been attached to a surface ship before, but it was a new Navy experience. It would give me a chance to get my Surface Warfare Qualifications done. Yes, I could do a surface ship. It would be good to back home again.

I remember how wonderful the flight home was. All I wanted was two things I couldn't get anywhere outside of the United States... a six pack of Zima and a Papa John's pizza. It was good to be home.

I had never thought about going to a surface ship. Why would I? I was a bubblehead, and bubbleheads live on submarines. I never even considered leaving the submarine community, so this was all new to me. No matter what happens, I will make the best of it. After all, the only reason I was nervous was because I didn't know what to expect. Maybe I would like it better.

A big change had just hit the USS Radford. Before this time, women were not allowed on any United States ships of the line that go into harm's way. Now, things had changed, and the Radford had just acquired thirty nine female sailors and added them to its ranks. I was really not looking forward to this change, since I had never been to sea with a woman before. This was going to get interesting to say the least.

When I arrived at pier four where the Radford was moored, I had to stop and marvel at it. It was larger than I expected. I walked up the brow and started up to the Quarterdeck, trying to remember the proper way to board a ship. If I screwed this up, I could just hear what they would be saying for the next four years "Look at that bubblehead trying to be a real sailor. What a looser!" No, this was going to have to go well. I marched proudly up to the top of the brow, then turned and saluted the Flag that was flying on the after deck. After that, I faced the Officer of the Deck and saluted him saying "Request permission to come aboard." He saluted me back and said "Permission granted." That only allowed me to take two more steps to the deck of the ship. The I handed the OOD my orders and said "MS2(SS) Westfall reporting as ordered." The OOD looked at me, smiled and said "A bubblehead cook. The Navy does have a sense of humor." I just kind of smiled and let that one go by.

As I stood there looking at everything surrounding me, the OOD called down to the mess decks for someone to come up and show me aboard. I had no idea what to expect, but I was excited to see what was in store for me.

Before too long, a young sailor entered the Quarterdeck and introduced himself. "Hi" he said sticking out his hand "I'm MS2 Olden, the Senior Galley Watch Captain. C'mon down and I will take you to the ships office." The Ships Office, formally the Personnel Office, is where all newly arriving personnel have to start out. This is when they read and process your orders, review your medical and dental status, and get your pay status situated. Once that was done, I no longer needed an escort.

The Ships Office was located on the forward port side of the ship, just up from the mess decks. Lucky for me there was really no way to get lost after leaving the ships office, as long as I followed the passageway. Soon, I came to the serving line where lunch was being served.

There was several Food Service Assistants (FSA's) standing in the galley, just across the serving line. I saw that they were being rude and mouthy with the customers. Now, there is a very important lesson my father taught me: Keep your mouth shut until you know what you are talking about. I had already seen a few things that I knew were not being done correctly, but now was not the time to say anything. I needed to wait until I was in position to correct the errors I saw.

My philosophy about serving the crew was a pretty simple one. If you are working under me, you will be polite and respectful. An E-1 will get the same courtesy and respect and an E-9. Every customer will be given the best possible service, and has the right to a tasty, nutritious meal, and we will do everything in our power to give it to him.

FSA's, or Food Service Attendants, are younger sailors who are temporarily assigned to the galley to help clean and serve food. They were usually attached for sixty days, and in extreme situations, they would come back later for a second tour. The Galley Watch Captain was in charge of the meal, the cleanliness of the galley and Crews Mess, and over all of the FSA's and junior cooks. Normally, there were twenty FSA's assigned to the Galley Watch Captain, and they were placed over certain areas. Some of the areas include the serving line, vegetable preparation or the deep sink, where the endless line of pots and pans were stacked and washed. The Chief Petty Officer's Mess (CPO) was just behind the Galley, and there were two FSA's, usually handpicked, who served and cleaned for the Chief's, Senior Chief's and Master Chief's.

Just past the galley was the Crews Mess. The crews Mess would hold about 75 people, and was manned by four FSA's. The crew would go through the chow line, pick up a desert, and then walk into the crews mess. To keep the chow traffic down, they would have a seat and the FSA would wait on them, getting them whatever drink they would want. This not only cut down on the traffic and mess, but it made the crew feel a little bit like they were out at a restaurant.

My Chief, MSC(SW) Powers, decided it would be best if I went under instruction for a couple weeks. That meant that even though I was senior, I would work under Petty Officer Olden and learn the ropes aboard a surface ship. After all, I had not been in a galley for several years, and I was a bit rusty.

The following morning I reported to the galley expecting to see a happy, smiling group of FSA's. Instead of the eight early FSA's I was expecting, I was greeted by only two. I looked at my watch and saw that it was about four thirty, one hour before breakfast was supposed to start. As a rule, the entire galley staff was supposed to be ready to roll one hour prior to the meal.

After sending one of the FSA's to wake up all of the late personnel, I started panning up the bacon in the galley. No matter where in the world you were cooking, the Navy breakfast was done pretty much the same way. I didn't really care if Olden showed up or not, because I was anxious to show this crew what I could do for them.

When Petty Officer Olden finally showed up, he was not in any hurry to get the meal out. He smiled at me and said "Dude, you are trying way too hard. This crew doesn't care how hard you work, as long as there is blood on the deck when you leave here at night!" Well, it was pretty obvious that the USS Radford's Senior

Galley Watch Captain had an attitude problem, and was burned out. I had seen this many times before, and knew that there was only one thing he cared about: leaving the Radford. I decided to leave him to his misery for a minute, and get a cup of coffee.

When I walked into the Crews Mess, I saw that some of the crew was already assembling. After picking up a coffee cup, I walked over to the coffee machine and saw that it was empty. I asked the FSA standing by why no one had made coffee yet. He said "Oh, no one on this crew drinks coffee." Ok, there are a few things in life that are certain. You will pay your taxes. You will one day die. Sailors drink coffee. I smiled and introduced myself to the FSA. "My name is Petty Officer Westfall" I said, offering my hand. As he shook my hand, I continued "Here is how we are going to do this. Go ahead and make one urn of coffee, and have the second urn ready to go when the first one starts to run out." He smiled and said "Ok Petty Officer, but they won't drink it."

I went back into the galley and saw that the serving line was being set up by two more sleepy looking FSA's. I found Petty Officer Olden and asked him if there was anything I could do to help out. He said "Nope, we are all good. I am going to sit in Crews Mess until these guys get the line ready to go" When I looked down at my watch, I saw that it was time for the line to open, but it was not ready yet. I started helping out the FSA's, and pushing them to quicken their pace. I was pretty annoyed by this time and decided that I was going to talk to the chief about standing my own watch instead of working with Olden.

Once the chow line was opened, the crew slowly walked by, sliding their trays down the line. No one said anything, they just all looked straight ahead and watched the FSA's slop food down on their trays. Petty Officer Olden would ask each passing crew member "What do you want?" Then they would say "Two over easy" or "Cheese omelet", and he would cook the eggs to order. I looked over to see what he had to offer for the omelets, and saw that he only had American cheese and ham. I was pretty disappointed at the way he was addressing the crew. Breakfast should be a time to wake up and get ready for the day to come. It should be a positive experience for everyone, and put the crew in a good mood. I could see that there was a lot of work to do improving the service.

As I walked back into the Crews Mess, I noticed that no one was drinking the coffee. I walked over and poured myself a cup, then tasted it. It was absolutely the worst stuff I have ever put into my mouth. I asked the FSA who had made the coffee who trained him in his skills, and he said "No one. I just taught myself." I asked him "Do you think it tastes right?" "Oh, I wouldn't know. I never drink coffee!" Problem ascertained. The coffee issue will be addressed after breakfast. "Drain out that coffee, and clean the urn. We will have training after breakfast."

I went into the galley, and I saw a couple of the new young ladies standing in the chow line waiting for their eggs. Just then a young sailor, Seaman Jonas, walked past the galley, and looking at them said "As-Salam Alaikum. Alaikum As-Salam." It was obvious he was trying to impress them with his Arabic greeting skills. They were not impressed at all, and pretty much ignored him. Then he looked at Petty Officer Olden and said "Hey man, can I have an egg white omelet?" Olden slapped his spatula on the grill and yelled "How many time do I have to tell you NO SPECIAL ORDERS! Now, do you want eggs over easy or a cheese omelet?" Nope, this was not going to work. I would talk to Chief Powers later this morning.

As chow secured, I walked over to the drawer where all of the recipe cards were kept and pulled out the recipe for coffee. After assembling all of the FSA's on the mess decks, I addressed them. "Do you realize that you should be going through about three urns of coffee each morning? The navy drinks coffee. If they are not drinking your coffee, it is because your coffee sucks." Then I asked them how many of them drank coffee every morning. Only three of them drank coffee, so I pointed to one of them and said "You are now in charge of the morning coffee. This recipe will be posted on the bulkhead next to the coffee urn, and it will be followed to the letter each morning. As soon as the coffee is done, you will have the very first cup. If it is not perfect, you and I will be having words. Any questions? Good. Now, let's get cleaned up."

After quarters that morning, I asked Chief Powers if I could start my own watch section opposite Petty Officer Olden. When he asked why, I told him about my morning and told him I would not be able to do it again without intervening, and that would cause problems. The chief said "Alright, you can start tomorrow and give Olden the day off. He is burned out because he has been ridden hard this past year, and he is at his breaking point."

Now that that was taken care of, I wanted to find the ships Qualification Officer. I had gotten my dolphins years ago, but now I had the opportunity to get my Enlisted Surface Warfare pin (ESWS). I knew it would not be as difficult as my Submarine Warfare quals, but it would still be a challenge.

Qualifying on a surface ship, especially a Destroyer like the Radford was easier because there were more people standing watch. With more people come more opportunities for getting checkouts and signatures. The central engineering nerve center on board was just two decks below the galley, and usually there was not too much to do there, so getting checkouts should be relatively simple.

The very first evening just before going home, I grabbed a plate of cookies from the galley and took them on down to Maneuvering. As I entered the Maneuvering control room, I asked the Engineering Officer of the Watch (EOOW) for permission to enter with cookies. He looked at me and said "Hey, aren't you the new cook on board?" "Yes Sir" I replied, handing him the plate of cookies "My name is MS2(SS) Westfall, and I am your new Galley Watch Captain. I just wanted to come down and introduce myself." The EOOW smiled and said "Yeah, I'll bet. You are here looking for a checkout." I just smiled and said "I was just heading home, and I thought maybe you guys would like a cookie. That's it. Now, I am leaving... have an awesome evening!" As I walked toward the door, the EOOW said "I think this is the beginning of a beautiful friendship." Life was still good!

Chapter Thirteen

The next morning I arrived on the ship at four o'clock, anxious to start my day. I walked into the galley and started the ovens, then walked around to make sure everything was as it should be. As four thirty approached, I noticed that there was only one FSA that reported to me for duty that morning. As I looked at the Watch Bill, I read off the names of all the missing FSA's. I asked him where all of the others were and he said "Oh, they just like to sleep in a bit." I smiled at him and said "Would you please do me a favor? Would you go and find these people and tell them if they are not here ready for work in five minutes, I will make sure that they are scrubbing decks until midnight!"

About four minutes later, seven sleepy, half shaven FSA's walked into Crews Mess. Once I had checked them all off the Watch Bill, I addressed them. "Good morning. My name is Petty officer Westfall, and I will be running the watch today. I have three hard and fast rules, and as long as you remember them, I promise you we will get along fine. First, the crew will be treated just like they were customers out in town. You will smile, be courteous and respect all of them, no matter who they are. If you can't smile and be nice, you will be moved into the deep sink where you can scrub pots and frown all day long. Second. You will follow orders. I am a really good guy to work with, but the Navy comes first. As long as you do what you are told and use common sense, we will get along fine. Third, take care of me, and I will take care of you. Our job is to serve the crew. Let's do it, and do it well. Oh, one last thing. You will be here on time, shaven and clean, wearing clean clothes. Period. Any questions? Great! Now, let's get to work."

My first order of business was the coffee. SN Wiggins was assigned to the coffee mess, and he was making the first pot exactly like the recipe card told him too. Today was going to be a better day. Next, was the galley. I called the four galley FSA's together, and established which one was senior. It seems that an SN O'Malley was going to be in charge of the galley and mess decks FSA's, and he will report to me. I learned long ago that if I put one FSA in charge, my problems go way down.

Looking down at my watch, I could see that it was just hitting five o'clock. Half an hour to go before the crew comes through. As the bacon, hash browns, corned beef hash, and doughnuts were being panned up, I set up my egg station. I really didn't care what Petty Officer Olden did the day before. This was going to be done my way. Omelets would be made with the following ingredients: American cheese, Swiss cheese, ham, mushrooms, onions, green peppers, olives, and tomatoes.

As the grill was warming up, I looked over the steam line. Everything was in order, and looked nice and neat. Life was good. Next, I went in to the Crews Mess for a cup of coffee. Wiggins saw me walking toward the coffee pot and quickly handed me a cup. Then he smiled and said "Wow! The coffee tastes great!" I added a bit of sugar to mine and took a swallow. "Hmmm. Your right. Good job! Now when the crew comes in, I want you to advertise your coffee and tell them it is a new kind of coffee. I want them to know the coffee on board the USS Radford is as good a cup of coffee as you can get anywhere in the Navy." Then I called out loudly "All FSA's meet me at the head of the chow line!"

Once all eight FSA's were at the head of the chow line, I walked into the galley and asked them all to line up facing me. Then I said "Alright. It looks like everything is ready. Grab a plate." SN O'Malley just kind of stared at me and said "I don't understand." I smiled and said "Ok. Here is how it goes. You guys are a part of this crew, and you deserve to be treated with the same courtesy and respect as they do. Now, one half hour before every meal, as long as your station is ready, you will be served and waited on, just like everyone else. So, how can I make your eggs?" The shock was evident, but they were soon sitting in the Crews Mess joking and eating breakfast. I walked onto the mess decks to the first table of FSA's and said "Hi, what can I get for you?" They just stared at me like I had two heads. Then one of the said "Coffee please." so I went and got his coffee. As soon as everyone was served, I reminded them what time I wanted them at their stations and asked them not to be late.

As five thirty rolled around, the chow line started forming. I reminded the FSA's who were serving to smile, and to be friendly to everyone. I told them if anyone got out of line, to let me know and I would handle it. Then I smiled at my first customer and said "Good morning, Sir. What can I make for you this morning?" It was obvious everyone was in a better mood today.

A few minutes later, a couple of the young ladies got into line, and sure enough, SN Jonas was right behind them. "As-Salam Alaikum. Alaikum As-Salam" he yelled out down the passageway. I just smiled at him and said "Do you even know what you are saying?" He looked at me with a bit of a puzzled expression and said "Uh, I think so." I looked at him, trying not to embarrass him too much, and said "'As-Salam Alaikum' means 'Peace be with you', and then it is answered with 'Alaikum As-Salam', which means Peace also be with you.' You are saying both parts of a greeting, and anyone who knows any Arabic at all will think you are an idiot." Then I pointed to the egg station and said "How about an egg white omelet?"

When chow was over, we started cleaning up and getting ready for the lunch prep. I walked out to the mess decks to see how the team was progressing, and everyone was quiet. Then the ten or twelve crew members who were finishing up their breakfast all started clapping for me. When I asked why, they all held up their coffee cups and said "thank you." It was nice to be noticed!

Throughout most of my years in the Navy, I smoked. The only place that you could smoke on the ship was on the smoking deck, which was located on the starboard side forward. Several times a day I would go up and have a smoke, taking a break from all of the goings on down below. It was a nice time to talk with people from other parts of the ship, or just gossip with some friends. Much of the feedback I received from the crew was from the smoking deck. The best part about the smoking deck was that everyone was kind of equal there. Normally, you wouldn't rub elbows with a Chief or a Senior Chief, but on the smoking deck you saw these people several times a day. That is also where I met my first female challenge, Seaman Anna Brown.

SN Brown was a debutant whose daddy had cut her off until she had a life of her own. She was a cheerleader, a homecoming queen, and everyone's sweetheart. Now SN Brown is in the Navy, and she was assigned as an FSA on the USS Arthur W. Radford. SN Brown was now my problem.

When she first appeared in the galley, she smiled sweetly and tried to charm her way into my good graces. I decided to bring her in slowly and put her on the serving line. I had O'Malley show her the ropes and teach her how to set up the line. Her first dinner service went well, although she spent more time flirting with the customers than working. When chow secured she actually asked me if someone else could clean up her station so she could get to bed early. I had to gently break the news to her that she was no longer in Kansas, and she was going to not only secure the serving line, but she and her fellow FSA's were also going to scrub and swab the galley deck. Don't look now SN Brown, you are in the Navy!

The next morning everyone showed up at four thirty. Everyone that is, except for SN Brown. When she finally arrived around five fifteen, she got into line with all the rest of the FSA's and actually asked for two eggs over easy. I smiled and said "Good morning. You are forty five minutes late, so please get out of the chow line and get your station ready. She put her hands on her hips and said "No. I want my breakfast first, or I am not going to work." I looked at her and said "Brown, in my office right now!" She saw that I was not kidding around, so she set her tray down and slowly walked into the Mess Specialist office.

It has always been a good idea to have a credible witness with you when addressing a subordinate, especially an immature female FSA. I walked out into the mess deck and asked one of the senior Petty Officers to come with me while I addressed SN Brown.

When I got to the officer, SN Brown was sitting in the Chief's chair. I yelled "Attention!" She popped to attention and looked straight ahead. "The next time you are late for duty, you will clean and secure the galley all by yourself. If you are late, you will not eat until after the meal, when your station is secured."

She turned toward me and started to say something, but I cut her off. "I don't want to hear it! This is the time for you to listen, not speak! Now, the next time you tell me that you are not going to do something, you had better damn well be wearing your swim suit because I WILL THROW YOUR ASS OFF THIS SHIP! Do you understand me?" At this point, she started crying. Now, I had seen a lot of things in my Navy career, and I had dealt with a lot of situations, but this is the first time anyone ever started crying after I chewed them out. I tried my best to act unaffected and said "Now get out of my office and get on your station right now!" "Yes, Petty Officer Westfall" she said, and ran out of the office.

About ten minutes later, chow started. I was making an omelet when I overheard SN Brown yelling "You will take what I give you, and you will like it. Now shut up and get out of this chow line!" I saw that she had been talking to one of the younger Radiomen, and he was angry. I said "Hang on a minute." Then I said to SN Brown "Get off my serving line and relieve the deep sink. No one talks to my customers like that. You will scrub pots until you learn how to act. Send O'Malley up here in your place." A couple minutes later, O'Malley showed up a bit confused and asked "Did I do something wrong?" I smiled and said "No, she did. Just enjoy your time away from washing pots and pans."

I liked working with O'Malley. He was a good, hard working fellow who took pride in whatever he did, even if it was just washing pots and pans. He quickly won my respect, and he and I became good friends. One of his buddies, SN Mayo, worked side by side with O'Malley in the deep sink. I enjoyed talking to them as we worked through the day and it all worked because they had the maturity to understand our relationship. They knew when it was time to stop playing, and start working. They could kid around and have fun, and then the next day they knew how to be respectful and work well.

After a few weeks in port, the good ship Radford got underway for a week or so. Now this was the first time I had ever been underway on a surface ship! I was very excited and anxious to get out of port. Just to set the mood, I started singing some old sea songs. "Fair well and adieu to you fair Spanish ladies... Fair well and adieu to you ladies of Spain; for we've received orders for to sail on to Boston, and so never more shall we see you again..."

The best part of going out to sea on a surface ship is the view. On a submarine, you never got to see anything until the boat surfaced and docked. Now I could actually go up for some fresh air while underway. Yes, I think I can live with this side of the Navy!

While a submarine had its maneuvering watch, a surface ship set a sea and anchor detail. It was not as complex as a maneuvering watch, and the Damage Control parties were not manned, but all the important watches on the ship were manned. I really enjoyed going topside for a smoke. The salt air was wonderful! I knew then that I was born to be at sea. There was nothing in the world like it.

My favorite time of the day was four o'clock in the morning. I would always wake up a couple hours before breakfast so I could grab a cup of coffee and head topside. I would sit there all by myself, just looking out into the ocean. There was nothing in the world like it. I liked to look out over the star filled sky and just watch the black waves as far as the eye could see. I would always pray, and ask God to guide me through the day, then I would pray for my family, and wonder what Mom and the rest of my family was doing right then. Just writing this is making me miss the sea. Man, I loved going underway. I loved the Navy.

The wardroom was located just above the galley. There was a dumb waiter that could be used to raise the food from the galley to the wardroom pantry, saving the poor wardroom cook from all those steps back and forth from the galley. As a rule, the wardroom cook would serve the same food to the officers that the crew ate down below.

Working in the wardroom had lots of perks. Not only did you get to rub elbows with the Skipper, but you always found out what was going on with the ships schedule long before anyone else knew about it. As long as you did your job, and kept up with the cleanliness of the wardroom and all the staterooms, life was good.

There were a lot of politics that went with the position. You were exposed to all kinds of departmental mail and correspondence. Many of the things that went on in the wardroom area were classified and subject to the privacy policy. I guess you could say that the wardroom cook was seen, but not seen.

I spent a lot of time in the wardroom. I was not assigned there, but if the officers were comfortable around me I could get away with being places that I probably shouldn't be, like certain engineering spaces during specific underway times. I wanted access for my qualifications, and this was the way to get it.

There were three basic warfare qualifications: Submarine, Surface, and Air Warfare. I had one, but I wanted the other two. I had only known two people in my entire career that had all three warfare designations, and they were both Master Chiefs. I wanted all three, and I wasn't planning on becoming a Master Chief.

My Surface Warfare qualifications were actually not that difficult. Compared to my submarine quals, they were downright easy. I had been given a qualification book written for the USS Radford that contained the breakdown on every system on board. This made it a lot easier because it was all compacted into one book, instead of all the Ships Service Manuals the submarine had. Since I was pretty much in control of my day, I could plan my learning sessions and checkouts whenever I needed them.

One thing I couldn't understand was why ESWS qualifications were not mandatory aboard surface ships. On the submarines, you have no choice, you either qualify or you get processed off. If the crew is 100% qualified on any ship, it means they are much more capable of operating the ship and handling shipboard emergencies. Out of a four hundred man crew perhaps only thirty enlisted people where actively perusing their warfare qualifications. I encouraged all the FSA's to pursue these qualifications, and offered extra time off during the day to assist them with scheduling their checkouts.

One of the ugly truths about ships is how they dispose of their trash. On extended deployments, the trash is thrown over the fan tail into the opened ocean, where it is torn apart by the fish and ultimately sinks to the floor of the ocean. Every evening around eight o'clock, the ships FSA's would assemble with the duty cook and dispose of the trash. This just happened to be the day we got our second female FSA, SN Romero.

Romero was also very pretty. When the ship was in port, Romero worked as a waitress at Hooters, and she was quite popular. Like SN Brown, she tried her best to seduce me into letting her do whatever she wanted, and make someone else do the dirty jobs. Needless to say, this didn't work out for her any better than it did for Brown.

As the trash was being assembled for disposal, I was organizing the passing line and telling the FSA's what they were going to be doing. When SN Mayo tried to hand her a bag of trash, she dropped it to the floor and said "I am not going to do this." When O'Malley saw what was going on, he told her to pick it up and start moving the trash to the aft section of the ship. Once again, she looked sternly at him and said "No! I am not going to do this, so just shut up and leave me alone!" then she walked off towards the female berthing area.

Just as Romero was reaching the end of the passageway, I caught up to her. "Where are you going?" I demanded. She ignored me and just kept walking. "ROMERO!" I shouted "Stop now and stand at attention!" This time she saw that I was not kidding around. As she popped to attention, I started in on her. "You are in the Navy now and you WILL follow my orders! Now, turn around and get back to the trash line." She hesitated, then looked at me and burst into tears. I have to say, this modern day sobbing sailor was starting to get on my nerves. "Petty Officer Westfall, I am sorry for being disrespectful. I didn't mean to be insubordinate." She was now crying uncontrollably, and reached out to hug me. Now, hugging the help was really not covered in the Radford handbook either, so I just kind of patted her on the back and gently pushed her away. "Romero, what's going on?" As she regained control of herself, so looked at me with her beautiful sad eyes and said "My whole adult life has been dedicated to helping and training dolphins. Ever since I was a little girl, I have loved dolphins. Now you want me to throw trash into the ocean where the dolphins that I love so much live. I can't do that. It goes against everything I believe in." Finally, an answer. "Romero, I understand what you are saying, and I can see your dilemma. I will tell you what; if you will promise the next time to bring your problem to me instead of openly rebelling, I will make sure you never have to be a part of throwing the trash overboard. You need to respect the fact that this is a Navy warship, and we have a job to do. Are we in agreement?" Romero looked up at me and smiled, and then she quickly gave me a hug. "Ok, now this has to stop." I said "I am sure there are regulations against making your boss feel this uncomfortable!" She smiled and gave me a mock salute and walked back toward the galley. Another tragedy averted.

Once the trash detail was secured, the ship grew quiet for the nightly routine. All the passageway lights were dimmed, and most of the crew settled down to their berthing compartments to watch a movie or read a book. I liked to go to the ships library and find distraction with a video game or a good book. Sometimes, I would meet topside with Mayo and O'Malley and just sit around and shoot the breeze. O'Malley would sometimes bring up his guitar and we would listen to him sing or just play a slow tune. When you add that to the warm, salty breeze of the ocean air, I have a hard time imagining anywhere in the world I would rather be. I loved being at sea.

I decided to take in a breath of fresh air before turning in, so I walked back to the fan tail to see who was out there. There was a small crowd of sailors sitting together, talking about this or that. As I came near, I heard one of the younger sailors asking Master Chief Morley if he had ever heard of a haunted ship.

Master Chief Morley rubbed his chin and said "Pull up a chair and pay attention, because you won't hear this story again. Back when most of you were still in grade school, I worked at the Puget Sound Naval Shipyard in Bremerton, Washington. That's where I first set my eyes and foot on the aircraft carrier, USS Hornet (CV-12). The Hornet had been decommissioned in 1970, and was in moth balls. We were assigned to keep up the many ships there, like the Hornet, in case they were ever needed again. They all just sit there at anchorage, quiet and unmanned. The Hornet is now a museum in Alameda California, and has been called Alameda's Haunted Aircraft Carrier for quite some time now. The stories go back for some time, and I didn't much believe any of them until I first stepped aboard the ship." The Master Chief paused for a puff on his pipe, and looked longingly out over the water.

"I guess I need to tell you a bit about the Hornet before you can understand how it became haunted. The ship I am talking about is the eighth ship to have the name Hornet. The one just before it was another aircraft carrier, the CV-8, which launched 16 Army B-25s to strike Tokyo in one of the most daring raids in the history of warfare, the "Doolittle Raid". Anyway, the eighth USS Hornet, the one currently docked in Alameda, was commissioned in 1943 at the height of the war in the Pacific. She quickly became one of the most highly decorated ships in the United States Navy. She was responsible for destroying over 1400 Japanese aircraft and destroyed or damaged over a million tons of enemy shipping. She supported nearly every Pacific amphibious landing after March 1944 and struck the critical first hits in sinking the Japanese super battleship, Yamato." Again the Chief paused. By the look on his face, you would have thought that he had been aboard it during the Great War.

"The Hornets impressive record didn't come without cost. An aircraft carrier, in times of war or peace, is a dangerous place. Sailors have walked into aircraft's spinning props, been sucked into their air intakes, and blown off deck by their exhaust. Dropped ordnance has exploded, burning and maiming sailors. Snapping flight arrest cables are known to have decapitated at least three men on the USS Hornet. I have been told that in almost three decades of active service, more than 300 people lost their lives aboard that ship. The majority claimed during combat, others from these horrendous shipboard accidents, still others from suicide. The USS Hornet has the dubious honor for having the highest suicide rate in the Navy.

"I think the ships history of tragedies and death is the reason it is now called America's most haunted ship. Doors opening and closing by themselves, tools that vanish only to reappear after a long search, objects that move across floors or fall off shelves without reason, spectral sailors that move through the ship as if carrying out orders from another age, toilets that flush themselves, eerie presences felt, and feelings of being grabbed or pushed when no one is around.

"I remember one weekend when I was attached to the Navy Yard maintenance detail, we were assigned to cycle some of the topside vents because of painting we had done earlier that day. One of the guys that were working with me at the time, Smitty, asked me if I would ever have the nerve to spend the night aboard the ship. I just smiled and said 'sure, how about tonight?' Taking my dare, we agreed to meet back on board around eight that evening.

"After meeting back on board, we decided to sleep in the pilots briefing room, because there was still some light coming in through the hatch. I'll have to admit, I was a bit nervous. It's hard to lie there, knowing that you are the only people on that huge ship and not get spooked. Anyway, we decided to go right to sleep. About three hours later, around eleven thirty, we were awoken by a loud hammering sound, like someone was trying to free a stuck hatch. I quickly jumped up and yelled 'Dammit, Smitty! Stop screwing around.' Just then Smitty, who had been lying right next to me the whole time, said 'What did I do?' Then, as we were looking at each other, the banging started again. That's when we decided to leave the ship and go home."

As the story took a pause, I looked around and saw that the group had grown. Now there were almost twenty sailors sitting there, listening to Master Chief Morley's story. One of the new guys, Seaman Watts, asked "Master Chief, is that the only thing that happened to you?" As the Master Chief sat back and puffed longingly at his pipe, he said "No… that's not the only thing that happened to me aboard the Hornet.

"A couple weeks later, I was painting topside on the flight deck. I was all the way over by the elevator, but I had left my tool bag over by the main ladder, about fifty yards away. As I stood up to fetch it, I saw a sailor reach into the bag and take something. Since I was the only person assigned to work on the Hornet that day, I yelled 'Hey… wait up.' The sailor looked at me, and then started walking toward the island (control tower). Just as he opened the hatch and entered the island, I noticed his rating badge was on his right sleeve. Now, any of you who know your Navy history knows that the Navy hasn't allowed rating badges on the right sleeve since 1949. Once I came to the hatch and looked in, there was nothing there but darkness and silence. Aye… the USS Hornet was indeed haunted, and I never set foot on her again…" After that, the Master Chief just closed his eyes and reclined, puffing away on his pipe.

Not to be outdone by the Mast Chief, Senior Chief Potter spoke up. "I have heard stories about the Hornet, but none of them compare to the legend of the 'Flying Dutchman.' Now, shut your yaps and I will tell you a story…"

The Senior Chief slowly looked around, sizing up his audience. After a moment or two, he started telling his story. "The Flying Dutchman is probably the most famous Ghost Ship ever. But what most people don't know is that 'The Flying Dutchman' refers to the Captain of the vessel, and not the vessel itself. Now there are many Spectral ships around the World that are known as 'The Flying Dutchman' but I am going to tell you about the original, located off the Cape of Good Hope, down in Southern Africa, way back around the year 1750 or so.

"The Captain of the vessel, Hendrick Van Der Decken, was voyaging around the Cape of Good Hope with a final destination of Amsterdam. He swore to round the Cape if it took him 'til Doomsday'. Even when a terrible storm blew in, Van Der Decken refused to turn the ship around despite the pleas of the crew. Monster waves pummeled the ship while the captain sang obscene songs, drank beer and smoked his pipe. Finally, with no options remaining, several of the crew mutinied.

"The Captain, aroused from his drunken stupor, shot the lead mutineer dead and threw his body overboard. Right then, just above him the clouds parted and a voice billowed from the Heavens. 'You're a very stubborn man' the voice said, to which the Captain replied 'I never asked you for a peaceful voyage; I never asked you for anything, so clear off before I shoot you too!' Van Der Decken made aim to fire into the sky but the pistol exploded in his hand. Then the voice from the heavens said 'Now you are condemned to sail the oceans for eternity, with a ghostly crew of dead men, bringing death to all who sight your spectral ship, and to never make port or know a moment's peace. Furthermore, gall shall be your drink, and red hot iron your meat'"

The Senior Chief spit a mouthful of tobacco juice over the rail, and then he continued "There have been many sightings of The Flying Dutchman, often by reputable and experienced seamen, including Prince George of Wales and his brother, Prince Albert Victor of Wales. According to a German Admiral, German U Boat crews logged sightings of The Flying Dutchman off the Cape Peninsula. For all of these crews, it proved to be a bad omen. On a calm day in 1941, a crowd at Glencairn beach in Cape Town saw a ship with wind-filled sails, but it vanished just as it was about to crash onto the rocks." With that, the Senior Chief got up, looked around and finally, walked back into the ship.

After an hour or so of swapping sea stories, I decided it was time to turn in. I walked down to supply berthing where my division was assigned to live. My rack was a middle rack in a quiet corner. Since there were already many people sleeping, I tried to be as quiet as I could be. I got out my shaving kit and walked into the head to brush my teeth and take a shower.

There were four showers in our berthing compartment, and in the morning there would be a line of guys waiting to get in. At night, it wasn't such a problem and I could get away with taking a "Hollywood" shower. It was so relaxing, and just what I needed for a good nights sleep. After saying my prayers and thanking the Lord for yet another safe day on the beautiful seas, I would lie in my rack and feel the movement of the ship as it rocked me back and forth. Soon, I would be totally relaxed and fall off to sleep. This was the way to end a day at sea. Life was good.

The next day was a rainy one, and the seas were a bit rough. Several of the FSA's were sea sick, and that is to be expected. That is one thing I can proudly claim... In twenty two years I have never been sea sick, not even once.

The meals can be a bit more stressful when there is bad weather and rolling seas. When you are on a ship at sea, the ship is constantly rolling back and forth. As it moves, the deck goes up and down, and your legs are constantly compensating for the changes, and this takes its toll on your body throughout the day. By the time dinner is over, you are wiped out and ready for bed!

Another problem is the ships rig for sea. Like the submarine, surface ships roll side to side, and anything that is not secured will fall or in some cases, fly out dangerously. The secret to a successful rig for sea is to always stay rigged, even in port. I didn't think it would be as bad on surface ships, so this is a lesson I learned the hard way.

I remember that we were doing a Tiger Cruise from Charleston, South Carolina back into Norfolk. A Tiger Cruise is where family members board the ship for a short cruise in order to see what their loved ones do at sea. It's a great experience for all ages, and usually they come off without a hitch. Usually. This time we boarded the families in Charleston, South Carolina after a three day liberty port. Approximately fifty civilians came aboard, and life was looking pretty good. That is, until we started cruising North. After about an hour underway, the ship received a weather forecast telling us that the hurricane that had just passed through decided to double back and make trouble. Now we were in no danger of hitting the hurricane, just the bad seas that came with it.

As it was drawing closer to lunch time, the waves started picking up. I noticed fewer and fewer civilians walking about, and heard that many of them were seasick. We had planned to have surf and turf that afternoon, as a special lunch for the families. The surf and turf that day was going to be fried shrimp and rib eye steaks, the crew's favorite!

After breaking out the steaks, I had them sitting out on the serving line to defrost. Now the serving line ran up the midline of the ship, so if the ship rocked far enough to one side, anything sitting on the serving line would fly off into the galley deck. I was very busy trying to get the meal ready, and with the loss of over half of my FSA's, I was running around like a chicken with its head cut off. I was in the Crews Mess setting up tables for the special meal when I heard a crash in the galley. I ran in to see what had happened and could not believe my eyes. There was blood everywhere! The ship had rolled heavily and threw the half thawed steaks all the way across the galley and into the wall on the other side. Once the steaks splattered across the deck, the ship shifted again and doubled the mess. It looked like Freddie Kruger's basement. What a mess.

As I looked for the remaining FSA's to help cleaning up the mess, I ran into the Ships Leading Corpsman, HM1 Yates. He told me he had sent my last FSA to the rack, since he was throwing up in a trash can. Doc said O'Malley did not want to leave his post, but when he saw him throwing up, Doc ordered him to his rack. It looks like it was just me now. Life was sucking in the galley.

After an hour or so, the galley started looking less like a nightmare and more like a floating kitchen again. I had flooded the deck with boiling water and scrubbed it down. The serving line was set up, and the steaks were on the grill. The shrimp was frying, and the salad bar was finished. It ended up being a single man mission, but it was almost done. For the first time in my Navy career I wished that I could have been seasick. But no, I had to be the rock.

As the chow line was opened for business, four of my seasick FSA's returned to their stations. Finally, a break! As I looked at the chow line, I could see only six people, where there would usually be a line stretching down the passageway. It seemed that everyone had lost their appetite, and was trying to recover from the violent voyage. The few people who had lined up asked for bread to make sandwiches. It seems that surf and turf tends to lose its luster when the seas are rough. With the day I was having, it made perfect sense.

A few hours later, the good ship Radford was moored back at pier four. The civilians disembarked and life was slowly returning to normal. It was Friday. After being away from Norfolk for the past two weeks, I was ready for a break. As dinner was secured that evening, I sent everyone home and wished them a good evening. As I slowly walked down the pier toward the parking lot, I looked back at the sea as the black clouds of the hurricane faded into the horizon. I closed my eyes and slowly drew in a deep breath of sea air. It was a bad day, but it was a bad day in the Navy. A bad day in the Navy was better to me than a good day anywhere else. As I walked down the pier, I started singing to myself "I'll sing you a song, a good song of the sea... with a way, hey, blow the man down..."

Chapter Fourteen

The USS Arthur W. Radford, a Spruance Class destroyer, was commissioned on April 16, 1977. It had a long and honorable history, and though it was getting old, it was still selected as the platform for the new advanced hybrid composite structure, known as the Advanced Enclosed Mast/Sensor (AEM/S) System. That sounds kind of complicated, but basically it means we needed to go into the shipyard and have a new experimental mast put on the ship. The stepping of a new mast is kind of a big deal in the Navy.

According to Navy tradition, Mast Stepping is a ceremonial occasion which usually happens at the end of a ship's construction. It involves placing or welding one or more coins into the mast step of a ship, and is seen as an important occasion in a ship's construction, which is thought to bring good luck. Although the coins were originally placed under the main-mast of a ship, they are now generally welded under the radar mast.

The practice is believed to originate from ancient Rome. One ancient sea story tells that, due to the dangers of early sea travel, the coins were placed under the mast so the crew would be able to cross to the afterlife if the ship were sunk. The Romans believed it was necessary for a person to take coins with them to pay Charon, in order to cross the river Styx to the afterlife and as a result of this; coins were placed in the mouths of the dead before they were buried.

Another old sea story told aboard fishing ships off the coast of Norway is that the insertion of coins under the mast of a ship was to serve as a sacrifice thanking the gods for a successful construction, or a request for divine protection in the future. If coins were not placed under the mast of a ship, the gods would become angry and it would mean certain doom for the vessel.

The Radford's mast stepping ceremony was held on May 17, 1997, at the Norfolk Naval Shipyard in Portsmouth Virginia. Twenty-one steel pennies, all minted in 1943, were placed under the Radford's new mast. Steel pennies were selected because copper is traditionally considered to bring bad luck. The steel pennies (Twenty-one cents) symbolized the "Twenty-first Century" technology embodied in this Advanced Technology Demonstration. Only the Supply Officer and I knew that three of the steel pennies that were used in this ceremony had a bit of a different origin than the rest.

While the ship was in the shipyard, I had been assigned to the wardroom mess. It was my job to shop for the food used to feed the officers, then bring it in and prepare the breakfast and lunch for them each day.

As the Mast Stepping ceremony quickly approached, the Supply Officer, Mr. Armstrong, explained the tradition to me. I asked him where the coins come from, and he said he was supposed to go to a local coin shop and purchase them. That gave me an idea. That night when I went home, I looked through an old coin album that I had had. It had been my father's for years, and after he died, my mother gave it to me. I remembered him telling me about the steel cents that he had put in the album. In 1943, the American war effort left the mints with very little copper. For that year, and that year only, the cents were made out of steel. All three mints, Philadelphia, Denver and San Francisco made steel cents that year. These coins were kind of special to me, and I decided to immortalize them in a really cool way. I took the three coins from the album and took them to work with me.

I saw Mr. Armstrong the next day and pulled him to the side. "Sir, can I ask you for a favor?" I handed him the three steel cents. "These were my father's before he died, and I think it would be cool if they could be used for the Mast Stepping ceremony next week." Mr. Armstrong smiled and said "Since it's my job to buy the twenty one steel pennies, I can promise you they will be used in the ceremony." So, on May 17, 1997, my dad's three steel cents became part of an American warship. I thought that was kind of cool.

A few weeks later we were back at pier four getting ready to go underway once more. Before long we would be heading out for a Mediterranean cruise, and I was kind of looking forward to that. Besides, there were still a few countries that I had not been to. Recently, our new MS1 checked on board. Her name was Cindy Harmon, and she just came from a Recruiting Command. I liked her, because she was very straight forward, and not afraid to get her hands dirty. I knew we would get along pretty well.

Before we knew it, we were underway towards the Mediterranean Sea. It was our turn, and that was just fine with me. There I was at four o'clock in the morning in the galley just a singing my heart out "Anchors aweigh, my boys, anchors aweigh... farewell to all these joys we sail at the break of day, hey, hey, hey..." As the crew would come through the chow line, many of them joined me in singing. Man, did I love getting underway!

The trip across the Atlantic took about two weeks, allowing plenty of time for plowing ditches in the water, or in other words, running around in circles. We spent a lot of time working on NBC drills (Nuclear, Biological and Chemical attacks), damage control party drills, and lots of flight ops. I almost forgot that we were on a surface ship! A destroyer is by definition a smaller ship, but it does have a Hilo (helicopter) deck and carries a Hilo and a small flight ops team whenever it deploys.

As we were nearing port in Brest, France, the pulse of the crew changed. Every attitude got a little bit better and the excitement was evident. We pulled in around four o'clock Friday afternoon, and since I had been around the world a couple times already, I volunteered for the duty. Usually, the younger, single sailors would be allowed to leave the ship as soon as liberty was down in foreign ports. Since, as a rule, the older married guys wanted more time off in the home port, the single guys took the duty there.

"Liberty call, liberty call. Liberty commences on board for all hands not actually on watch to expire for duty section three tomorrow morning at zero six hundred. Now liberty call." As the OOD's order rang out throughout the ships passageways, the crew scattered. Within minutes, the ship was quiet, and we continued getting ready for chow.

O'Malley and Mayo were on duty with me, along with several other FSA's. Since I didn't have any plans in France, I figured after the meal was secured I would just head on out and find a place to get a quiet drink. O'Malley and Mayo asked if they could tag along with me, and I thought it would be fun, so I agreed.

Chow was secured and the galley was cleaned in record time. After a quick change of clothes, the three of us were on the beach and heading out to the town. As we walked down along the harbor wall, you could see the World War II German Submarine pens still standing out in the harbor. Since I was interested in submarine history, I couldn't help but stare and wonder what it looked like back in the day.

The French port at Brest was occupied on 18 June, 1940 by the German 5th Panzer Division. The building of the U-boat bunker started in January 1941 and in September 1941 the first boat, U-372 used the first ready pen. Brest was captured by the allied forces on September 21, 1944 after a fierce month long battle which cost United States forces over 10,000 casualties and almost wiped out the entire town. Brest is still a submarine base, now serving the French Navy of course, and the old German bunker is still in use today. The pens still look just like they did back in 1940. Being a navy guy and a bubblehead, I really enjoyed seeing the pens.

Brest was nice, but we really weren't there long enough to see much. I was grateful that the ship arraigned for us to convert our money earlier that day, so we could get right on down to the business of drinking.

After walking across the base and up the hill, we found ourselves at the front gate. Since it was a very nice evening and we were on the edge of town, we decided to walk to the nearest club. The town was kind of fast paced, and the roads were very narrow. It seemed to have a grey haze around it, and there really wasn't many touristy things to do, so we asked directions to the nearest bar or club. Soon, we came to this place called... oh who am I kidding? I couldn't pronounce it if I wanted to. Anyway, we decided to go in a have a drink.

The bar was very small, but it was packed with people. It reminded me of one of the dorm rooms back in sub school, where we would hold huge parties on the weekends. O'Malley and Mayo quickly found girls to dance with, but I was content just sitting at the bar enjoying my bourbon and coke. A few minutes later, one of the locals came over and introduced himself. I remember that his name was Asange, and he knew almost no English at all. It was kind of fun attempting to communicate with him, and after several drinks, we seemed to be communicating just fine.

As the evening flew by, Asange kept trying to teach me French, but I was a lost cause. Finally, I gave up, and he said something to the Bartender. The Bartender smiled and beckoned me to come closer, and then he whispered in my ear "this guy is gay, and wants you to come home with him." Well, that explained a lot. I asked the Bartender to politely inform my new friend that I was not homosexual, and although flattered, I must decline his offer. I decided not to share this incident with O'Malley and Mayo, and moved to a noisier part of the club. After about twenty seconds, a very young girl came up to me and said "If you give me twenty dollars, I will be your date for the night." Well, that just about did it for me. I politely declined her offer, and explained that I was not looking for a date. I decided it was time for me to find O'Malley and Mayo and suggest that we find a different, less friendly club.

About a mile down the road we found what looked like a sports bar. Inside there were several of our Shipmates, so we decided to make our stand there. I am not too sure how the evening ended, but I did remember getting out of a taxi cab back at the French Naval Base a few hours later.

As I was boarding the ship, I was greeted by about twenty of the guys from Engineering. It seems that they were all very hungry, but there was no place to eat at two thirty five in the morning. I made the command decision to open the galley a few hours early and cook breakfast. I fired up the grill and made about fifty grilled ham and cheese sandwiches, and served them with French fries. I knew the Chief wouldn't mind as long as we kept the noise down and I cleaned up the mess. By three thirty, everyone was fed, and life was good once again.

The following day was a kind of slow day. Everyone who was not on duty had gone out the night before and gotten hammered, so the hair of the dog was the status quo for the day. The Chief had arranged for the ship to get fresh French pastry's delivered, and they were excellent!

A bit later in the morning, the Skipper informed us that he had invited some French VIP's to come to the ship later that evening. Every time VIP's came to the ship, it was our department that had to jump through all the hoops and put on a good show. I knew then that the night was going to be a long one.

The Hilo hangar is where the reception was going to be. We had to have a huge cake ready, along with hors devours for two hundred guests. There would be champagne, wine and lots of tiny French beers. Everyone had to be dressed perfectly, and ready to jump at a moment's notice. This was not going to be fun.

My job was to be the go-between man, working from the wardroom pantry. I had to run the galley operation, which included all food preparation and clean up, and the distribution from the pantry. No matter what went wrong, it was going to be my fault. As you could imagine, there was a lot of preparation to be done, so the rest of the afternoon was spent in the galley. O'Malley and Mayo were the only FSA's I had in the galley, because all the others had been pulled up to play as waiters. It looked like this was going to be a long night.

A few hours later, the VIP's arrived and behind them was half the population of Brest. In record time they blew through the hors devours and they were drinking wine like it was going out of style. I was doing everything I could to keep the food flowing. The thing that was worrying me was the flow of dirty dishes going down to the galley. It was way too quiet down there, and the food had stopped coming back up. I quickly excused myself and ran down the ladder to the galley to see what was going on. As soon as I got to the galley door, I heard pans hitting the floor, and cussing that would have embarrassed half of the crew. This part of the machine was starting to fall apart.

When I walked into the galley, O'Malley came right up to me. His shirt was soaking wet, and he had a long shallow cut up his arm. He looked at me and it was obvious he was just about to blow. I looked behind him and there was Mayo with what seemed to be tomato sauce all over his pants. He pointed at me and said "Petty Officer Westfall, with all due respect..." At that point I said "STOP! Both of you, go into the office right now!" As they were walking to the office, I picked up the sound powered phone and called the wardroom pantry. I had an idea...

When I walked into the office, I pushed the button to lower the dumb waiter. I looked at O'Malley and said "Ok, let me have it." (Now, once again, for the sake of my mother who will be reading this book, I have 'softened' the language a bit.) O'Malley was bright red "How the heck are we suppose to feed seven thousand mostly furry people, when there are only the fudging two of us?" As he said it, he kicked the desk. The Mayo started in "And what about that stupid flicking dumb waiter, that has done nothing but bring in dirty fluffy pans!" It was obvious these guys were stressed out, so there was just one thing to do.

I reached over and locked the door, and then I opened the dumb waiter and pulled out a twelve pack of cold beer that was reserved for the VIP's. As O'Malley and Mayo looked at me with disbelief, I popped off the top on two of the bottles and handed them to the overworked FSA's. O'Malley said "You know this is illegal, and we could all get Captains Mast for this". I thought for a moment and said "OK, the regulations say that you can't drink while on duty. If anyone suspects that you are drinking, tell them I gave you the evening off, and I will say the same thing. That being said, don't get caught and don't operate any equipment from here on out without asking me first. I will leave the beer in the office, and you are allowed to have one every half hour, as long as you pretend to be in a good mood!"

As I walked back out of the office, I couldn't help but wonder if I was just pouring water onto a sinking ship. Oh well, there is an old submarine saying "You can chew me out in the sunshine" (translation) "If we live through this moment, I will be happy to get chewed out later".

As I returned to the wardroom pantry, I could see that the reception was starting to die down. The VIP's had starting moving off the ship, and had invited the Skipper and rest of the officers to go with them to another reception somewhere on the base. Now, all we had to do was clean up.

The next hour was pretty quiet. If you walked by the galley, you could hear O'Malley and Mayo singing happily while cleaning up. You know, the British Navy has been serving beer on their military ships for centuries. Perhaps the British Navy has the right idea.

As I was putting the finishing touches on the pantry, I saw that there were still about four cases of beer left. The Skipper said I needed to keep a close eye on the beer, and make sure none of it was taken without my express authorization. I decided to 'authorize' myself to empty out ten liter bottles of Ginger Ale and refill them with beer. I called down to the galley to get a progress report and Mayo told me they were just finishing up. I told him as soon as the decks were swabbed, to meet me on the back of the ship, or the 'fan tail' as we called it.

When the guys finally show up on the fan tail, I handed each of them a bottle of 'Ginger Ale' and told them to take a load off and have a seat. O'Malley looked at me and said "Uh, thanks boss, but we kind of wanted to climb into a different kind of bottle." I smiled and said "Indulge me. Have some Ginger Ale." O'Malley cracked open the bottle and took a sip. Then he smiled and whispered something to Mayo, and then they decided to sit and chill out for a bit. We sat there for the next couple of hours, watching the sun set over the English Channel. Life was good.

I had duty the following day, but as soon as I secured the galley, I headed off into town. Since they had been working so hard lately, I let my drinking buddies O'Malley and Mayo off earlier in the day. They were supposed to be in one of the bars off the main highway, so I was pretty sure I would find them.

By the time I had gotten into town, the sky had grown dark. It was really odd that there was nobody in the street. No traffic, nobody walking down the sidewalk, no one anywhere.

Now, I am not a sports kind of guy, and I don't pay attention to any of the professional teams at all. I did find out why the streets were empty though. This was the night of the World Cup, and France was hosting in 1998. Everyone was watching the game, except for me.

I decided it would be a good time to call my mom, so I entered a phone booth that was on the sidewalk. As I was talking to her, I heard a piercing scream coming from down the street. Then I saw three totally naked men running down the road as fast as they could. Just as I was trying to explain what I was seeing to my mother, I saw a police car with lights and siren blazing going after the men. As they were about to run past my phone booth, the police car swerved in front of them and the cop got out. Just when I thought nothing else could surprise me, the three naked men jumped onto the police car and started yelling. The cop also jumped on the police car and he started yelling too!

As I was trying to make sense of what was going on, the bars on both sides of the street started emptying out. People were flooding the street and screaming like there was no tomorrow. As I looked out from the safety of my phone booth, two girls noticed me on the phone. That's when they both pull up their shirts and started pressing certain parts of their bodies on the glass of my phone booth. I decided that I should probably get off of the phone, since I couldn't hear anything anyway. No wonder the people went crazy... France had won the World Cup!

When I finally was able to get out of the phone booth, I took a good look around and couldn't believe what I was seeing. There were naked people running around, people hanging from balconies, women with their shirts off... you name it, it was going on. I decided with all the chaos, maybe I should lay low and find a now empty bar to slip into.

No matter what bar you were in that night, the beer was free. It was like nothing else in the world was important. I never found my drinking buddies, but it didn't matter. That night, everyone was drinking buddies! It was a great day to be in France.

The next day was our last day in Brest. I was off, so I decided to stay close to the ship. After eating breakfast, I took a slow walk down by the waterside. Since the very first time I saw the ocean, I fell in love with it. The smell of the salt in the air was one of the best smells I had ever experienced.

As I walked down along the harbor wall, I looked out at the submarine pens and imagined how they looked sixty years before. I pictured the allied war planes flying low overhead, dropping bombs on the German occupied naval base. I thought about the ten thousand allied troops that were killed here, and what it must have looked like after it was all over. Now, all that was left was the submarine pen in the lonely harbor. It just makes you think.

As I looked on down the sea wall, I saw that a new ship had pulled in the night before, so I decided to go over and have a look. It was just about the same size as the Radford, and was moored just a few yards down from it. "H.M.S. Wellington" I read on the gang way. 'Her Majesties Ship' just sounded so formal.

As I was standing there looking at the ship, two men walked up behind me. "Good morning Mate" one said is a sharp British accent. "Are you from the Yank ship?" He asked, pointing at the Radford. I smiled and said "Yes, hello. I'm Clay Westfall, a cook aboard the USS Radford. How long are you guys in port?" "We will just be in the day, and then we will be heading back over to Portsmouth. Would you like to come aboard and have a look?" I quickly accepted, and soon we were walking down the main passageway.

The H.M.S. Wellington looked a lot like our ship, although there were some differences. The Wellington was a communications ship, so it was much cooler that the Radford. Electronics tend to heat up, especially when they are running constantly. Keeping the ship at a cooler temperature makes the systems run smoother. It reminded me of life aboard a submarine. Those things were like iceboxes.

After the tour, I was invited down to the Crews Mess. It looked pretty much like our Crews Mess, with a few differences. They had a beer refrigerator with a list on the front of it. I asked one of the guys how the beer rationing worked, and he explained it to me.

There are more than one mess aboard most British ships and submarines. Each of these messes had what was called a 'tic' list on the refrigerator door. On this list was the name of each crewman. Next to each name was a column for beer and a column for pop. Every time you took something from the refrigerator, you had to mark it down on the list. When the ship came into port, the crew would gather in the accommodation room to receive their subsistence allowance, about seventy dollars a day. As they passed through the pay line, they would also pass by the Mess Treasurer, and he would deduct whatever they owed.

Normally, underway you were allowed to have three beers, or 'tins' as they called it per day. You could only consume alcohol when you were coming off duty and not required back for a sufficient time. It was a very serious offense to be drunk on duty. You were not allowed to have anyone else's tins, but on special occasions like birthdays or channel rights, it was not uncommon for your mate's to slip you a couple of their tins.

One of the guys who I met on the pier introduced himself as Liam. He reached over to the fridge and pulled out a tin of dark beer, and then he handed it to me and said "Here's to the Yanks... May the good Lord always keep them on our side!" It sounded good to me, and the beer was free, so I toasted to it. Then, Liam's mate Artis stood up and said "Here is to the all the Yanks who live on the USS Radford." That also sounded good, so I drank to it. As my tin was coming to an end, Artis grabbed another one out of the fridge and popped the top for me. "Here's to Clay the cook... May his haggis never hang limp!" I wasn't sure what that meant, but who was I to judge? I drank to it anyway.

As I came to the bottom of my second tin, I was finding it easier to toast to things. As I started a toast, Liam yelled "NO! Your tin is empty. Hang on... Ok. Here's a fresh one. Now, what were you saying?" I smiled and started again "Here's to the H.M.S. Wellington... May she never run out of beer!" Actually, I could have toasted to my Aunt Molly's pet goat and no one would have cared.

As we toasted and cheered, I noticed that more and more British sailors piled into the mess. It was only ten thirty and I was already hammered. As we started singing the British National Anthem, the Senior Enlisted Man came into the Crews Mess and told us we were getting too rowdy. It was time to break it up and get off the ship.

As I was being walked off the Wellington, Liam asked if we were going to be in Portsmouth, England any time soon. When I told him we would be there sometime in the near future, he said "Perfect, mate! My mate's and I will be drinking at Phantom's Pub every night for the next three weeks. Everyone knows where it is, so it will be easy to find. The pint's are on me!" After shaking hands and saying our goodbyes, I headed back to the Radford. Since I was pretty well drunk and it was only eleven thirty, I decided the rack was the best place for me, and that's where I spent the next eighteen hours.

The following morning the ship's company was busy making preparations to leave port. Our next stop, Portsmouth, England, was only a half days cruise across the English Channel. As far as liberty ports go, Brest was alright, but we were looking for a bit more scenery and entertainment. The crew was actually looking forward to Portsmouth, because our British brethren had a wonderful reputation for drinking and getting every "Yank" they come across shnockered.

Once we shoved off and got underway, I decided to put my time off to good use and get some of my qualifications out of the way. So far I had been doing very well on my quals, as I was about three months ahead of schedule. This time I was looking to get some of my engineering points signed off. I had already talked to the night baker and obtained a couple dozen brownies to grease the wheels a bit. At the rate I was going, I would be qualified Surface Warfare before we arrived back at pier four.

As I was walking through the Hilo hangar, my Division Officer, Lt. McCarthy was walking by and stopped me. "Hey Westfall, I forgot to tell you something at quarters this morning. I nominated you for the Command Advancement Program." The CAP program, as we called it, was something that happened on every ship in the Navy. Every year the Commanding Officer had the authority to advance one person of his choosing to the next highest pay grade. Usually, the hard chargers aboard the ship would be nominated by their Division Officers. "Thank you Sir. I appreciate the nomination."

The problem with the CAP program was that too many times it was used to help out Sailors who were about to be kicked out of the Navy for high year tenure. High year tenure means the person has gone as far as they can at the present rank. If they are not promoted, they are not allowed to reenlist.

This CAP period was just like all the rest. The next day Lt. McCarthy walked into the Crews Mess and pulled me aside. "Westfall, the Skipper really wanted to CAP you to First Class, but SK3 Thornton has four children and is at high year tenure. He had to give it to Thornton." And that was the story of my life. I had been nominated for CAP on every ship I had ever been on, and every time they would give it some poor slob who couldn't advance. That's just great.

Chapter Fifteen

As we were being tied up alongside the sea wall at the Portsmouth, England naval base, I could already tell that it was going to be a better port. The Portsmouth naval base was located a few miles from town, but there were lots of taxies parked outside the base, so life was good.

I wanted to wait around until O'Malley and Mayo got off watch, so we headed out a little bit later. Just outside the base was an old English tavern called the "Wounded Fox". I loved this place as soon as I walked through the door because it looked like the perfect place to drink and swap sea stories.

The one thing that made this pub truly authentic was the drunken guy with the red beard. He was just about two hundred years old and sitting at the end of the bar. When he looked over at us, I nodded at him and said "Hello, Sir." He smiled and said "Americans! I love Americans! Thanks for your help back in the war." Then he yelled toward the bar "Danny... Give the Yanks a pint on me!" "You still haven't paid your tab from the last round you bought, old man!" the bartender answered.

I laughed and asked Danny for a round of draft ale, and we pulled up some stools at the bar. There was something to be said about drinking a pint in an English pub. Looking around the room and seeing all the many things that were displayed there was so cool. No matter where you looked, there was a Coat of Arms with the entire family history under it. I mean, they went back centuries, all the way back to the dark ages.

After an hour or so, I asked Danny if he had heard of the club called 'Phantom's Pub' and he said "Yeah, I've heard of it. It's just inside town, but be careful... it's haunted." Now I ask you, what could possibly be better than drinking a pint with your buddies in an English pub in England? Drinking a pint with your buddies in a haunted English pub in England!

We picked up a cab outside the Wounded Fox and were heading into town. The roads were so narrow it was hard to see how two cars could pass each other without hitting. When I commented about it, the taxi driver said "Well, the town is very old. The buildings were mostly built in the 17th century, so the roads that ran between them at the time were narrow, because the only traffic was an occasional horse and buggy. Now, even though the traffic is an issue, the buildings are still in the same place, thus, the roads are narrow." That made perfect sense to me. The United States was a much younger country, thus, the buildings are more modern and they are further apart. See? Once again, it is wonderful to be an American!

Soon we arrived at Phantoms Pub, and we paid the driver. The pub was located under an old hotel that looked like it had been closed for many years. Like most buildings in the old section of Portsmouth, this one looked like it had a long history.

As we walking into the pub, O'Malley started checking out the ladies. Mayo and I just walked around, looking at all the wonderful things that were hanging on the walls. Over in the corner across from the front door was a huge painting of an old man in a Royal Navy uniform. It looked like it was well over a hundred years old and it had an engraved plaque under it: "Here stands Captain Patrick O'Laughlin, Commander of the mightiest fleet that ever sailed." Then, in a smaller inscription under the plaque were the words "His ships are in port, but his heart will forever be lost at sea..."

Just as I finished reading, I hear a loud voice behind me "Who let those damn Yanks into our humble pub?" I turned and there was Liam and about thirty of his buddies sitting in the center of the room. Before I knew it, there were four pints standing tall in front of me. I knew then this was going to be a good night! Liam's friend Artis and another guy named David started asking me questions about life on the Radford. While I was answering their questions as well as I could, O'Malley walked up and asked "Hey, who is the dude in the painting?" I smiled, held up my pint and said "That's Captain Patrick O'Laughlin, commander of the mightiest fleet that ever sailed."

As my words echoed through the room, the bell that hung above the bar starting ringing loudly, and everyone was silent. After several sharp strikes, the bar tender stood on the top of the bar and said "Hear-ye hear-ye. We will now commence the telling of the story of the legendary Patty O'Laughlin, for our American mates. Everyone will be silent and pay the proper respect."

The bartender started speaking to the silent room "The year was 1621, and the winter squalls were upon His Majesty's waters we now call the English Channel." The bartender, Nolan, paused for dramatic effect. "Patrick O'Laughlin, or our beloved Patty O, as we have come to call him, was in command of the Flagship, HMS Nelson."

Nolan stopped for a deep drink of ale. Then he wiped his mouth on a bar towel and started speaking again. "The HMS Nelson had orders to sail to India with the Kings attaché to deliver a Royal dispatch. Three hours before they were to depart, Captain Patty decided to go home quickly, and have a word with his wife Althea." Just then there was a knock on the bar. As Nolan looked down, he saw a young man holding his empty glass "Another pint, mate." "WHAT?" screamed Nolan. "Who dares interrupt the telling of the tales of Patty O?" The young customer's eyes were wide. He said "Please forgive me sir. I meant no disrespect." Then, the young man went quietly back to his seat.

"Where was I? Oh yeah. It seems that the Captain and Ms. Althea..." "WAIT!" A scream came from the bar room. It was David, Liam's friend "Nolan, wasn't her name Samantha?" "No, you uneducated wanker. And if you ever again interrupt the telling of the tale of Patty O, you will be banished from the Phantoms Pub forever!" A nasty look from Nolan to David confirmed that David was out of line. Note to self: Never interrupt Nolan when he is telling a story.

"The Captain and Ms. Althea had been arguing earlier that day, and when the Captain left, he was very angry. He told her he was tired of her taking in all kinds of men while he was away, as it was; she was what we call a bit of a tramp. Well, the Captain felt like he had more to say, so he went back to his house, where he found the lovely Ms. Althea in the arms of a woodsman who was new to Portsmouth. The Captain grabbed him and pushed him into the fireplace, where his knickers caught fire. As the Captain was reaching to give him a wallop, Althea struck him from behind with a piece of stove wood, and then ran up to the top floor where she hid on the balcony. As she was looking down to see where her angry husband was, she slipped and fell off the balcony, to her death on the rocks below.

"As the Captain was trying to subdue the woodsman, he heard the scream of his lovely bride, and then he turned and started up the stairs. The woodsman, who had been severely burned, quickly ran out the door and was never seen again. As far as Althea goes, the Captain couldn't find her. It seems her body washed off the rocks, and out to sea. Captain Patty never knew what became of his beautiful Althea." Nolan stepped back and took a long drink from the pint he had been holding. Then he took a deep breath and said "As far as Captain Patty goes, well he went to sea on the Nelson that night, and headed to India.

"As the weeks passed, the HMS Nelson encountered a terrible storm off the coast of South Africa, and was lost at sea. As the ship was going down, Captain Patty made a vow to Neptune, the god of the sea. 'I will find my Althea, and I will find the woodsman; this a swear by the sea and he who lords over it.' And that was the end of Captain Patty... or was it?" Nolan stepped off the bar and there was silence throughout the room. Then Liam stood up tall and raised his glass, yelling "To Patty O!" Everyone in the room stood up and held up their glasses "To Patty O!"

As the cheers died down, I slowly stood up and raised my hand. "Excuse me" I said, nervously "With all due respect to Captain O'Laughlin, where does the story end?" Once again, the room was silent. Once again, the bell sounded. Nolan stepped back onto the bar and shouted "Hear-ye hear-ye. We will now commence in the telling of the conclusion of the story of Captain Patrick O'Laughlin. As the years past, Portsmouth grew. Buildings were torn down, and buildings were built. The home that Patty O knew with his lovely wife Althea was torn down in the early eighteenth century. In its place was a modern hotel standing over a modest pub called 'Donny lads.' Well, about once a month, usually when the sky is the darkest, Captain Patty still wonders the hallways of the hotel, looking for his beloved Althea. He has been seen from time to time looking out of the windows on the top floor. Sometimes you can hear him moaning down the stair well in almost a whisper 'Alllltheeeaa...' and then he is gone."

Nolan paused for a drink. Liam stood up and said "Nolan, may I have the honor of finishing the story for our new American friends?" Nolan bowed deeply and said "The honor is yours, mate."

Liam walked over behind the bar, the stepped up to the same place that Nolan stood. "As far as the quest for the woodsman goes, Captain Patty still looks for him. You see, after Captain Patty had been seen walking through the hotel and pub all those years, they changed the name of the place. It's now called 'Phantoms Pub,' the very pub in which you are sitting at this moment." Liam paused for a drink, and then went on

"Now, when Patty pushed the woodsman into the fire, the woodman was badly burned on his thighs and upward towards his stomach. Patty sometimes wonders into the loo after a customer. As you stand there, doing your business, you may feel the warm arm of a friend across your shoulders. When you look to see who it is, you will be looking into the hollow eyes of our very own Captain Patty O'Laughlin, looking down to see if you are the scarred woodsman he is cursed to one day find." Liam slowly lifted his glass and said "Cheers to you, Captain Patty." Then everyone in the pub jumped to their feet and held up their glasses "Cheers to Patty O!" yelled the room.

The next couple hours were spent drinking and swapping sea stories. Every now and then someone would challenge someone else to a game of darts or arm wrestling, even though it didn't matter who won or lost.

After a few pints, Mayo had to go visit the loo. A couple minutes later, he came running out of the bathroom, white as a sheet! He grabbed me and shouted "Clay... It's true. Patty O'Laughlin was just in the bathroom. Come on, let's grab O'Malley and get the hell out of here!" I had never seen Mayo like this, so I was enjoying it. He started getting angry at me and said "Go in there if you don't believe me!"

I walked into the loo and while I was standing there doing my business, I felt something hitting the top of my shoulder, kind of like someone putting their arm around my shoulder. I slowly looked to see who it was but there was nobody there. Then, as I started to wash my hands, I heard a soft whisper "Alllllltheeeaa..." After washing my hands, I noticed a small speaker just over the light above the sink. I looked closer at the ceiling above the urinals and found a small air duct that blows down as you go. It was classic! I couldn't wait to tease Mayo about being such a chicken. Of course, the whole ship would eventually hear about it!

Not too long after that, we headed back to the ship. Since we had breakfast the following morning, we knew we shouldn't stay out too late. As we got back to the ship, there was our faithful following of drunken sailors, waiting for someone to feel sorry for them and open the galley. I quickly threw together about fifty grilled ham and cheese sandwiches and everyone was happy. Since it was already after midnight, the boys and I closed up shop and headed off to the rack.

The next morning came quickly, but the day dragged on. Most of the crew was off the ship, since this was a liberty port. Usually we would feed at least three hundred, but with so many people out in town, our numbers were more like a hundred or so. Once we finished serving dinner and cleaning up the galley, O'Malley, Mayo and I met up on the smoking deck. Since we were due to pull out the next day, we knew this would be our last night in England.

At this time I was married, so I only took a little bit of money with me for the liberty ports. We did have an awesome time last night, so I knew I didn't have very much money to blow. I reached into my pocket and pulled out one English pound. "Well guys, I have one pound. How much do you guys have?" Mayo shrugged his shoulders and said "I ran out of money yesterday." O'Malley smiled and said "Dude, I was drinking your beers last night." Well, that meant one pound was all we had. I smiled and said "Ok guys. We are going to take this pound and we are going to head out into town and have an excellent night. I don't know how we are going to do it, but I know that this pound will be enough!"

We quickly got dressed and headed out across the base. As we were walking, O'Malley asked "How are we going to get to town?" I just shrugged my shoulders and said "I have no idea. We will see." A couple minutes later, we came across the Supply Chief, Chief Barret, walking slowly out toward the town. "Hiya Chief. Are you heading out this evening?" He smiled and said "Yep, just going out here to catch a taxi. You want to ride with me?" I looked at Mayo and O'Malley and smiled. "Yes, Chief, we would like that. Much obliged." Our luck was already coming through.

Once we arrive in town, we started walking toward the Phantoms pub. As we started to cross the street, we heard a familiar voice coming out of a corner club. "Hey Cookie, where are you guys going?" It was Jones, one of the Leading Mechanics from the ship. "Oh, we are just taking it easy tonight, heading on down to the Phantom." "No, you won't be taking it easy tonight." He said "You have been taking such good care of us on the ship, especially the past few nights. Nobody else would ever open the galley for us after hours. You guys come in here and drink some pints!"

Well, my one pound plan seemed to be working out just fine. We got a ride into town and now we were drinking free pints. Life was good!

After a couple hours, the mechanics started to head back to the ship. We really weren't ready to go back, but since they had to start up the main engines early, they had to call it a night. Once we parted ways we started heading uptown towards the Phantom. After a short walk, we arrived at the pub and went inside to see if there was anyone there from the ship.

"Oh, hell, it's those damn yanks again!" The familiar voice was that of Artis, one of the British sailors. There they all were, some of them were still wearing the same clothes they wore the day before. Liam threw me a twenty pound note and yelled "Yank money is no good here tonight. You are guests of the Queen! Go buy us a round, mate."

I would have to admit, this was a night to remember. Before I could get a half a pint down, more money was being thrown at me. And just when I thought the evening was coming to a close, I found an envelope under my beer glass. I looked around but it seemed like no one was paying attention to it, so I am not sure where it came from. I opened it up and found a one hundred pound note. I read the letter to O'Malley and Mayo "Dear Yank, Here is a hundred quid... Buy a couple rounds for the house. GOD SAVE THE QUEEN!" It was signed "Captain Patrick O'Laughlin". Well there you go. If a dead man buys you a drink, you have to respect the gesture. I bought the whole pub a round, and then I stood on my chair and yelled "This round is on Patty O'Laughlin... GOD SAVE THE QUEEN!" Every one cheered so loud, the noise was deafening.

After another hour, the party started dying down. It was quarter to four in the morning, and we needed to head back to the ship. Just when I was wondering how we were going to get back to the base, Liam yelled from the door of the pub "Hey Clay. Do you and your mates want a lift back to the ship?" Well, what do you know? "Sure, that would be great!" Soon, we were crossing the gang plank and back on the ship. As I was getting undressed and just about to climb into my rack, I emptied my pockets and looked down at my hand. There were four one pound coins. Not only did I have one of the best party nights of my life, but I also made a three pound profit. Life was good.

The next day we pulled out nice and early. I was actually looking forward to this underway so I could get rolling on my ESWS qualification. I only needed a few more signatures, and then I would be able to finish up my qualification book. Just a few more days and it would all be over. One of the things I liked best about being underway again was the fact that every space was manned. Whatever system I needed to check out on, there was an expert standing by with time on their hands.

My immediate supervisor, Cindy Harmon, was also working toward her ESWS. We worked together on some of the systems, and shared notes on some of the checkouts we had gone through.

Finally, it was time for my ESWS board. I was excited about it because I had been studying very hard and wanted to get it over with. Promptly, at 1400, I went into the Chiefs Mess where my board was convened. The Command Master Chief invited me in and offered me a cup of coffee. I was then seated at a table where some of my friends were also sitting. These people were experts in their field, and would be asking me various questions. Since I knew the material, I wasn't too worried about anything.

The first question was asked by the Master Chief about the sea whiz, and I knew all about it. "The sea whiz is actually the MK15 Phalanx CIWS (Close in Weapons System), an anti-ship missile defense system." I further explained that it was a fast-reaction, rapid-fire twenty millimeter gun system that provides United States Navy ships with a terminal defense against anti-ship missiles that may have penetrated other fleet defenses. Designed to engage anti-ship cruise missiles and fixed-wing aircraft at short range, The Phalanx automatically engages functions that are usually performed by separate, independent systems such as search, detection, threat evaluation, acquisition, track, firing, target destruction, kill assessment and cease fire."

As I was sitting there being proud of myself, the Master Chief said "That very impressive. Can you tell me about the updates that were incorporated into the system last year?" Updates? What was she talking about? As far as I knew, there were no updates. "Master Chief, I am not aware of any updates." She smiled and made a note on her decision pad. Ok, this could be a trick. Sometimes they try to bait qualifiers and shake them up. I was not going to fall for that!

Sitting next to the Master Chief was a smoking deck buddy of mine, BM1 Linda Hartley. She smiled and said "Congratulations on your board. We all can't wait to see you wearing your new warfare pin." I smiled back and thanked her. Then she said "What can you tell me about the United States' fleet of Spruance Class Destroyers?"

I took a sip of coffee and started digging back in my memory "Well, at the end of the 1960's the United States Navy started a competition for a new class of guided missile ships which would be more suitable for missions in carrier battle groups then the ships of the previous class. This program was called DDX and once all the bidding was over, Ingalls Shipbuilding in Pascagoula, Mississippi was awarded the contract to build all ships of that class." I took a sip of coffee and could see that she was impressed with the answer so far. I continued "The thirty-one Spruance class destroyers were developed for the primary mission of anti-submarine warfare, including operations as an integral part of attack carrier forces.

"The Spruance-class ships are more than twice as large as a World War II destroyer and just as large as a World War II cruiser. Utilizing highly developed weapons systems, these destroyers are designed to hunt down and destroy high speed submarines in all weather, but can also engage ships, aircraft, and shore targets. These multi-purpose combatants are also capable of providing naval gunfire support in conjunction with Marine amphibious operations worldwide."

Petty Officer Hartley said "Wow! You have had your nose in the books, haven't you? Two years ago, the designers found a structural weakness in the superstructure of the Spruance class. Can you tell me what that was, and how did Ingalls Shipbuilding overcome the problem?" Uh, No, I couldn't. I had no clue what she was talking about. "I am unaware of any issues with the design." She nodded and wrote something down. "I am done for now."

The next question came from my buddy Tim Oleander, a Senior Engineman. He looked at me and smiled, saying "Ok, Clay. Tell me about the USS Radford's propulsion system." I smiled back because I knew all he wanted to know about the Radford's engines.

"The Spruance class destroyers were the first class of ships in the United States Navy to have gas turbine power. The ship has four General Electric LM-2500 engines that are marine shaft power versions of the TF39 turbofan used on DC-10 and C-5A aircraft. Producing a total of 80,000 shaft horsepower, they can drive the ship in excess of 30 knots, but we usually don't operate all four engines at the same time. One engine is able to accelerate the ship to 19 knots, two engines reach 27 knots. The two other engines are only activated when the ship shall reach its high speed of 33 knots. From the cold start of the engines to the high speed it takes just twelve minutes." Ha. Take that Tim!

Petty Officer Oleander smiled again and said "It's obvious you know what you are talking about. Now, can you tell me what updates we received during the past shipyard period?" More updates? What the hell is he talking about? I didn't hear about any updates! "As far as I know these systems are state of the art, and there were no updates." Ok, now I was getting nervous.

The next question came from Senior Chief Haskell. "Petty Officer Westfall, what can you tell me about the Spruance Class Destroyers' other weapons systems?"

"Well Senior, when the Spruance class was first developed, the ships were equipped with a Mk-112 launcher for ASROC located behind the #1 Mk-45 lightweight gun mount. After the designers installed the Tomahawk cruise missile, seven of the destroyers', including the Radford, got two Mk-143 armored box launchers for Tomahawk. Both launchers were placed next to the ASROC launcher. Three years ago all the other ships were equipped with the Mk-41 VLS and the ASROC launcher was removed." I could tell he was very impressed with my knowledge of the systems. I continued "Early in the 1980's, each ship was equipped with two Phalanx close in weapons systems. All ships that were in commission also got a RAM (Rolling Airframe Missile) launcher with 21 missiles each. That, by the way, is a very bad ass system." I took a sip of my coffee, and smiled. How could they not pass me? I obviously knew everything there was to know about this ship.

"Well, you have been studying." the Senior Chief said. "So tell me, how was the RAM system modified to work better with the ships anti-submarine warfare systems?" OK, now this was pissing me off. "Senior, I am not sure."

At that time, the Master Chief said "Petty Officer Westfall, will you hand me your qualification book?" I angrily handed it to her, and after looking at the cover she said "This is the old book. We got new books about a year ago, why don't you have a new book? There are no updates in this book." Trying my best not to scream I said "Master Chief, this was the book I was given as I came aboard the Radford. I thought it was the latest version." She looked at me and said sadly "You need a new book."

"At this time, I don't see how we can pass you. Look through your new book and we will reschedule for next week sometime." I was so angry I could have spit. After summoning all the political correctness I could muster, I stood up and addressed the room. "Thank you all for your time. I will research all the system updates and request a new board next week."

As I left the Chiefs Mess, I quickly walked aft to the fan tail. I walked past several of my shipmates, and as I passed they all had the same question "Hey Clay, how did the board go?" Ignoring their questions, I calmly walked to the guard rail at the end of the ship and looked out over the beautiful sea. The ships screws were churning up the waves, and there were three dolphins following the ship. I looked down at my ESWS qualification manual for a moment, and then I drew back and threw it as far as I could, and then I watched it disappear into the black waters. Maybe Davy Jones could figure it out.

One of the training events the Navy had planned for us was an underway replenishment (UNREP) with the USNS Laramie (T-AO-203). An UNREP is a method of transferring fuel, munitions, and stores from one ship to another while under way.

The alongside connected replenishment (CONREP) is a standard method of transferring liquids such as fuel and fresh water, along with ammunition and bulk goods. The supplying ship holds a steady course and speed, generally between 12 and 16 knots. The receiving ship then comes alongside the supplier at a distance of approximately 30 yards. A gun line, pneumatic line thrower, or shot line is fired from the supplier, which is used to pull across a messenger line. This line is used to pull across other equipment such as a distance line, phone line, and the transfer rig lines. As the command ship of the replenishment operation, the supply ship provides all lines and equipment needed for the transfer. Additionally, all commands are directed from the supply ship.

Because of the relative position of the ships, it is possible for some ships to set up multiple transfer rigs, allowing for faster transfer or the transfer of multiple types of stores. Additionally, many replenishment ships are set up to service two receivers at one time, with one being replenished on each side.

Alongside connected replenishment is a risky operation, as two or three ships running side-by-side must hold to precisely the same course and speed for a long period of time. A slight steering error on the part of one of the ships could cause a collision, or break the transfer lines and fuel hoses. For this reason, experienced and qualified helmsmen are required during the replenishment, and the crew on the bridge must give their undivided attention to the ship's course and speed.

The risk is increased when a replenishment ship is servicing two ships at once.

In case of emergency, crews practice emergency breakaway procedures, where the ships will separate in less-than-optimal situations. Although the ships will be saved from collision, it is possible to lose stores, as the ships may not be able to finish the current transfer.

Following successful completion of replenishment, many US ships engage in the custom of playing a signature tune over the replenished vessel's PA system as they break away from the supplying vessel. That is the wardrooms method of celebrating a successful and safe UNREP... the crews way of celebrating was a bit different.

Sitting inside of the Hilo hanger was a 'reception' team consisting of about eight pre-selected crew members. All of them were armed with potato guns and water balloon launchers, just waiting for the signal. This form of 'reception' has been practiced by the crews of replenishing ships since the cold war ended. To my knowledge, no Skipper has ever approved of this action.

When the breakaway song was played over the ships loudspeaker, the Hilo hanger doors were opened and all the USS Radford UNREP reception team opened fire. Just when the first potato splattered against the USNS Laramie, the doors to the Laramie UNREP locker swung open and about twenty crewmen came out with some kind of fruit launchers. As grapefruits splattered all over the side of the Radford, our balloon brigade started shooting water balloons and potatoes at the bridge of the Oiler.

As the Officer of the Deck aboard the Laramie took fire, he quickly ordered a turn to starboard. Now, the OOD obviously wasn't worried about his mighty ship being pelted with water balloons, but for the safety of the ships and the combatants it was in everybody's best interest to end the festivities before someone fell overboard.

The celebration of our apparent victory was cut short by the Skippers angry voice coming over the ships PA system "You just couldn't resist your tradition, could you? Now clean those busted grapefruits off my ship before I break heads!" It was fairly obvious that the Skipper wasn't as thrilled with our victory as we were. But what was he going to do to us? Make us leave our families and go to sea? As we cleaned up the mess, I reflected on the events of the past few hours. I knew that once it was all over, I was going to miss all of this.

Chapter Sixteen

The next week was spent making ditches in the water. No drills, no operations, just making circles. That's usually what happens when Junior Officers are learning how to drive the ship. After a few days I got over my bad attitude about the ESWS, and got the new qual book. There were about fifteen new changes to the ships major systems in the past couple years, and before I knew it, I had it all down pat.

My ESWS qualification board was rescheduled, and I blew it away. Now that it was done, I could relax and take it easy.

One thing I really liked about surface ships was the fact that you could take a day off even if you were at sea. On the submarine, you worked all day every day. If you were at sea for ninety days, you worked for ninety days. On the Radford we worked a rotation underway, and that usually meant two or three days off a week. Oh, and Sundays were always a holiday routine. Movies, books, computer games... whatever you would do to relax, you could do on Sunday. It was so nice. I would wake up around ten o'clock, walk down to the Crews Mess and have a cup of coffee and maybe grab something to eat. Then go to the weather deck and have a smoke or two, and shoot the bull a bit with my buddies up there. Then, I would go down to the Ships Library and play some computer games. Before I knew it, it was time for a movie, maybe two, then dinner and off to bed again. Much better than the submarine!

Well, the Navy was having trouble finding people who wanted to be Recruiters. My tour on the Radford was supposed to be three years, but it looks like the Navy had other plans for me. While we were underway, I received a message from personnel informing me that I was going to be transferred to the Navy Recruiting Command later that year. The note further stated that if I refused these orders, I would not be allowed to re-enlist at my 18 year mark. That meant that I would not be allowed to make my twenty years and retire.

I was pretty angry at the Navy when I first heard this, and headed on up to the weather deck. My boss Cindy was up there, since she was my boss, she knew why I was so angry. She said "It's all good, Clay. Recruiting is a piece of cake. All you need to do is bring in your quota of recruits, and life will be good." The problem I had with Recruiting was that most Recruiters would sooner or later have to sell their souls. They would soon stretch the truth or bend a rule to make their quota. I couldn't do that, so I knew that I would not make a good recruiter.

Two days later we found ourselves running headlong on into a storm. We tried to go around it, but it looked like we were going to hit the rough weather anyway. I remember standing on the bridge, watching the forecastle, (the front of the ship) going under the water. It was awesome! Something about watching the waves come over the sides of the ship just seems so unnatural.

I had the watch that day, and I was preparing the breakouts for the following day. There were several cases of meat in the chill box, thawing out for the following day. As I was reaching up to the top shelf pulling out two sixty pound cases, the ship shifted violently to the starboard side. As the cases shifted, my back popped very loudly and it felt like I had been stabbed in the back. I fell to the floor and the cases of meat fell on top of me. I had never felt anything like it.

Mayo was in the deep sink and he ran over to help me. After putting away the meat and helping me to me feet, we walked down to the medical bay.

"Looks like you may have popped a disc out of place." The Doc said. "Get off your feet, take two of these and call me in the morning." Well, I guess that was that. The Doc had given me some Motrin 800, so I was off to bed. I had the next day off, so hopefully I would recover before I had watch next.

A few days later we pulled back into Norfolk. I had tried hard to get out of my orders to go recruiting, but there was just no way. The only way I could retire from the Navy was to go Recruiting. I was so angry; there was nothing that could put me in a good mood. Nothing, that is, except a trip to St. Croix! We were scheduled to do sound trials down South in a week or so, so the Skipper asked for one more liberty port before winter and that's what we got. Life was going to get better soon!

About ten days later, we were haze grey and underway once again. We would be spending two days in Fredricksted, after about a week's worth of sound trials.

For the past year or so, I had been telling the FSA's about my days with the submarine force. More than once I told them about the Salt Lake City and its fabled attempt to take over the Island. I was the envy of everyone under twenty years old! O'Malley and Mayo made me promise to take them and the rest of the FSA team on a tour of Fredricksted. Since I had been on the Radford, I had made a pretty good name for myself. I had lots of friends, and I had won the respect of the entire crew. I would miss the Radford.

Things were different in St. Croix. A couple years ago a hurricane had come through and took out the pier. Now there was a much wider, newer pier. The Radford tied up in the same place the cruise ship had tied up a few years earlier. I was also sorely disappointed to find out that Sadie one leg had passed away, so there was no beer truck. We were all kind of bummed out about that.

Once again, I had both days in port off, so life was good. I spent all morning on the beach, chilling out with a couple buddies from engineering. We barbequed some hamburgers and drank some rum, just taking it easy. What a perfect day it was! O'Malley and Mayo had the duty, so I was just going to lie low until they got off of work.

A couple of the guys and I took a walk after lunch, just going up the beach to see what was there. We found a small bar about a mile from the ship. It was the coolest spot! There was nobody in the place, except for us. The front of the place was open, so the cool ocean breeze was constantly blowing. There were a couple of dart boards there, and all the rum in the world. Just writing this is making me miss the islands.

I got a bit hungry after a while, and I started looking around the place to see what they had to eat. In the corner of the bar there was a heated glass case with some kind of small turnover's in it. I asked the Rasta behind the bar what it was, and he smiled and said "These are homemade, man. We catch them and cook them and make the pies. Try one for free, man. If you don't like it, you don't have to pay for it." That sounded like a good deal to me, so I agreed.

He handed me a pie on a small paper plate, and watched me eagerly. I took a bite and it was wonderful! I had never tasted anything so good. I wanted another one. And then I wanted another one. When I had eaten my fourth pie, I asked him what it was. He said "Do you know what a conch is, man?" I soberly thought about the ugly, snotty looking sea creatures that I had boiled and unscrewed from their shells. Often guys would find them while snorkeling and ask me to 'de-conch' them so they can bring the shells aboard as souvenirs. "Uh, yeah." I said, kind of hesitantly. "That is what it is made out of man." Note to self: If you don't want to hear the answer, don't ask the question.

After a few hours of darts and drinks, I left my buddies and went back to the ship. It was time for me to meet up with Mayo and O'Malley and begin our night of festivities.

When I got to the Quarterdeck that evening, I was a bit surprised at the liberty party that was standing there waiting for me. I was expecting Mayo and O'Malley, but not the twelve other FSA's that were standing there. "We are ready for our historic tour, Petty Officer Westfall" said Seaman Arnold, one of our newest FSA's. She had only been in the ship for a couple weeks, and now she was hanging around with us. I was not sure if that would be the proper indoctrination for this young Sailor.

"Alright" I said, addressing the crowd "from this moment on, as long as we are off duty and off the ship, you will not address me as Petty Officer Westfall. I am Clay... got it? Good. Now, let's hit the beach."

As we walked down the pier, I would stop from time to time and point out things, like where old Sadie one leg would park her truck, or where the old Rastafarian speared and skinned the sand shark. Every time I stopped to point something out, the gang hung on my every word.

There were several new bars in and around Fredricksted, so of course we had to check them all out. The first bar had a nice outdoor dining room, so after drinking a few rum and cokes I started telling the story of the Salt Lake City and the battle for St. Croix.

As the story progressed, we started walking down to the Brandy Snifter. Once we arrived we had a few more rum and cokes and then the story went into full play. As the story progressed, we walked through the town and back to the pier. We made a pit stop in front of an old closed down store, where I told the story of Old Hank Bilko and his infamous tattoo. The chair he bravely sat in was still sitting in the corner of the shop covered in dust.

Once we returned to the pier, I carefully described how the police cars were parked half way down, and the ships force with all its guns drawn had formed a line. Every ear listened intently as the story unfolded, and no one said a word. Once the story was over, there was only silence.

It was almost ten thirty by this time, but nobody was ready to slow down. I suggested we hit the all night rum store, then head on out to the beach to spend the night.

The night was perfect for hanging out with the galley folk. The next day was Saturday, so most of the FSA's were off. The few that did have to work headed home and left the rest of us to sit up all night and swap sea stories.

I guess it was about two in the morning when the party started to die down. There were about twenty people sleeping around the cabana, and a few shooting the bull around a fire. I had taken a bottle of light cruisan rum and a couple bottles of soda and was sitting down by the water, looking out over the ocean. The breeze was perfect, and I was feeling no pain.

I heard a noise behind me and there was one of the FSA's, Seaman Fallon, walking up behind me. She asked if she could join me, and I said it would be nice to have some company, so she sat a couple feet from me.

Jennifer Fallon was about nineteen years old. She was a good sailor, but not that popular with the other FSA's. She had long brown hair, and a pretty nice body, but she had acne, and wasn't very sought after by the boys. I had no doubt that in a couple years she was going to be quite the catch.

"You looked like you could use some company" she said with a smile. I smiled back "Yeah, I guess I could. I love looking out over the ocean and smelling the salt air. There is nothing as wonderful as the sea." As I looked out over the horizon, I felt Jen looking at me. I knew that she had been drinking with the rest of us, and she was pretty much tanked. I have to admit, she looked very pretty in the moonlight. If I would have met her on this beach a few years ago, things would have been different.

As I was looking out over the ocean, thinking about times past, I didn't notice that Jen had moved over next to me. When I turned toward her to say something, she tried to kiss me and put her hand in my lap. I quickly jumped up and said "Whoa now. I think it's time you and I went for a walk."

I took her hand and led her away from the beach. As we were walking, I explained to her that I was married, and as flattered as I was, I was not going to sleep with her. She just smiled and said "We will see" and rubbed my hand. After a couple minutes of walking, she said "If you are such a good husband, why are you holding my hand and leading me up the beach?" I just smiled and said "I want you to meet some friends of mine."

As we arrived at the head of the pier, the USS Radford Shore Patrol was standing there shooting the breeze. I stopped right by where they were standing and

I looked at Jen. "You are a very special women, and I know you are pretty toasted right now, because you are a lot friendlier than usual, so I am sending you back to the ship." She looked at me with surprise and said "You're a jerk!" I just smiled and said "Tomorrow you will thank me for being such a jerk." Then I asked the Shore Patrol to see that she got back to the ship safely and make sure she went to bed so no one would take advantage of her. After that I made the long, lonely journey back to the beach. Yes, if it had been a few years earlier, this story may have ended differently.

The next morning I woke up with sand and sun in my eyes. I could smell something wonderful cooking, and I saw one of the natives cooking over our fire. O'Malley and Mayo were already up and were sitting by the fire talking to the Rasta.

"Good morning, guys" I said as I took a seat "Wow! That smells really good!" Then I looked at the man cooking and offered my hand "Hi, I'm Clay." The man smiled and shook my hand "Good morning, man. I am Joseph. Would you like some fish chowder?" I quickly accepted and Joseph handed me a plate of what looked like chunky oatmeal. I was a bit leery until I tasted it, but it was quite good.

As we were kicking back drinking coffee flavored with spiced rum, we look out at the Radford. The water around the ship was so clear and calm; you could drop a quarter off the pier and see it a hundred feet down. That's when I decided that I wanted to dive off of the ship.

"Hey guys, I think I am going to dive off the ships O-4 level!" The O-4 level was about fifty feet off the water, and this probably wasn't the best idea in the world. But, I would soon be leaving the ship, and this may be my last opportunity to be in St. Croix. I wanted to do something fun with the guys, and this seemed like as good an idea as any.

"I don't think that's allowed, Clay" Mayo said. "I remember three guys went to Captains Mast and were busted a couple years ago for jumping off the weather deck, and that's a lot safer than the O-4 level." I looked at him and smiled "You know, sometimes you just have to say 'ah, what the hell' and go for it." I decided I would do it around lunch time.

The next couple hours were spent drinking rum and playing football in the sand. Several of the off going FSA's re-joined our ranks, and were sitting around the beach enjoying their day. I know I just keep on saying this, but it was a perfect day!

Around one o'clock that afternoon I decided to head to the ship. I really didn't expect too many people to go with me, but when I looked back there must have been thirty people behind me. As we started walking up the pier, O'Malley said "I don't care about the rest of these guys; I am jumping off with you." Several of the others also said they wanted to jump, but I doubted their bravery. "Look, you guys could get into a lot of trouble for this." Mayo smiled and said "I seriously doubt that the great Clay Westfall would ever get into trouble. You know you are untouchable aboard the Radford. Now we may burn, but you? Never!"

As we arrived at the ship, I started up the gangway. As I looked back I saw that most of my brave followers were now having second thoughts. When I got to the Quarterdeck, I found that my boss, Cindy was on watch. "Request permission to come aboard" I said, standing at attention. Cindy saluted me and said "Granted." The she said "Westfall, what are you doing here? You have obviously been under the influence of a lot of rum, and chow is over. You had better not be planning any excitement on my watch!" I smiled at her and said "Petty Officer Harmon, I promise I will be off the ship before you know it!" I quickly turned and headed for the O-4 level.

When I got to the opened deck on the O-4 level, I was surprised to find the Roving Watch, Petty Officer Nelson standing there enjoying the sunshine. He looked at me and said "Hi, Clay. Shouldn't you be off drinking rum or swimming or something?" I smiled at him and said "That's an excellent idea!" Then I yelled "Geronimo" and dove over the side of the boat.

As I hit the water, I quickly remembered that grace was not my strong point. I landed on my side, and it hurt. Perhaps that is why this event is so ill advised.

When I came to the surface, I saw three bodies flying over the rail after me. My faithful drinking buddies, O'Malley and Mayo were hot on my tail, and one other FSA named Domingas bravely followed. Once we all came up to the surface, we gave a victory cheer and swam toward the pier.

After climbing up the ladder just aft of the ship, we stood on the pier and took a breath. The Duty Chief, Chief Butler, came to the after rail of the ship and said "Westfall that was the stupidest thing I have ever seen. That being said, it was pretty cool!"

The rest of the day was spent at the beach swapping stories and enjoying the beautiful weather. Before we knew it, the sun was down and liberty aboard the ship had expired. The next day we were haze grey and underway again. Soon, St. Croix was but a memory.

The next morning I had just finished up serving breakfast when Petty Officer Harmon came into the office. She looked at me and shook her head. "I honestly have never seen anything like this." I was not sure what she was talking about "Good morning. What's the problem?" I asked. "You are" she said. "After that stunt you pulled yesterday, the duty section started talking about you and the FSA's and soon the Duty Officer found out about it. He told the Skipper this morning, and during the morning briefing, the Skipper pulled me aside." Well, I could just imagine what was happening now. Is it going to be restriction or Captains Mast? "Oh no, what did he say?" She shook her head and said "He asked if all of you were alright, then he said 'That Westfall, nothing he does surprises me' and that was it! I honestly believe he could catch you in bed naked with his fourteen year old daughter and he would just shake his head and say 'Oh, that Westfall'. I have never seen anything like it. You know, you are actually untouchable aboard this ship!"

After watch that evening, I went down to the supply office to check my email. At that time, we had just gotten the capability to send and receive email at sea. The more popular email was from the ships social network. It was kind of a way to let off steam, and you could talk to anyone or everyone, depending on what you want to say.

As soon as I logged in I saw many posts from the people who had been partying the past couple days. As I was reading through them, I kept seeing the same references to me and Seaman Fallon. It seems that lots of people saw us sitting on the beach together, and then leaving together. Obviously that was enough for the ships gossip fence. I felt that I needed to address the issue before it got too far out of hand.

I decided the best way to address this would be by sending out an email to the entire crew, E-6 and below. I wrote "Dear everybody, it has come to my attention that there are many rumors going on about me and a certain young lady and what may or may not have happened on the beach of St. Croix. These rumors need to stop. Now I have been around a long time, and I can handle things like this, but this young lady is new on board the ship and the last thing she needs is a reputation. I am a married man, and I have not and will not cheat on my wife. Nothing happened between us, so please, let's put this to rest. If you are still interested in my sex life, well buy me a beer and we can discuss it. Thank you for your compassion and your cooperation, and have a fine Navy day! MS2(SW/SS) Clay Westfall." And that was that.

The next few days were spent testing the five inch gun. That pretty much consisted of taking the radar readings and putting them into the fire control system and shooting as close to the target as we could. The Radford was very good at this, and scored with very high marks.

While we were out, the Skipper authorized a cook out and a swim call. A cook out is a good thing because it's a change from the daily norm. The crew gets tired of the same old routine, and anything to break it up is a good thing. We put the barbeque grill on the fan tail, and loaded it with hot dogs, hamburgers, chicken and ribs.

The Boatswains' Mates brought out some kiddy wading pools, and several of the crew members changed into their shorts and sat in them. The Skipper stopped the ship and opened up the railing on the fan tail so everyone could go swimming. There is something special about swimming in the Caribbean... the water is so wonderful! You can swim down about ten feet and see the entire ship! It looks like it is floating in the air.

We always have a couple Gunners' Mates with M-16's standing by as shark watches. Every now and then there would be a couple sharks coming by, but they usually turn away long before they are seen as a danger. Once on the Salt Lake City the shark watch took a shot, but it turns out it was only a tuna.

The picnic turned out to be a great success. Everyone was happy and well fed, and even if it did take forever to clean it all up, it was a lot of fun. Once the dishes were done and the galley was swabbed, it was almost nine o'clock.

After everyone left the galley, and everything was shut down for the night, I went up to the weather deck. I walked back aft, where it was all quiet. I sat on a cleat by the after railing and just looked out over the ocean. It was so peaceful and quiet. There was nothing but endless stars in the sky and the sound of the screws, churning up the water. I knew that this was going to be my last underway.

As I was looking out over the water, I couldn't help but think about the past fifteen years. I knew that I was going to miss all of this. There was nowhere else in the world where I could feel such peace of mind, and be alone with my thoughts. I thought about how many times I would sit here in the darkness and pray, or just talk to God. This solitude is the thing I would miss the most.

Before hitting the rack that night, one of my Hull Tech buddies, HT3 Echols, stopped me in the passageway. "Hi Cookie" he said. "Would you do me a favor and come down the HT shop before you turn in? A couple of us have something for you.

After dropping down two decks we walked into the HT shop, where the Chief HT and a couple others were standing by. "Petty Officer Westfall" the Chief said "We know this is your last underway, and that you will be leaving soon. We just wanted to take a second and let you know how much we have enjoyed sailing around the world with you." As the Chief nodded to him, Echols reached into one of the workbench drawers and brought something out that looked like an ashtray. After looking a bit closer, I saw that it was the end of a spent five inch gun shell, which had been polished to a brilliant shine. The Chief read "To MS2(SW/SS) Westfall, the best MS that we know. From the repair division." As I accepted this unique award, I thanked each one of them. This was such a cool trophy, and would look good on my mantle. I was going to miss these guys.

I had the galley watch the following day. As the ship set the sea and anchor detail, one of the newest members of the crew came to the galley to see me. He handed me a piece of paper and said "Hello, Petty Officer Westfall. The Engineering Officer of the Watch asked me to generate the paperwork so that we could lower the mast before we get into port. He said we would need about fifty yards of chow line to do it."

I carefully looked at the paperwork. This guy seemed like a nice guy, but obviously, he was not very smart. I asked him "Did you route the mast lowering paperwork to the Bridge?" "Uh, no, I didn't know I needed to." I quickly signed the paper and handed it back to him. "Before I can give you the fifty yards of chow line, you are going to have to go back to the engine room. I need at least a quart of relative bearing grease so the line can be greased properly."

Before leaving, he looked at me and said "Can I ask you a personal question." I stopped wiping the counter and said "Sure, go ahead and ask." "Have you ever regretted joining the Navy?" he asked. I smiled and said "Once, for about ten minutes. Then I started thinking... I was in the world's finest Navy. My job was to work on a United States Navy ship, and by doing the best job that I could, I was helping to protect the men, women and children back home. As we pull into port this afternoon, take a look at the shoreline and all those people standing on the pier. They are here prospering because you did your job. You should be very proud of being part of such a wonderful thing."

As he thought about it, the Seaman smiled and said "Yeah, your right. I am proud of what I am doing. Thank you." As he started to walk off, I said "One day you will look back and remember this day. You will remember that it was you who was sent to get the chow line and the relative bearing grease."

I remember around the beginning of February the next year, at around eleven thirty at night, something noteworthy happened. The Radford was about twenty five miles out from Virginia Beach running some calibration tests on some of the new electronics that had been installed. The tests required the Radford to circle an electronic buoy, taking specific readings on every pass, so everyone was pretty much bored to death. Most of the time, tests like these require the attention of five of six people, so the rest of the crew just goes through the motions.

That same evening that Saudi Arabian ship, the Saudi Riyadh, a 29,258-ton, 657-foot-long container ship, was heading up the Chesapeake Bay bound for Baltimore. As the Saudi Riyadh was approaching the mouth of the bay from the northeast, it prepared to line up in the shipping lanes before it took on the marine pilot for its eventual trip to Baltimore. It was late, and the transit up the Chesapeake was a slow, routine cruise.

Everything was quiet aboard the Radford, until one of the Damage Control Petty Officers saw a large shadow coming closer and closer. By the time he had alerted the bridge, it was too late. Most of the crew had been sleeping soundly below deck, blissfully unaware of the oncoming danger.

When the Saudi Riyadh struck the Radford on the forward, starboard side (right side), it ripped a pie shaped gash about thirty feet behind the bow of the ship. The impact penetrated about twenty five feet into the centerline of the RADFORD, and left a hole from the deck to the waterline. The impact was so great, it toppled the Radford's' five-inch, fifty four-caliber gun and damaged its Tomahawk cruise missile tubes. One sailor aboard, MM3 Willows, suffered a broken arm.

The Saudi Riyadh sustained a four-foot-high, 30-foot-long gash along the port and starboard sides of its bow, with most of the damage to its port side.

The Radford sustained an estimated $32.7 million in damages and the damage prevented the Radford from leaving on a scheduled six-month deployment to the Mediterranean Sea with the carrier Theodore Roosevelt battle group.

Saudi owners deny culpability In Navy crash, and put the blame squarely on the shoulders of the Radford. The United States Justice Department blamed the Saudi ship for the accident, but proceeded to notify the Radford's commanding officer that it had lost confidence in his ability to command as a result of the collision and would relieve him of his duties. He was reassigned to shore command. That was one of the dangers of being the Skipper... even if you are in bed and have nothing to do with the incident; you are the one who is at fault.

Chapter Seventeen

Since there was nothing I could do about being sent to a Recruiting Command, I decided I might as well embrace it. The Recruiter school was in Pensacola Florida, and that wasn't too bad. Our class consisted of about forty people from all over the United States. About half of them hated being there as much as I did.

Basically, the school was all about regulations and memorizing scripts. I have never been any good at memorizing scripts or public speaking. Worse than that was the fact that everything we did was recorded so we could watch ourselves and see how badly we were screwing up. I have to admit, as many things as I had done over the years, this was the most difficult.

There are several steps to being a successful recruiter. First, you have to make people like you. If they don't like you, they won't trust you. If they don't trust you, they won't listen to you. Getting people to like me has never been a big problem for me.

The next thing you have to do is to get them to tell you what they want out of life, and write it down on a piece of paper. You need to help them to make a mental picture of what they want, then place themselves and their family in that picture. After that you show them how they will get all the things they desire when they join the Navy. You have to make it an emotional decision so they can see it and feel it. They need to own it! Once they own it and they see it applied to their life, most of the work is done.

The thing that bothers me most about recruiting is that there is great pressure put on Recruiters to make their quota. Sometimes when you are on the boarder of a grey area, the Recruiter will make a bad decision to keep from getting chewed out. I was constantly in trouble for not selling my soul.

My first Recruiting assignment was in Huntington, West Virginia. Huntington is a fairly big city, with a nice base for recruits. Marshal University is there, and there are always young people dropping out of school and joining the service.

Since recruiters have a data base with 99.9% of all the graduating students in the county, we could keep tabs on everyone. We also had the line on every high school in the county, complete with every student's ASVAB score. If a student had a score lower than the minimum score of thirty one, then we would usually pass them over. One of my problems was that I wanted to help everyone, and sometime I would beat the same old dead horse.

The Huntington Recruiting Station was considered a large station due to the number of Recruiters that were based out of it. Every station had a Recruiter in Charge, or a RINC as we called him.

Huntington had three Recruiters, one for the Nuke candidates and two junior Recruiters. Since I was brand new to the game, I was one of those junior Recruiters.

Just like being on a ship at sea, Recruiters have qualifications to do. The first thing that any competitive Recruiter needed to do was to get his Gold Wreath. Every Recruiter was entitled to wear his "Rookie Cookie" which was the basic issue recruiting badge. The Golden Wreath was just that, a golden wreath that fit around the rookie cookie, showing that you were on top of your game. There were many Recruiters who never obtained their Golden Wreath, even after months of recruiting.

The basic job of any Recruiter was sales. You had to sell the Navy. I had no problem with selling the Navy. I loved the Navy! But it wasn't that easy. There were hours and hours of telephone cold calls, where you basically just went down a phone list and called people attempting to fill up your appointment book. Usually, the odds were against you. Out of every twenty cold calls you would set maybe one appointment if you were lucky. Then, every morning the Rinc would want to know what appointments you had set for the day.

Once you set an appointment, you have to make sure your client keeps it. You would be surprised how many people will quickly set an appointment just to get off the phone with you. We would have to call back a day before the appointment to make sure they would be there. Usually, out of ten appointments set, you might keep four of them.

Just because someone shows up for an appointment, doesn't mean your job is finished. The next thing you had to do was give them the practice ASVAB test. The ASVAB usually took about three hours to complete, and we didn't want to waste time on people who couldn't pass the test. If we gave them the pre-test, we could find out how well they would do in just a half hour or so. Once they took the pre-test and passed it, we would have to get them to commit to going to MEPS and taking the actual ASVAB.

MEPS stands for the Military Entrance Processing Station. This is where applicants going into all branches of the military would go for medical screening, academic testing and choosing their job assignment. Once you get them to MEPS, you were about ninety five percent certain they would be going in the Military.

The Recruiting office was located in a large strip mall just off the main highway in Huntington. Next to us were the Army, Marine Corps and Air Force Recruiting offices. All of the Recruiters had an unspoken agreement to leave each other's prospects alone. If the Army was talking to a student, and the student was thinking about joining the Army, we would support that and try not to change their mind. Recruiting was hard enough without being attacked by the competition.

I remember my first day in the Huntington office. I was wearing my dress blue uniform with all my ribbons and warfare devices. Standing tall and looking good, I knew that anyone who saw me would want to join the Navy.

The day was absolutely beautiful! It was a perfect fall day with a cool breeze blowing. I stepped out of the office and started walking down the sidewalk in the direction of the University. As I was walking through a small outdoor picnic area, I was stopped by a young man. "Are you the Navy Recruiter?" I smiled and said "Yes, I sure am. I'm Petty Officer Westfall. How are you?" I asked, sticking out my hand. He smiled and shook my hand. "I'm Oscar Sampson. I think I want to join the Navy." Wow! This job couldn't be easier!

As Oscar and I walked back to the Recruiting office, I found out a little bit of his background. He had recently graduated from school and was now unemployed. He said he tried to get into the Army, but the Recruiters didn't like him. When I asked him when he would be willing to go into the Navy, he said "I am ready to go right now!" That should have made me a bit suspicious, but since I had only been a Recruiter for about ten minutes, I didn't pick up on it.

Once we got back to the office, I looked around at the other Recruiters. I was so proud of myself... here I was walking in with my first Recruit on my first morning. Life was good, or so I thought.

Tim Waller was the Rinc in the Huntington Recruiting office, and as soon as he saw me coming in he called me into his office. "Who do you have there?" he asked. "This is Oscar Sampson. He just walked up to me and asked to join the Navy. Not too bad for ten minutes work, is it?" Tim looked at me and smiled "Well, maybe you should test him before you measure him for uniforms." I smiled at him and headed back to my desk.

I explained to Oscar about the ASVAB pre-test, but he said he already knew about it. I showed him to the testing station in the back room of the office and started the clock. He had forty five minutes to take the test.

When I walked back to my desk, I sat down and drank some of my coffee. When the other Recruiters looked at me, I smiled and said "I thought you guys said this was hard." Danny Ellison was the Nuke recruiter, and usually tested the smarter applicants. He shook his head and said "Clay, let me tell you a story about a man named Oscar... One day about a year ago, he walked into this office and said he wanted to join the Navy. Then we tested him. He scored a six. Not a ninety six, or a thirty six, just a six. First I thought he just had a problem with the test, so I told him to try back in a couple months."

Uh oh. I started to feel something slipping. Then the other Huntington Recruiter, Arthur Harris spoke up "A couple months later, Oscar comes back into the office. Danny was on leave, so I decided to test Oscar again for him. This time Oscar scored a whopping five. That's right, a five. We pretty much decided at that time that he was just dumber than sack of doorknobs."

Tim had stepped out of his office and joined the conversation. "My turn" he said. "I was walking through the plaza one day about six months ago, just minding my own business and enjoying the fresh air. Oscar came up out of nowhere and started talking to me about how his luck had run out and how he really needed a break. He begged me to help him get into the Navy. I felt bad for him, and brought him back into the office. I worked with him for a few days, and then I tested him again. That time he busted out a big old eleven. He was actually quite proud of doubling his score."

Now I could see why they were all having such fun with me. It was my turn to feel bad for Oscar. A few minutes later, Oscar came out from the back room. I asked him how he thought he did, and he said "I busted that test wide opened this time. I know I passed it!"

After a few minutes I had his test graded. This time Oscar cut a nine. I talked to him a few minutes about what books he could study to possible do better, and then I walked him out of the office and wished him my best. I had just learned the hard way that there were no easy days in Recruiting. Man, I really missed the Radford.

Every other Friday we had a zone meeting in Charleston. All the Recruiting Stations in our district would meet in that central location and go over what happened the week before. Things like who recruited the most people, or who had the best new idea for recruiting. The Zone Supervisor, Chief Platt, stood in the middle of the room and called out all the Rinc's one at a time. Once they gave their report, he moved on. When he would finish grilling the Rinc's, he dismissed everyone and we would head on back to Huntington.

That first Friday when we arrived back at the Huntington Station, there was a young man waiting to see me. He said I had left a note on his answering machine, and he was interested in learning more about the Navy. Remembering the runaround that Oscar gave me, I was a bit more cautious this time.

"Hi, I'm Petty Officer Westfall. Come on in and have a seat. Can I get you a soda or a cup of coffee?" I asked. He introduced himself as Roger Cohen, and asked for a soda, and then we started talking. "So Roger, what brings you in to see me today?" I asked. "I want to have a life somewhere out of West Virginia" he replied. That was something I could work with. After looking him up in my high school data base, I saw that he had graduated from Smithdale High School that past year, and he had already taken the ASVAB test and scored a 99, with was the highest score anyone could get. My day was getting brighter.

As we started discussing job possibilities, Petty Officer Waller came out of his office and started listening to our conversation. "I think I would like to work with electronics" Roger said. That's when Tim stepped in and said "Roger, let me show you something." Tim showed him what it would be like to work with nuclear power, and that only the smartest people can become Nukes. Once Roger learned about the twenty thousand dollar enlistment bonus, he started getting interested.

"When could I go in?" Roger asked. "Did you bring your duffle bag? You can go right now!" I said. He looked at me kind of surprised, and then I said "Well, right this second may be too soon. How about Monday? That way you have time to say good-bye and have one more party weekend before starting the rest of your life." Roger smiled at me and said "Yeah that sounds more like it. Let's do it on Monday."

The rest of the afternoon was spent preparing the package for Roger's enlistment. Since it was my first package, Danny was helping me to put it all together. The main parts of the package were things like the birth certificate, high school diploma and social security card. You might take those things for granted, but there have been many cases where small issues like that have kept people from joining the service. Sometimes these documents are destroyed in house fires, or lost in divorce proceedings. Since they are official documents, they take time to replace.

Medical records are another issue. There are many everyday conditions that people have that can keep them out of the service. Things like being bipolar, diabetic or having a past head injury. Recruiters have been trying to sweep things under the rug for years to get their "bones on the bus".

Some of the other things I needed to obtain for Roger to get into the Navy were a copy of his work history, names of references, and a complete background on any and all police involvement. That was another problem area. Kids are always getting into trouble. They think since they are juveniles that nothing they do matters after they are eighteen. That is not true when it comes to joining the Armed Forces. A couple misdemeanors can be more than enough to keep you from enlisting. A drug mention opens new doors for trouble.

Every applicant that walks through our door has to be tested for drugs. Recruiting offices usually carry cheap instant drug test kits that will tell us if an applicant is clean or if they have recently used drugs. If the test is positive, we tell them to stop doing whatever they are doing and then we will test them a month later. If they are clean, we send them to MEPS for processing.

Roger told me that he had smoked marijuana a couple times, but just for experimental purposes (like we all did). A quick urine test confirmed that he had not used any detectable drugs in the past thirty days, so all was well.

Once the package was complete, Roger was off to tell his folks about his decision. He said they had talked about it often in the past, so it would not come as a surprise to them, and everything would be fine.

As Monday morning rolled around, Roger came into the office at eight o'clock, just as I had asked him to. He had brought a small overnight bag with him, because the MEPS process usually took two days, so the Navy puts the applicants up for the night. Tim told me to go through the package one more time to make sure all the signatures were where they needed to be.

Whenever we had any applicants going to the MEPS station, we had them take a shuttle to Beckley, which was about eighty miles away. Once they were on the shuttle, they were on their own. Sometimes, if the applicant was a particularly important one, we would meet them up there the following day for the counseling and job selection session.

At that time, our Recruiting Station had a three recruit monthly requirement. That meant that we were required to put at least three people into the Navy, or we would be a failing station. You did not want to be a failing station. One of those three recruits was supposed to be an upper class Recruit, or a Nuke. Since my man was a Nuke, we needed to make sure he went in with no problems.

Tim drove up to Beckley the following day, just to make sure there were no problems with Roger getting his job. We didn't hear from him for several hours, and I was getting a bit nervous. Finally, around five o'clock that afternoon, Tim called and said Roger had just been sworn into the Navy! I did it! My first Recruit!

The following morning, Tim called for everyone's attention. Then he said "Petty Officer Westfall, front and center." I marched up to him smartly, not really knowing what to expect. As I stood at attention, he addressed the rest of the room. "As everyone knows, the desire of every Recruiter is to obtain his or her Golden Wreath in their first month of recruiting. Petty Officer Westfall is now getting presented with his first Golden Wreath for Putting his first Recruit into the Navy within his first week of recruiting. He is also getting presented with his second Golden Wreath for putting in an upper class recruit in on his first month. He is also getting his Third Golden Wreath, as the rest of us are, for the Huntington Station getting selected for Station of the year. Congratulations!" He then handed me a Golden Wreath with two silver stars in it, for the subsequent awards. Wow! Three Golden Wreaths in my first week of Recruiting. Life was good.

In Gallipolis, Ohio, just an hour away from Huntington, is a small satellite Recruiting Office. There was also a small Army and Marine office in the same building, each of them only big enough for one desk, one bookshelf, two chairs and a coat rack. It was an important station, because although Gallipolis only has a population of around five thousand people, there are four high schools in the surrounding area. The Gallipolis station was under the Huntington office. Any Recruits that were brought in through Gallipolis fell under Huntington's monthly quota.

The long time Recruiter in Gallipolis, Steven Branch, was retiring. Since I was the newest Recruiter in Huntington, I drew the short straw and became the new Gallipolis Recruiter. The next month was spent taking a crash course in single Recruiter station operations. Life sucked, but it was moving forward.

As soon as the office was mine, I started going through the ASVAB books, looking for the smarter students. I worked late nights the first couple weeks, making phone calls and trying to schedule any appointments that I could. I wasn't making much headway, but I was not going to give up.

I remember one evening I was working late, and just as I was getting ready to head out for the night, I heard someone crying out in the corridor. I walked out and found a young girl about seventeen year's old sitting outside of the Army office, sobbing into her hands. When I asked her if I could help her, she looked at me and said "I don't want to join the Navy." I smiled and said "Ok, then I don't want to put you in the Navy. Why don't you come into my office and tell me why you are crying, and maybe I can help you." We stepped into my office and she sat down in one of the chairs. I handed her a box of tissue, and she started to calm down. She said her name was Amanda.

"Now, Miss Amanda, what's the matter?" I asked. She told me that her Grandfather retired from the Army. Her father retired from the Army. Her two brothers and her sister were in the Army. Now, she wanted to join the Army, but she couldn't pass the ASVAB test. "Ok, it's not the end of the world. Let me look up your information, and then we will see what we can do about that test score." "But, I said I don't want to join the Navy. I want to join the Army." I smiled at her and said "Yes, but it's the same test. You can come in here after school for an hour or so each day, until you are ready to take your test. Then I will talk to the Army Recruiter and get him to take you back down to re-test."

The next couple weeks seemed to go by pretty quickly. I had brought six applicants into my office, and signed up three of them. Since I only needed to get one a month, life was looking up.

Amanda studied very hard, but she was the kind of girl who had a hard time concentrating. She had been trying to get the minimum score, just to get into the Army. I showed her a couple tricks I learned in Recruiting school that taught people how to read and process information a bit differently. Some people responded better to these methods, so I figured it wouldn't hurt to show her. After borrowing the Army's job placement book, I showed Amanda that if she got at least a fifty on her ASVAB, she could go in as an E-3 and get a better job. Sold on the idea, she decided to study for another week and see if she could do better. David, the Army Recruiter, said he would take Amanda back down to MEPS to take her test again the following week. He told me that I was wasting my time with her, and that she would never pass the test. I asked him to test her again for me as a favor, and he said he would.

The next Thursday finally arrived, and Amanda left for the MEPS station. I knew that she would not get back until that evening, so I stayed in a local school for most of the day, talking to possible applicants. As dinner time rolled around, David finally arrived from MEPS. Just as I was about to ask him how it went, Amanda ran through the door and tackled me, almost knocking me to the floor. She kissed me on the cheek and said through her tears "I made a fifty six... thank you so much!" I was very glad to hear that all went well. David shook my hand and said "Dude, I owe you one. You got me a Recruit and saved my tail. Thank you." I went home that evening feeling really nice. It felt good to help Amanda get into the Army.

The following week was our bi-monthly meeting in Charleston. I was feeling really good, since I had put three people into the Navy that month. I was two recruits over quota, which was good, but not that smart, as I found out. Tim pulled me aside and said "Clay, man you're messing up. You are supposed to put one in, then string the next one along until the next month. That way you make goal every month. Now what will you do if you have a dry month next month?" That made sense all right, but it seemed kind of selfish. These people wanted to start their careers, and it just seemed wrong to string them along.

As we all started moving our chairs into a circle, and got ready for the meeting. Chief Platt stood in the middle and started reading off a list. "Ok, let's see where everyone stands as of now. Huntington made their quota, with one extra. Tim looked at me and smiled, making me feel good for having such a great month. I couldn't wait to see if Chief Platt mentioned me to the others. Just then he said "Petty Officer Westfall, please stand up." I stood up, modestly putting my hands behind my back. "Petty Officer Westfall has a quota of one up there in Gallipolis. He put three Recruits in the Navy this month!" Just as everyone started applauding for me, Chief Platt stopped them and continued "Wait, I have more. Charleston Station did not get its quota, and neither did Beckley Station. Our Zone did not make its full quota, so we failed. Do you know why we failed? We failed because Petty Officer Westfall spent all his time putting a Recruit into the Army!" He stared at me and looked very angry "But Chief, I got three people in..." He cut me off and started yelling at me "You should have spent your time putting more people into the Navy, then we would have made goal for the zone!"

I was so angry, I could spit. Everyone was staring at me. I stood up and said "Chief, that's not fair. All I did was help a student achieve her dream. I don't deserve this." That was a mistake. I should have just kept my mouth shut, and left. "Your job isn't to help students achieve their dream... your job is to put people in the Navy. If you can't do the job we trained you for, then get the hell out of my zone." That was it. I walked to my car and left. As I drove home I was thinking about how much I hated Recruiting. I had a wonderful career in the Navy, and then they forced me to do something I did not want to do. Chief Platt was a jerk, and he didn't care about anyone but himself.

When I arrived at the house, it was still pretty early. I made a drink and drank it fast, and then I made another one. I just couldn't get Chief Platt out of my mind. A few minutes later, a car pulled into my driveway. It was Tim and Danny, heading back to Huntington. I met them at the door.

"Tim, I am sorry I left. I was just so angry, and I knew I was going to get put on report if I said what I was thinking." Tim smiled and me and put his hand on my shoulder. "Don't sweat it. I talked to Amanda at MEPS that day, and she told me what you did. She never would have joined the Navy, and you helped her get what she wanted. Platt is an ass, and we all know it. Now, since you are half way drunk anyway, take the rest of the weekend off. Come see me on Monday, and we will set your plan of attack for next month." I thanked him, and then they left. At least Tim understood. Life was blurry, but better.

Chapter Eighteen

The next few months were a lot tougher than the first ones. I missed goal once, then I made goal three times. It was December, and with Christmas on the horizon, I knew that nobody would want to join the Navy that month. I had concentrated on students that would be graduating in May, trying to get them to enlist in the Delayed Entry Program. This way they would sign up today, and go into the Navy after they graduate.

One day, Harrison Nassir walked into my office. Harry was a senior at Wilmot High School and was due to graduate in May. He had been looking at the Navy for a few months now, although his dad had been pushing him toward the Marine Corps. Now there is nothing at all wrong with being a Marine, but Harry loved the ocean, and liked the idea of seeing the world from an aircraft carrier.

Harry had taken his ASVAB test at school earlier that year, and he had scored a ninety nine, the highest score possible. After I showed him what his life would be like as a Nuke, he couldn't wait until he graduated!

Harry didn't want to join the Delayed Entry Program, because it seemed immature to him. He wanted to sign the papers and leave as soon as he had that diploma.

As the end of the month drew near, Chief Platt was having trouble getting his quota filled for the zone. A couple of the stations were going to be alright, but it was clear to him that there were about four stations that were going to fall short. He was calling me every day to see how I was going to help him. I had already gotten one Recruit to MEPS, so my personal goal was met. But, it was never that simple with Recruiting.

Harrison was eighteen years old. Normally, you had to have your diploma and your parents' signature to join the Navy, but if you were eighteen and had a good ASVAB score, you could join right away. This is where my next problem came from.

One morning, around the seventeenth of the month, Harry came into the office, very upset. Seeing that he was upset, I closed the door and asked him what was wrong. "I got in a huge fight with my dad, and I told him I never wanted to see him again" he said. After a few minutes, he went on. "My dad thinks that I am still a child, and when I told him I wanted to stay out with my buddies tonight, he said as long as I lived under his roof, I would do what he said!"

I talked to Harry for a while and attempting to calm him down, but it was no use. He was pissed! He looked at me and said "Petty Officer Westfall, I want to join the Navy now. I don't need my diploma, and I am eighteen years old. I want to go today." I put my hand on his shoulder and said "I'll tell you what. Why don't you go to lunch and we will talk about this when you have calmed down a bit more." After Harry left the office, I tried to contact his dad.

As I was waiting for Harry's dad to call me back, I received a call from Chief Platt. "What are you doing for the United States Navy today?" he asked. After explaining to him what was going on, he started laughing. "Well, it looks like you are going to be able to save the zone! Get his ass down to MEPS and get that boy in the Navy!" I hesitated for just a minute and said "Chief, it would be best if he stays and graduates, then he can join the Navy after he graduates."

After a couple minutes of silence, Chief Platt said "Petty Officer Westfall, your job is to put people in the Navy. Not the Army. Not in school, but in the Navy. Who cares if this kid is mad at his dad, or why he wants to join the Navy? Now this is what you are going to do. Tell him to go ahead and drop out of school and get him to MEPS today. Do you hear me? Stop trying to be everyone's friend and do your damn job!" Then he slammed down the phone.

A few minutes later, I received a call from Mr. Nassir. I asked him if he could come down to my office today, and get to the bottom of all the fuss. He said he would be down a little bit later that afternoon. After that I called the Guidance Counselor at Harry's school, and let her know what was going on.

When Harry came back in to the office, he was much calmer. I brought him a soda, and asked him to hear me out. "Harry, you have the world at your fingertips. You are smarter than most kids, and your future is looking excellent! If you were to drop out of school, you would be limiting your options. Let's say you decide after a few years to leave the Navy and work for a civilian company. You don't have your diploma, so you can't get the job."

"Yeah, but my dad is pretty upset with me. I think it would best if I just joined the Navy and got out of town." He said. "Harry, your dad and your mom love you. Now, as long as you live under their roof, you are going to have to follow their rules, and that means not staying out late on school nights." "Well, it's too late now anyway." He said "I already told my Guidance Counselor." I smiled and said "I already talked to her, and she is going to forget about your request to drop out of school."

Just then there was a knock at the office door, and Harry's father walked in. "Petty Officer Westfall, can I talk to my son for a moment?" I smiled, and walked out of the office. As I stood outside of the office, I thought about the ass chewing I was going to get from Chief Platt. If that man didn't hate me now, he sure would after today.

After a few moments, Mr. Nassir came out and asked me to join them in the office. "Well Petty Officer Westfall, I have decided to wait until I graduate, then I will join the Navy. Thank you for helping me get my head screwed back on right." I shook hands with both of them, and wished them a good day. Then, I stood back and waited for the hatchet to fall.

A couple hours later, Chief Platt called and asked me how the situation was going. I told him what had happened, and he said "Let me get this right... you went out of your way to get him to change his mind, and not join the Navy?" I said "Chief, he needs to graduate from high school first. If he was your son, what would you want him to do?" The scream that came across the phone next almost made me drop it "HE'S NOT MY SON, YOU IDIOT!" That's when I slammed down the phone. I was done with Chief Platt and his evil ways. My next call was to the Huntington Station to talk to my immediate Supervisor, Tim Waller.

"Petty Officer Waller, I am done with this!" I said, and then I explained everything that happened in Gallipolis that day. After a moment of silence, Tim said "Clay, you did not do the popular thing, but you did do the right thing. Now, take the rest of the day and drive around looking for Applicants." That was Tim's way of saying go home and don't come back until Monday. That was the best advice I had gotten in a long time.

The Christmas holiday was nice, but soon it was over and it was back to the old grind. That following Monday morning the drive to Gallipolis seemed a lot longer than before. I remembered back when I enjoyed coming to work. As much as I hated Recruiting, I put my best foot forward, and tried to do a good job. But Chief Platt had sucked the life out of me. Now, I could honestly say that this was the worst job I had ever had. I hated everything about Recruiting.

When I got to the office, I was greeted by a young lady in at the door. Before I could even unlock the door, she stuck her hand out and said "Excuse me, are you Petty Officer Westfall? My name is Brittany and I want to join the Navy right now." I started laughing and said "Well, why don't you wait until I get the door opened first." When she didn't even crack a smile, I started noticing that she was acting strangely. She kept looking back and forth down the road and she acted very impatient.

When we finally got into the office, I made a pot of coffee and started interviewing her. "So, how old are you, Brittany?" She quickly told me she was twenty years old and graduated from Mesa Valley High School a couple years before. I looked at her ASVAB score from three years before and she had scored a thirty six, so I was sure she would do well on the test. "What kind of job field are you thinking about getting into?" I asked. "I really don't care, as long as I can go today." She kept looking out the window, like she was waiting for someone.

I got Brittany started on the ASVAB pre-test, even though she really didn't need it. I needed a couple minutes to try and figure out why she was so nervous. I asked David, the Army recruiter to keep an eye on Brittany until I had gotten back.

Gallipolis was a small town, and I had gotten to know many of the locals and shop owners. I knew that my friend Chuck, a Gallipolis Police Officer, would be sitting at Mrs. Kitty's coffee house just down the block. When I walked in I saw Chuck sitting at a booth facing the front door. "Good Morning, Chuck." He looked up from his morning newspaper and smiled "Hi, Clay. How's tricks?" I quickly told him about Brittany and gave him a description of her, and then I left and went back to my office.

When I got there, Brittany was just finishing her test. I graded it slowly, keeping one eye on her. She just kept looking out the window and looking nervous. "Well, you got a thirty two, so it looks like you should be good to go. Have you decided what you want to do yet?" "Look, I don't care. Just give me a job and let's get out of here" she said, almost yelling.

Just as I was trying to figure out what to do next, I heard a radio squawk. If you have ever been a Police Officer, you know exactly what that sound means. Before I could sit back down at my desk, Chuck was at my office door with two other Police Officers. As the men entered the small office, Chuck said "Don't move. Brittany Foster, you are under arrest for aggravated assault, attempted murder and child endangerment." Well, there goes my Recruit. The two officers that came in with Chuck hand cuffed Brittany behind her back, and then the female Officer frisked her and led her out of the building to a waiting squad car.

"Thanks for the heads up Clay" Chuck said. "She and her husband got into a big fight last night over bills or something. After he fell asleep, she smacked him a couple times with a golf club and set the apartment building on fire, with her kids still in bed. This lady has issues." I shook my head and thanked Chuck and the other Police Officers, then I handed him a pamphlet on Navy job selection. "What is this for?" Chuck asked. "Give it to Brittany. When she comes out of prison in fifty years she will need a job." "Will do." Chuck laughed, and then he gave a quick wave as he was leaving.

The rest of the day was pretty quiet. I had one other interview and a DEP meeting (Delayed Entry Program,) after lunch. Gallipolis had about eight Depper's at that time, and the monthly meetings kept them primed up and ready to go. Sometimes we would go for a run around the park, or just hand out business cards in the local mall. Every month, each Depper was required to bring in at least one name of a person who is interested in joining the Navy. Since these guys were all current students, they had access to the student body of several schools. This is where I would get a lot of my leads from.

Just before I left for the night, I checked my email to see if I had any leads. After going through the list of the usual spam and garbage, I noticed an email that I didn't recognize. It was from someone called "Lilmissamy", and it read:

Dear Petty Officer Westfall,

I was in your office at a DEP meeting once, but I didn't do very well on the test. I would like to come back and try it again, if that's alright. Also, I will be getting out of school soon, and I would like to help out around the office, if you would like. I can call my friends and tell them about the Navy. I hope to be in this week, love Amy.

The seemed ok, except for the 'love Amy' part, but it was probably just a force of habit. I looked through my DEP meeting log, to see who this Amy person was. Finally, I found an Amy Mulford who had tested a couple months ago, but didn't to very well. Amy was a seventeen year old senior at Mesa Valley High School, and was due to graduate soon. I remember she was nice, and very talkative   I replied to her email and told her I would appreciated any help she could give me. Then I signed it as I always do, 'MS2 (SW/SS) Westfall, United States Navy.'

The next morning I had a medical Doctors appointment, so I came in to the office a bit later. When I walked in, a young lady with long blonde hair was waiting for me by my office door. "Hi Clay" she said. I recognized her this time "Hello Amy. How have you been?" She smiled and gave me a quick hug, which kind of caught me off guard. "Oh, please, call me Petty Officer Westfall. It helps you to get ready for the real Navy." I smiled, so as not to hurt her feelings. Then I reached out my hand to shake hers "And we don't hug, we shake hands." She looked at me and smiled. "Oh, I thought we were closer than that." I was a bit puzzled by that comment, but I shrugged it off as a bad joke.

The rest of the afternoon was spent going down the school lists looking for qualified people that we hadn't talked to yet. As it was getting closer to the end of the work day, I mentioned to Amy that we needed to start shutting down for the day. As I was putting the books away, Amy came over to me and touched my hand, and then she smiled at me and moved closer. "Whoa, Amy. Let's stop and talk about this. Not only am I a married man, but I am old enough to be your father. Not to mention the fact that I am your Recruiter and you are a student. This is not going to happen." She smiled and said "But no one will ever know." I quickly stepped into the door way and looked into the Army office. "David, can you please come in here."

When David walked in, he looked a bit surprised. I said "Sergeant Hollings, this is Amy Mulford, an applicant from Mesa Valley High School. I need to explain something to Amy and I would like for you to officially witness it." As I went back over everything I had told her previously so David could hear it. "Amy, I would like to continue being your Recruiter, but only if you promise me that this will stop." Amy was visibly embarrassed by David's presence, and quickly apologized for getting out of line. Then she turned and ran out the door. Great. This was all I needed when my Zone Supervisor already hated me. I asked David if he could write an official statement for me, telling about the incident. He said he would, and I thanked him and left for the day. On the way home, I called my Rinc, Tim Waller, and explained everything to him. He said I had done everything just as I should have, and told me to go home for the day. Did I ever mention that I hated Recruiting?

The next day was rainy and nasty. I sat in the office most of the morning and cold called all of my lists. When I was done with that, I checked my email to see if there were and interested applicants. After weeding through the usual garbage, I found another email from "Lilmissamy". It read:

Dear Clay,

I am sorry about what happened yesterday. It was stupid of me to show you my feelings when the Army and Marine Recruiters were there. I do understand why you did what you did. I will stay away for a few days so people will not suspect us. I love you. Amy.

Well there you have it. Just when I thought my enlistment couldn't get any worse. I forwarded the email to Tim and Chief Platt, and then I stood by and waited for the phone call. It took a couple minutes, but sure enough, Chief Platt called. "So, I guess I should have expected this" he said. "First, you help a girl join the Army, and then you talk a Nuke out of joining the Navy. Now, you are sleeping with your applicants!" That was the last straw. "Chief Platt" I said "I am not sleeping with my applicants. If you have any doubts about my abilities or my integrity, then send me back to the fleet! I am sick of this crap." Before he could answer me, I hung up the phone. I really didn't care what happened after that. I know I had four more years until I retired, and I was not going to let Platt screw me out of my retirement. I was just about done with this.

That night it snowed and it snowed. I made my way to Gallipolis, but it wasn't easy. I figured after the way I hung up on the Zone Supervisor the day before, I would probably be on report today.

As I was walking through the snow drifts to my office, I felt a sudden pain in my back. As I reach around to grab my back, it felt like someone hit me with an ax. The pain was so terrible I fell to the ground. After lying there for what seemed like forever, I slowly climbed to my feet, and walked back to my car. As I drove myself to the hospital, I called Tim to tell him what was going on.

After two hours and one MRI, I found out that my lower back was the problem. I had hurt it pretty bad back aboard the Radford, and I never really followed up on it. Now, when you look at the MRI, you can clearly see massive bulging between the L4 and L5 vertebra. The pressure on my spinal cord caused the severe pain that dropped me in the parking lot. When I asked the Doctor what could be done to fix the problem, he told me I would eventually have to have spinal surgery. Well that's just great. The Doctor gave me one week's bed rest and told me I needed to get to a specialist. I could just hear Platt now...

After a week of lying on my back, the pressure in my spine subsided. I was cleared to go back to work, but I was told that this problem would not just go away.

When I arrived back in Gallipolis, I knew I had a lot of catching up to do. I was scheduled to meet with a former high school drop out that morning, and see what I could do with him. He was running late, which gave me time to sort through the mail. Besides the usual advertisements and notices, I found seven get well cards, one from my buddies the Marines next door, and six from Amy Mulford.

My applicant, Josh Yates, came into the office about half an hour late for his appointment. Josh was nineteen years old, and dropped out of school in the tenth grade. Now that times were hard and he needed a job, he greatly regretted his decision. I had set him up to take his General Equivalency Diploma Test, or his GED, the week before, and it seemed that he had passed it with flying colors. Now, it was time to take his ASVAB pretest and see how he would do.

As Josh was taking his test, Tim Waller called to see how I was doing. I told him I had an applicant that I was planning on sending to MEPs the week, and I had a line on two others. He told me to keep up the good work and to stay out of Charleston and away from Chief Platt. Well, at least Tim appreciated what I was doing.

A bit later, Josh came back in and handed me his test. "How do you think you did?" I asked. He smiled and said "I'll bet you the lunch of your choice that I made at least a forty five." I looked at him and said "Deal." It took a few minutes to grade the test, and when I was finished, I looked at Josh and slowly shook my head. "Hmmm.... Where do I want to eat lunch? Maybe that big crab and lobster place, or perhaps a huge sirloin steak..." Josh was looking very worried. "Well, at least tell me how I did!" he said rather desperately. "Ok, but first, how much money do you have for lunch?" As he took out his wallet, I decided to let him off the hook. "Ok, fine. You made a sixty one! Outstanding job! Now you can go into a much better field of training. Congratulations, Josh!"

Just then, Josh's mother came in to pick him up. After he told her the good news, he said "Well Mom, I have to go to lunch now. Petty Officer Westfall is about to buy me a big steak!" He smiled and nudged me. I smiled back and said "That's right. Mrs. Yates, would you please join us? Your lunch today is on the United States Navy!" She accepted, so we walked down the block to the steak house. Lunch was a small price to pay for making goal this month. Life, finally, was better.

Charleston, West Virginia was our Recruiting zone, and it was a part of Naval Recruiting District, Richmond. That's where the Skipper and all the politics were. As a rule, I tried to stay as far away from Richmond, Virginia as possible. Since I needed surgery on my spine, I was going to be out of commission for a long time. Chief Platt wanted me to drive up to Richmond so I could talk with the classifier, and see how they wanted to deal with my surgery.

Once I got there, the Doctor started asking all kinds of questions, and read over my diagnosis two or three times. For a minute there I wondered if I was dying. When he finally finished going over my records, he started going through some books that were on his desk. After what seemed like hours, he actually started talking to me. "Petty Officer Westfall, here is the problem. You are under orders now not to sit or stand for too long. You are a Recruiter, and that's what you do... sit and stand. I am afraid this may be the end of your career as a Recruiter." No more Recruiting? Resisting all my urges to kiss this man, I tried to look bothered by what he was telling me. "No more Recruiting? What?" I wasn't sure if he was buying my award winning performance, but I did try to look convincing.

When I left the Doctor, I went off to see the Master Chief. As I got to his door, he was just hanging up the phone. "I just spoke to the Doctor about you. I guess you are done Recruiting for the Navy. Now, get the hell out of my office. I have work to do." I didn't wait for a hug, I just left.

As I was driving back to West Virginia, I called Tim and told him what was going on. He had already talked to Chief Platt and they had decided that I will keep running the office in Gallipolis up until the day I have to report to the Naval Hospital in Norfolk, Virginia. Since my appointment was only a week away, I had time to tie up some loose ends before leaving.

When I got to the office the next day, I was shuffling through my email, where I found several emails from Amy. Each one was just a little cozier than the last one. I had to do something about her, but I wasn't really sure what to do. Then, I had an idea.

I called Josh Yates up and asked him if he could come in and work with me the following day. Since he was out of school and had no job, he said he was looking forward to it. Then, I went back to my storage locker in the rear of the building to find some Recruiting posters. After hanging the posters in the office, I called

Amy and asked her if she was interested in making some phone calls the next day, and she was more than happy to do it. Since Josh would be here the next day, I knew she wouldn't be a problem.

The next morning Josh arrived at eight thirty, just as I asked him to. I told him about my problems with Amy, and I asked him if he would mind working with her so she could better understand the ASVAB test.

Amy arrived a few minutes later, and was very disappointed to see Josh. She looked at my recruiting poster, three very pretty women working on an airplane. "Why did you put this old poster up?" she asked. "I like watching women fixing airplanes. There is just something sexy about women fixing airplanes." I said, smiling at Josh. Amy was paying close attention to what we were saying. Then she asked me "Petty Officer Westfall, how high do I have to score to work on airplanes?" Well, you have to score at least a thirty one. Then I can guarantee that you can be one of those sexy women in that poster." Then I pointed to Josh and said "He just scored a whopping sixty one. I'll bet he could help you." That was all it took, and they started studying.

The next two days were spent cleaning up my office and helping Josh to teach Amy how to take the ASVAB. While I was watching them, I noticed Amy had a different way of thinking. She had to write the problem out, when most of us could just see it in our head. I started showing her different ways of working some of the problems, to see if it would help her out with some of the tougher ones. She seemed to be getting the hang of it.

The next day I decided to close up the office and drive all the way to Beckley. I wanted to take Josh and

Amy down to take their actual ASVAB test and find out once and for all what they could do. Amy had made a twenty eight on her pretest, so it would be touch and go with her. Sometimes people do better, and sometimes they do worse. Since I was taking Josh down anyway, I really had nothing to lose.

The test started at ten o'clock, and took three hours. You needed to use those three hours wisely in order to complete the test, and when you were done, depending on how well you did, you could negotiate for a job. Josh was the first one finished, and he cut a fifty nine. That was an excellent score, and won him a seat at the negotiation table. He decided to be a Fire Control Technician, and was going into the Navy as an E-3.

Amy finished her test about half an hour later. I asked her how she did "I think I blew it. It was really hard." I told her to wait until she sees her score before she beats herself up. A few minutes later they told me her score. I looked at her sadly and said "Amy, you scored a thirty eight. YOU DID IT!" She screamed and gave me a big hug. As we were walking over to the classifiers, I told her that I really wasn't that fond of female airplane mechanics, and she should pick out a career that she would enjoy. She chose to be a cook, just like me. Who would have thought it?

As the three of us were driving home that evening, I called Tim and told him the good news "Amy Mulford scored a thirty eight, and signed up as a cook. It looks like Gallipolis is at two hundred percent again this month." Tim started laughing "So, I guess you won't have to marry her to get her into the Navy, huh?" I had to admit, I was very relieved that she was going away. Before he hung up, he asked me to come into the Huntington office the following morning. Since the next day was Friday, and it was the last day I would ever spend as a recruiter, I didn't mind at all. When I dropped Amy and Josh off at the office in Gallipolis, I cleared out my desk, picked up my computer and locked the door for the last time. As I drove out of town, I couldn't help but smile as I looked through the rear view mirror.

The next morning I walked into the Huntington Station with a dozen doughnuts. I turned my computer in to Tim and sat down with him for my check out. He just smiled and shook my hand and said "Clay, I am sorry it sucked as much as it did. For the record, thank you for your hard work. Tell the fleet we said hello." With that, I left the Huntington office and drove out of town.

Thank God, it was all over. Did I ever mention I hated recruiting?

Chapter Nineteen

When I arrived at the Norfolk Naval Hospital in Portsmouth, Virginia, I went right to the personnel building to check in. Since my spinal appointment wasn't until the following week, I would be working at the Personnel Support Detachment, or PSD. That's where the personnel records for the entire command, a few thousand people, are maintained. The dispersing office and the ID card lab were also at PSD, as well as the military travel office.

I went into the main office and knocked on the door of the PSD Officer in Charge. "MS2 (SW/SS) Westfall, reporting as ordered" I said, standing at attention. I was standing in front of a large oak desk with an equally large black name plate that read "PNCS(SW) Boatman." A short man with a thick black mustache stood up and stuck out his hand "Hi, I'm Senior Chief Boatman, the dude in charge of this whole place. Welcome aboard!" I instantly felt better.

The Senior Chief took me around and introduced me to all of his staff. There were about forty people who worked in all the areas of PSD, and many of them were civilians. I knew I would like it there, because everyone was so friendly. Besides... it wasn't Recruiting.

The following week I reported to my Surgeon. He looked at all my x-rays and my MRI and explained my procedure. Basically, there is a swelling inside of my L-5 vertebra. The pressure pushes on my spinal cord, and causes great pain. He would have to cut two arches in my vertebra, kind of like a big "M", and that will relieve the pressure on both sides and should make the pain go away. I guess it sounds easy enough, unless you're worried about stuff like permanent paralysis or wheel chairs. My Surgeon, Dr. Michaels, schedule my procedure for early the next week. He explained that I would have thirty days of convalescent leave, which would commence as soon as I got out of surgery.

Ok, let's skip ahead. I had my surgery. Now, I was on convalescent leave. The first week was pretty brutal. I was in pain, so I took these really good pain killers. When they wore off, I took more. That and some pretty lights kind of sums up my first week.

The second week was a little better. I moved away from the good pain killers, and started on some that I could actually take and still function. I had been sitting around the house for a while now, and I was going a bit stir crazy. Since I needed to check in with the Doctor Michaels anyway, I decided to go see the Senior Chief.

"We have some problems, Clay." Senior said. "The Navy is taking your back issue very seriously. Here, read this." He said, handing me a letter. It was from the Naval Medical Board in Bethesda, Maryland. It said that my back injury was serious, and they had decided that at the end of my convalescent leave, they were going to give me a medical discharge from the Navy. It further stated that I would be receiving a ten percent disability pension.

"Senior Chief, this is unacceptable. I will be retiring with twenty years soon, and I will have a full pension. I don't want to be medically discharged!" I knew that if I was allowed to retired with a full pension, I would not only get fifty percent of my base pay for the rest of my life, but I would also get full medical benefits for me and my family as well. If I was medically discharged with a ten percent disability pension, I would get about one hundred and ten dollars a month, and the only medical coverage I would get was for my back.

"Ok, Senior, what can I do about this?" Senior Chief looked down at the medical manual on his desk and said "Well, they don't write these letters until after they have established a board and carefully weighed out all of the options. According to the findings of that board, your body is permanently damaged, and you are no longer physically able to do the job the Navy is paying you to do. They feel that if they were to let you stay in until retirement, you would be a detriment to the Navy." Then he looked down at his desk and said "I'm sorry Clay. In the Navy's eyes, this is a done deal."

Wow. I had been working towards my retirement for a long time, and now it was gone. This was not right. I drove back home and had no idea what I was going to do. Life was starting to suck again, big time.

I spent the next two weeks recuperating, and trying to figure out what I was going to do. Once my leave was over, I reported back to PSD. I had plenty of time to think it over, and I needed to talk to Senior Chief Boatman.

"Good morning, Senior" I said after knocking on his door. "I have decided that I am not going to take it. I refuse to let the Navy medically retire me. There has to be an appeal process, and I would be very grateful if you could help me find it."

The next few days were spent going through the books, trying to understand the criteria that the Navy used to make their decisions. According to the Medical Procedures Manuel, the board could be addressed in person, and has in rare, extreme cases reversed its decision. If there was even the smallest chance of me being able to retire, I was to going to try it.

Senior authorized a set of orders for me to drive up to Bethesda and challenge my board. A couple days later, I arrived in Bethesda and checked into the enlisted barracks. After putting my things in my room, I went over to the hospital and checked in with the Medical Review Counsel.

As I was sitting in the waiting room silently praying and asking the Lord for guidance, a very attractive young lady with long blonde hair walked up to me and said "Excuse me, are you Petty Officer Westfall?" I stood up politely and said "Yes ma'am. How can I help you?" She smiled and offered her hand "Hi. My name is Sandra Corning. I am your legal counselor for the procedure. Can you please come with me?"

As I followed her down the hall, I was wondering how experienced she was. She couldn't be older than maybe twenty eight or so. I wanted to have the best legal counsel I could get. Actually, I didn't even know I was going to have a legal counsel until she introduced herself to me.

When we walked into her office she offered me a chair and started to explain the procedure to me. She said there would be three medical doctors and one regular Line Officer, usually Navy or Marine Corps. All of them would be senior officers. The decision to discharge me from the Navy had already been made, so we would be doing all of the talking. It was our job to convince the board that they were wrong, and they really didn't like to second guess themselves.

On her desk were my medical record and my service record. As we went through the entries, year after year, we jotted down anything that we thought would be helpful. After a couple hours, Ms. Corning said "Why don't you take the rest of the day off and try to relax. I will finish this, and meet you here at nine o'clock tomorrow morning." I agreed and left for the day.

The following morning came quickly, and as I dressed in my sharpest Crackerjacks, I couldn't help but wonder how the day would go. Seventeen years in the Navy, just to be cast out at the last minute. It wasn't right. I started praying again.

Ms. Corning was in her office going over the last minute details of her case. As I walked in she smiled and said "Good Morning. We are the first case on the docket today. You look great!" I knew she was only trying to boost my confidence. I smiled and asked her what my chances were, and she told me we had as good a chance as anybody. That really wasn't very reassuring.

When we were called into the board room, we were ushered to a long table with some files on it. There were five men sitting at the head table, four board members and the reporter. The man who addressed us first was a Marine Colonel. "This proceeding will come to order. Counsel, do you have an opening statement?" Ms. Corning stood up and addressed the board "Sir, Petty Officer Westfall has had a long and distinguished career in the Navy. His evaluations are excellent, and his conduct has been exemplary. This board has ruled to separate him from the Navy prematurely, due to a lower back injury. We feel that this ruling is unwarranted and unnecessary, and Petty Officer Westfall would like to remain in the Navy until he can retire with full benefits in three more years."

The doctors and Ms. Corning discussed various topics in my medical record, and they went over every line of their report. Once all of the finding had been reviewed, the Colonel looked at me and said "Petty Officer Westfall, would you like to make a statement?" I stood at attention and said "Sir, yes I would Sir." I paused a minute, then I continued

"I remember back when I first thought of joining the Navy. I was walking through a mall back home and I saw a 'Heritage' poster hanging on the wall. I just stood there and stared at it, wishing it could be me. Then, I joined the Navy and became a part of something I really loved. The history, the tradition... I loved everything about the Navy. With all due respect Sir, I think you are wrong to discharge me. I can still do everything that I could do before my injury."

"Petty Officer Westfall" one of the board members said "Your back is injured. We have to keep your health in mind. I realize you want to stay in the Navy for the next three years." I smiled at him and said "Sir, my job isn't finished yet. I made a promise to myself eighteen years ago, and I am not finished yet. When I was in the Gulf, my team handled the broken bodies of our war dead; the ones who will never come home. If I leave now, I will always feel like I took the short cut in order to get back home. Sir, the Navy is not just what I want to do, it's who I am. Please, allow me to retire from the Navy and complete my mission. Let me leave on my own two feet."

After sending us out for a brief recess, the board called us back in. They told me that they had come to a conclusion. "Petty Officer Westfall" the Colonel said "I don't think we have ever had anyone in here that seemed to love the Navy as much as you do. We are happy to inform you that we have reversed our decision. You are welcome to retire in three years with full benefits. Congratulations." I quickly thanked them, and walked out before they could change their minds. Ms. Corning shook my hand and said "You know, I have been doing this for over a year now, and this is the first time I have actually seen them reverse their decision. Congratulations!" As I walked back to my room, I said another prayer thanking the Lord for letting me win. Life was good...

When I arrived back at the Hospital, I received some wonderful news. I had finally been promoted to First Class Petty Officer! The Navy's process for advancement at that time was terrible. You could be perfect in your field, and do excellent on your advancement exam, and still not get promoted. If the Navy only had room for a hundred E-6's, then you were not getting advanced. What they would do was to send you a PNA notice, which meant passed, but not advanced. A PNA notice was about as useless as tits on a bull, and usually just made people angry. In the past fifteen years, I had received fourteen PNA notices.

Another thing that set me back was my broken service. When I got out of the Navy the first time, I was an E-4. When I came back into the navy a couple years later, I had to start all over again. This put me about six years behind schedule for advancement. Actually, this advancement was a surprise to me, since the odds of me getting advanced were so slim.

I remember on Tuesday morning, September 11, 2001, things became very hectic at PSD. As soon as the World Trade Center attack had happened, the phones started ringing. The USNS Comfort (T-AH-20) was activated from its slumber in Baltimore Harbor, and it was our job to get it manned.

USNS Comfort (T-AH-20) is the third United States Navy ship to bear the name Comfort, and the second Mercy-class hospital ship to join the navy fleet. The USNS prefix identifies the Comfort as a non-commissioned ship owned by the U.S. Navy and crewed by civilians. In accordance with the Geneva Conventions, USNS Comfort and her crew do not carry any offensive weapons. Firing upon the Comfort would be considered a war crime and the ship does carry weapons for self-defense.

Like her sister ship USNS Mercy, Comfort was built as an oil tanker in 1976 by the National Steel and Shipbuilding Company. Her original name was SS Rose City and she was launched from San Diego, California.

Her career as an oil tanker ended when she was delivered to the Navy on December 1, 1987. Now, as a hospital ship, Comfort's new duties include providing emergency, on-site care for U.S. combatant forces deployed in war or other operations. Operated by the Military Sealift Command, Comfort provides rapid, flexible, and mobile medical and surgical services to support Marine Corps Air/Ground Task Forces deployed ashore, Army and Air Force units deployed ashore, and naval amphibious task forces and battle forces afloat. Secondarily, she provides mobile surgical hospital service for use by appropriate U.S. government agencies in disaster or humanitarian relief or limited humanitarian care incident to these missions or peacetime military operations. Comfort is more advanced than a field hospital but less capable than a traditional hospital on land.

Comfort was activated the afternoon of September 11, 2001, in response to the terrorist attack on the World Trade Center and sailed the next afternoon to serve as a 250-bed hospital facility at Pier 92 in midtown Manhattan. The ship arrived in Manhattan at about eight thirty on September 14. That evening a small number of relief workers arrived aboard the ship. As word about the ship spread, more workers began arriving over the next few days. The ship's clinic saw 561 guests for cuts, respiratory ailments, fractures and other minor injuries, and Comfort's team of Navy psychology personnel provided 500 mental health consultations to relief workers. Comfort also hosted a group of volunteer New York area massage therapists who gave 1,359 therapeutic medical massages to ship guests.

Every passing day at PSD brought me a little bit closer to retirement. Since I never really thought I would make it this far, it was kind of strange to think about. One day the Senior Chief asked me "So Clay, what kind of retirement ceremony are you going to have? I mean is it going to be big, or just a small private thing?" Now that's something I had never given any real thought to. "I don't know Senior, I never really thought about it."

A few days later, I was talking to a buddy of mine, Lee, about my retirement. When he asked me what I was planning to do, I told him I thought I would just retire quietly and just go away. He pulled me into an empty room and said "Clay that would be a mistake. I retired from the Navy ten years ago and I did nothing. I have regretted it ever since. You have to do something; something really cool. I promise you... if you don't, you will regret it." Now I had a great respect for Lee. This was something I had to consider. Ok. If I did have a retirement ceremony, how could I do it in a way that would accurately reflect my love for the Navy? I just couldn't see it happening.

Then I remembered something incredible that I had seen a while back. The Portsmouth Naval Hospital sits along the Elizabeth River. I used to love sitting there on the point watching the boats go by. Sometimes a nice big ship would come down the river, usually heading in or out of the shipyard. I used to smell the air and imagine that I was on those ships, just like the old days. I never realized how much I loved and missed being underway. There was no way to deny it... I loved the Navy. As I was sitting there on that Thursday afternoon, watching the little boats go by, all of the sudden all the boats disappeared. They all just kind of vanished. As I turned to see why they had all left, I saw a huge shadow coming up the river.

On Thursday, December 7th, 2000, the Battleship USS Wisconsin (BB-64) was towed from the Philadelphia

Naval Shipyard to its new home in Norfolk, Virginia. To see this awesome ship in all its size and glory coming down the Elizabeth River was something special.

USS Wisconsin (BB-64) is an Iowa-class Battleship, the second ship of the United States Navy to be named in honor of the state of Wisconsin. She was built at the Philadelphia Naval Shipyard in Philadelphia, Pennsylvania and launched on 7 December 1943 (the second anniversary of the Pearl Harbor raid), sponsored by the wife of the Governor of Wisconsin.

During her career, the Wisconsin served in the Pacific Theater of World War II, where she shelled Japanese fortifications and screened United States aircraft carriers as they conducted air raids against enemy positions. During the Korean War, Wisconsin shelled North Korean targets in support of United Nations and South Korean ground operations, after which she was decommissioned into the United States Navy reserve fleets, better known as the "mothball fleet". She was reactivated 1 August 1986 and modernized as part of the Reagan 600-ship Navy plan, and participated in Operation Desert Storm in January and February 1991.

Wisconsin was last decommissioned in September 1991, having earned a total of six battle stars for service in World War II and Korea, as well as a Navy Unit Commendation for service during the January/February 1991 Gulf War. She currently functions as a museum ship operated by Nauticus, The National Maritime Center in Norfolk, Virginia.

Ever since the first day I laid eyes on the Wisconsin, I wanted to go to sea with her. Now I have been on others Battleships, such as the USS New Jersey, the USS Iowa and the USS Alabama. There is something about the Wisconsin that really touched me. The first time I set foot on her, I fell in love. I knew now that this is where I was going to end my Navy career.

There are lots of things to do when preparing for a retirement ceremony. First off, as hard as this is to believe, I was not the only person who wanted to retire aboard the USS Wisconsin. My actual retirement date was June the 1st, 2005, but with the terminal leave I had saved up, my ceremony would be on the 18th of March. Although the USS Wisconsin had a very busy schedule, I was able to book the date I needed.

A couple weeks before the ceremony, I was invited down to the Wisconsin so they could show me how the ceremony would go. Since the ship was now part of a museum, there were lots of tourists walking around on it. I mean, who could blame them? The ship was awesome! When they asked me where on board I would like to actually retire, I told them I was thinking about doing it under the after sixteen inch guns.

As I walked aft down the length of the mighty ship, I looked down at the wooden deck. Battleships were the only ships in the active Navy that still had wooden decks. The deck was now weathered badly and dinged up. I could just imagine how many times divisional quarters had been held there.

I really don't think it is possible to walk by those huge guns without staring in awe. While looking down the length of the barrels, I started thinking about some of the stories I had read about the mighty Battleship.

Hitting a tank with a sixteen inch shell from a battleship's main battery is something like shooting a mouse with an elephant gun. It doesn't happen often. When it does happen, there isn't much left of the mouse.

Here is a story I read once in the Navy Times. It had been written back in 1951. "One night last week the 45,000-ton U.S. battleship Wisconsin (which relieved the New Jersey last month) lay off Korea's east coast, firing her secondary batteries of five inch guns in support of United Nations ground troops ashore. Finally there came a call for heavier fire. The Number two turret crew swung into action and five sixteen inch shells, weighing a ton apiece, whistled into the target area, eight thousand yards away.

"The result was direct hits on two Communist gun emplacements and one T-34 tank. An observer said "with what's left of that baby (the tank), they can't even make carpet tacks." Now those are guns. I wish I could have been there to see them in action. Yes, under the sixteen inch guns of the USS Wisconsin is where I will give my last Navy salute.

As I was walking back toward the bow of the ship, I remembered something I had read in the ship's deck log. Now here is something most people wouldn't know. The bow of the USS Wisconsin is not really the bow of the USS Wisconsin. It is the bow of the USS Kentucky (BB-66) which was never completed.

On Sunday, May 6, 1956, at approximately three fourteen in the afternoon, the USS Wisconsin collided with the USS Eaton (DDE-510). This happened off the Virginia Coast during heavy fog. The USS EATON almost lost her entire bow. The forward engine room of the Wisconsin was flooded and she was towed stern first to Norfolk. Norfolk Naval Shipyard workers fitted a 120-ton, sixty-eight-foot bow section from the unfinished Iowa-class battleship Kentucky to the Wisconsin in record time. Wisconsin was ready for service 16 days later and she departed for Spain on July 9th.

I honestly did not want to leave the ship, but I had to get back to work. Yes, Lee was right. This was going to be the perfect sendoff after an awesome career. Life was going to be good.

The next thing I had to do was to send out invitations. The most important guest at my ceremony was going to be my mother. She was there at the beginning of my Navy journey, and it was very important to me that she be there at the end. Another really cool thing was my brother Toby was driving up with her. I hadn't seen him in a while, so that was going to make it even better.

On Friday, March 18th 2005, I arrived onboard the USS Wisconsin (BB-64). The weather was calm and clear on this bitter sweet day. The uniform of the day was dress blues, and the crew was assembled for the ceremony. My mother and brother were seated in the front row, with all the other guests seated behind them. I still couldn't believe that it was me, Clay Westfall who was retiring.

The three sixteen inch guns stretched out proudly from the rear gun mount, as the ceremony started. The flag was folded and passed by my shipmates from PSD, and my good friend Lee sang the Star Spangled Banner. He sang it so beautifully; I could feel the tears welling up in my eyes. To be on that ship, in that uniform, under those guns... I have never been so proud to be an American.

As the Boatswains mate piped me ashore, I saluted my last time in uniform. I slowly walked along the Starboard side of the ship, thinking back about my life in the Navy. I thought about the USS Salt Lake City, my first submarine. It was on the list to be decommissioned early next year. Then it would be scrapped and chopped up. Then I thought about my second sub, the Baton Rouge. She had been decommissioned ten years ago, and now she was razor blades. My last sub, the Norfolk, was still on active duty a couple miles up the Elizabeth River. She was moored on pier twenty two with the rest of Squadron Six.

My favorite command, the USS Radford, was decommissioned exactly two years ago, on March 18th, 2003. The rumor is that she is going to be stripped and scuttled as part of a three-state artificial reef system just 30 miles from the Ocean City Inlet, off the coast of New Jersey. This is tentatively scheduled for May 2011. The Radford will be the largest ship ever sunk on the East Coast as an artificial reef. The wreck will lie in approximately 140 feet of water with the top deck of the ship around 60 feet deep allowing for the whole range of divers from recreational to the technical diver. It's always sad to see your old ships decommissioned.

As I was leaving the ship, I stopped at the brow and turned back. The wind was blowing slightly from the ocean, giving off that wonderful salty smell that I had grown to love over the years. I looked back and gazed longingly at the bridge of one of the mightiest ships the world had ever known. I looked back at the past twenty two years and the wonderful adventures that I had. The Navy was my life. I wouldn't trade that adventure for the world. It was a love I had for the sea, and a love for the Navy. It was my Navy.

The End

Made in the USA
Charleston, SC
05 November 2013